The Virgin Birth According to Temple Christology

The Virgin Birth According to Temple Christology

David H. Wenkel

LEXINGTON BOOKS

Lanham • Boulder • New York • London

Published by Lexington Books
An imprint of The Rowman & Littlefield Publishing Group, Inc.
4501 Forbes Boulevard, Suite 200, Lanham, Maryland 20706
www.rowman.com

86-90 Paul Street, London EC2A 4NE, United Kingdom

British Library Cataloguing in Publication Information Available

Library of Congress Cataloging-in-Publication Data

Names: Wenkel, David H., author.
Title: The virgin birth according to temple Christology / David H. Wenkel.
Description: Lanham : Lexington Books, [2025] | Includes bibliographical
   references and index. |
Summary: "This study of the virgin birth affirms the doctrine of the Apostles' Creed
   and seeks to follow in the footsteps of Athanasius of Alexandria by using exegetical
   typology. It builds an exegetical, theological, and catholic case for understanding
   Jesus' incarnation as an act of divine temple construction"—Provided by publisher.
Identifiers: LCCN 2024032960 (print) | LCCN 2024032961 (ebook) |
   ISBN 9781666970708 (cloth) | ISBN 9781666970715 (epub)
Subjects: LCSH: Virgin birth—History of doctrines. | Apostles' Creed. | Incarnation.
Classification: LCC BT317 .W454 2025 (print) | LCC BT317 (ebook) |
   DDC 232.92/1—dc23/eng/20240814
LC record available at https://lccn.loc.gov/2024032960
LC ebook record available at https://lccn.loc.gov/2024032961

For Nathan and Chris,
who remind me that every good gift is from above

Contents

Preface

This study focuses on the intersection between the doctrine of the virgin birth and the theological category of Temple Christology. It attempts to explain why Jesus-the-temple had to have a virgin mother by considering Jesus' unique status as the temple of God who was "made without human hands." The central thesis is this: *Jesus had to be conceived by a virgin mother by the immediate act of the Holy Spirit because of his identity as the heavenly temple of God.* According to this argument, the virginal conception of Jesus was necessary because the incarnation was a divine act of temple construction.

This study answers the call to reintroduce the nexus between Christology and typology as they were originally bound together by theologians such as Athanasius of Alexandria. Unfortunately, for most of church history, Christology and typology have gone their separate ways. This divergence is so stark that the imagery, phraseology, and words of scripture have lost their voice in the context of systematic theology and dogmatics. The approach of this study demonstrates that a typological study of biblical persons, events, and institutions can increase our understanding of Jesus, especially his virginal conception.

This constructive consideration of the virginal conception of Christ is rooted in the church fathers but engages with a range of modern thinkers. This study goes beyond the theology of the Apostles' Creed but not against it. It does not seek novelty for its own sake but doctrinal augmentation through theological formulation and exegesis. Thus, this study is a resource for those interested in Christology across a wide range of Christian traditions.

List of Abbreviations

AD	Anno Domini (=CE)
ANE	Ancient Near Eastern
AT	*Acta Theologica*
AUSS	*Andrews University Seminary Studies*
AYBRL	Anchor Yale Bible Reference Library
BC	Before Christ (=BCE)
BCBC	Believers Church Bible Commentary
BDAG	Arndt, W., F.W. Danker, W. Bauer, and F.W. Gingrich. *A Greek-English Lexicon of the New Testament and Other Early Christian Literature*. Chicago: University of Chicago Press, 2000.
BECNT	Baker Exegetical Commentary on the New Testament
BHS	*Biblia Hebraica Stuttgartensia*
BNTC	Black's New Testament Commentary
BSac	*Bibliotheca Sacra*
BTB	*Biblical Theology Bulletin*
BTCB	Brazos Theological Commentary on the Bible
BTS	Biblical Tools and Studies
BZAW	Beihefte zur Zeitschrift für die alttestamentliche Wissenschaft
CBC	Cornerstone Biblical Commentary
CD	*Church Dogmatics*, Karl Barth
CTC	Christian Theology in Context
CTR	*Criswell Theological Review*
DSS	Dead Sea Scrolls
ECC	Eerdmans Critical Commentary
EGGNT	Exegetical Guide to the Greek New Testament.

ERCT	Explorations in Reformed Confessional Theology
ESV	*English Standard Version*
ExpTim	*Expository Times*
HALOT	Koehler, L., W. Baumgartner, M.E.J. Richardson, and J.J. Stamm. *The Hebrew and Aramaic Lexicon of the Old Testament.* Leiden: E.J. Brill, 1994–2000.
HBT	*Horizons in Biblical Theology*
HTR	*Harvard Theological Review*
IJST	*International Journal of Systematic Theology*
JAT	*Journal of Analytic Theology*
JBL	*Journal of Biblical Literature*
JEH	*Journal of Ecclesiastical History*
JETS	*Journal of the Evangelical Theological Society*
JMP	*Journal of Medicine and Philosophy*
JRT	*Journal of Reformed Theology*
JSJ	*Journal for the Study of Judaism*
JSNTSup	*Journal for the Study of the New Testament Supplement Series*
JTI	*Journal of Theological Interpretation*
JTS	*Journal of Theological Studies*
LATCS	Los Angeles Theology Conference Series
LNTS	Library of New Testament Studies
LSTS	Library of Second Temple Studies
LXX	Septuagint
MJT	*Midwestern Journal of Theology*
MNTS	McMaster New Testament Studies
NAC	New American Commentary
NeoT	*NeoTestamentica*
NETS	New English Translation of the Septuagint
NICNT	New International Commentary on the New Testament
NICOT	New International Commentary on the Old Testament
NIGTC	New International Greek Testament Commentary
NovT	*Novum Testamentum*
NovTSup	Novum Testamentum, Supplements
NSBT	New Studies in Biblical Theology
NT	New Testament
NTM	New Testament Monographs
OECS	Oxford Early Christian Studies
OT	Old Testament
OTM	Oxford Theological Monographs
OSHT	Oxford Studies in Historical Theology
PCNT	Paideia Commentaries on the New Testament

PNTC	Pillar New Testament Commentary
PG	Patrologiae cursus completus. *Series Graeca.* ed. J. Migne
PL	Patrologiae cursus completus. *Series Latina.* ed. J. Migne
PRJ	*Puritan Reformed Journal*
ResQ	*Restoration Quarterly*
SBET	*Scottish Bulletin of Evangelical Theology*
SBJT	*Southern Baptist Journal of Theology*
SGBC	Story of God Biblical Commentary
SHST	Studies in Historical & Systematic Theology
SJT	*Scottish Journal of Theology*
SNTSMS	Society for New Testament Studies Monograph Series
SSBT	Short Studies in Biblical Theology
SST	Studies in Systematic Theology
SRT	Studies in Reformed Theology
STI	Studies in Theological Interpretation
RRCT	Retrieval and Renewal in Catholic Thought
TBT	Theologische Bibliothek Töpelmann
Them	*Themelios*
THOTC	Two Horizons Old Testament Commentary
TOTC	Tyndale Old Testament Commentaries
TrinJ	*Trinity Journal*
TRS	Thomistic Ressourcement Series
TynB	*Tyndale Bulletin*
UBCS	Understanding the Bible Commentary Series
VT	*Vetus Testamentum*
WBC	Word Biblical Commentary
WCF	Westminster Confession of Faith
ZECNT	Zondervan Exegetical Commentary on the New Testament

PRIMARY SOURCES

Acta Conc. Oec.	Cyril of Alexandria, *Acta Conciliorum Oecumenicorum, I., Council of Ephesus, 431*
An. Post.	Aristotle, *Posterior Analytics*
Ant.	Josephus, *Antiquities of the Jews*
Apol.	Justin Martyr, *First Apology*
C. Ar.	Athanasius, *Orations against the Arians*
Contra gent.	Aquinas, *Against the Gentiles*
De corona	Tertullian, *On the Military Garland*
De grat.	Augustine of Hippo, *On Grace and Free Will*
De Inc.	Athanasius, *On the Incarnation*

Dial.	Justin Martyr, *Dialogue with Trypho*
Ep.	Augustine of Hippo, *Letters*
Gent.	Athanasius, *Against the Gentiles*
Haer.	Irenaeus, *Against Heresies*
IEph.	Ignatius of Antioch, *The Letter to the Ephesians*
In Ps.	Augustine of Hippo, *Expositions on the Psalms*
Inst.	John Calvin, *Institutes of the Christian Religion*
LAB	Pseudo-Philo, *Liber Antiquitatum Biblicarum*
Phys.	Aristotle, *Physics*
Quaest. in Hept.	Augustine of Hippo, *Seven Questions Concerning the Heptateuch*
Ret.	Augustine of Hippo, *Retractions*
T.Jos	*Testament of Joseph*
Wars	Josephus, *Wars of the Jews*

Introduction

A Case for the Necessity of the Virgin Birth

This study offers a constructive dogmatic case for the necessity of what is commonly called the "virgin birth" of Jesus.[1] The precise phrase should be "virginal conception," but I retain the traditional Protestant expression and meaning.[2] The argument of this study proceeds with a categorical syllogism in three parts. This form of reasoning is deductive because it arrives at a specific and necessary conclusion by considering two premises. The first or major premise is that a heavenly temple must be constructed directly by the Holy Spirit. Second, the minor premise of this argument is that Jesus is a heavenly temple. Third, the conclusion is that Jesus had to be conceived of a virgin directly by the Spirit because of his identity as God's heavenly temple or dwelling place. According to this argument, the virgin birth of Jesus was necessary because the incarnation was a divine act of temple construction. *Jesus had to be conceived by a virgin mother by the immediate act of the Holy Spirit because of his identity as the heavenly temple of God.*

Despite its sparse appearances in canonical Christian scripture, the miraculous virginal conception (hereafter, "virgin birth") of Jesus to Mary has been a core tenet of the faith since the fourth century, perhaps even earlier than that. For the follower of Jesus—the implied reader of the New Testament—this event is both historical and important.[3] However, explaining its historicity may actually be easier than explaining its significance.

Christians across the catholic spectrum are regularly encouraged to believe this event took place through creeds, confessions, and catechisms. But Christians are not often directed toward resources that might help them understand *why* Jesus had to be conceived in this way. As a result, there are a range of questions that may not have robust answers. One of the particular problems that attends this doctrine of the virgin birth is one of necessity: why did it have to happen in the way that it did? Why did Jesus have to be conceived through the Holy Spirit in the womb of the virgin Mary? In order to offer a systematic and constructive theological answer that sheds more light on such questions, this study argues that Jesus had to be conceived to a virgin mother by the immediate act of the Holy Spirit because of his identity as the heavenly temple of God.

The two major texts for the doctrine of the virgin birth of Jesus come from the Gospels of Matthew and Luke.[4] There are more infancy accounts than this, but they are excluded from this study because they appear outside the canon and are dated as late as the second century.[5] Matthew narrates this event in the following manner:

> Now the birth of Jesus Christ took place in this way. When his mother Mary had been betrothed to Joseph, before they came together she was found to be with child from the Holy Spirit. (Matt. 1:18)

Matthew is keen to explain that this pregnancy took place before Mary and Joseph had come together in sexual union—that is—"before they came together."[6] The Gospel of Luke approaches this from a different vantage point. Luke first introduces Mary as a "virgin" by repeating this appellation twice, identifying her as "a *virgin* betrothed to a man whose name was Joseph, of the house of David. And the *virgin's* name was Mary" (Luke 1:27). Luke's narrative repeats Mary's status a third time when she exclaims, "How will this be, since I am a *virgin*?" (Luke 1:34). Next, Luke provides the content of the angelic speech from Gabriel to Mary:

> The Holy Spirit will come upon you, and the power of the Most High will overshadow you; therefore the child to be born will be called holy—the Son of God. (Luke 1:35)

Although Matthew and Luke offer different perspectives, their accounts are complementary.[7] For all the variations across the Gospel testimonies, they agree on one point that "the conception of Jesus took place by a miraculous intervention of the Holy Spirit in the womb of a virgin."[8] It is also noteworthy that no other New Testament writer contradicts their testimony.[9] The theology of the New Testament canon presents a united front about the miraculous nature of the virgin birth of Jesus.[10]

Beyond Matthew and Luke, the scope of the ancillary texts which traditionally support the doctrine of the virgin birth is rather small.[11] One of these is the prophetic text of Isaiah 7:14 ("Behold, the virgin shall conceive and bear a son, and shall call his name Immanuel") with its reference to a virgin (Hebrew *'almâ* and LXX *parthenos*) giving birth to a son.[12] This prophecy should not be entirely surprising to the reader of the canon. The roots of the expectations that a human will arrive to bring salvation are found in Genesis. The proto-evangelium (Gen. 3:15) offers hope for a Skull-crusher who will defeat the Serpent ("he shall bruise your head, and you shall bruise his heel").[13]

Other New Testament passages identify Jesus as sharing in the "flesh and blood" of his brothers (Heb. 2:14; similarly, 9:14). The letter of 1 Peter (1:18) also refers to the ransoming power of the "precious blood of Christ." Paul's letter to the Philippians (2:7) states that Jesus was "born in the likeness of men," and his letter to the Romans (5:14) identifies Adam as "a type of the one who was to come."[14] Paul also summarizes the entire incarnation event in the letter to the Galatians (4:4): "But when the fullness of time had come, God sent forth his Son, born of woman." There is no disputing the relevance of these texts, and there is much profit in considering how these passages are related to the variegated matrix of messianic expectations.[15] But this corpus of passages offers a data set that is far too narrow in scope for articulating a robust doctrine of the virgin birth.

Traditionally, there is a fixed, small number of biblical texts that are used to articulate a catholic doctrine of the virgin birth. But this was not always the case. As early as the fourth century, Athanasius of Alexandria (*c.* 293–373) was using a much wider swath of biblical texts to understand the incarnation. He utilized passages that referred to the imagery of the temple and the motif of God's dwelling place among his people. His volume entitled *On the Incarnation* was the first work devoted to the topic.[16] Unfortunately, this path was lost as the early Christian battles over Trinitarian doctrine progressed, and more emphasis was given to precise statements of orthodoxy backed up by Greek words. While the fixation of doctrinal formulae clarified doctrine for the church, it also tended to limit the scope of relevant biblical texts for dogmatic formulations. Motifs such as temple imagery became less important. This limitation in scope is evident in several recent studies of the virgin birth that do not consider the relevance of temple Christology at all.[17] This study seeks to resume Athanasius' task and consider how temple building in the Old Testament and clear references to Jesus' identity as the Messiah-temple form a much wider constellation of biblical texts to explain the incarnation.

According to the argument of this study, the incarnation of Jesus was an act of divine construction and analogous to the way in which one would construct a building. Jesus is not just any kind of building or even any kind of temple; he is the *heavenly* temple of God. This is why the adjective "heavenly" modifies Jesus in the central thesis of this study. In the central thesis and the related argumentation supporting the categorical syllogism, the word "heavenly" refers to Jesus being a temple made without human hands.

There are, as this study will demonstrate, two ways to build a temple. Temples which are built immediately by God or without instrumental means are called "made without hands" (*acheiropoietos*). And those which are made normally according to the standard practice of human instrumentality are earthly or "made with hands" (*cheiropoietos*).[18] Even those temples built by human hands were constructed in such a way so as to anticipate a climactic and final temple where God would dwell permanently among his covenant people.[19] In other words, temples built "with [human] hands" pointed toward a temple "made without hands." This means that the way in which the temple in Jerusalem and its antecedents were built explicates the mode of the Son coming into the world: he was constructed as a building would be for the full indwelling of God's presence, yet without human hands.[20]

When Jesus spoke about the destruction and resurrection of the "temple," John indicates that he was referring to himself and his identity: "But he was speaking about the temple of his body" (John 2:21).[21] Jesus predicted that his own body would be resurrected after his death as a raised temple.[22] In other words, Jesus' resurrection from the dead was a temple-resurrection. This point was initially lost on the original audience, even the disciples, for they only understood it as they remembered these words after he was raised from the dead (John 2:22). The power of the Spirit after Pentecost and the clarity provided by Jesus' resurrection from the dead enabled the disciples to remember his words and interpret them. John clearly identifies Jesus as the temple of God—he is the Messiah-temple where the fullness of the Godhead dwells bodily.

Theologically, John's Gospel indicates that Jesus' body was the temple of God before his Passion *and* after his resurrection. The text of John 2:21 provides a hermeneutical justification for this study because it "could be used as a kind of lens through which to see other Johannine references to the Temple that might not otherwise be detected."[23] This means that there were other instances in Jesus' teachings where he was referring to himself as the fulfillment of the tabernacle and/or the temple. This conclusion can be extended so that the prologue of John's Gospel (1:1) about the incarnation of the Word offers a hermeneutical lens for understanding Jesus' identity as the temple of God across the canon of scripture. At the very least, John's temple Christology offers a selection of clear passages about Jesus' identity which may be then used to theologically interpret passages about temple Christology which are more obscure.[24]

The reference to divine "hands" in acts of temple building is an anthropomorphism that attributes physical hands of a corporeal body to God, who is spirit.[25] The use of divine "hands" (but not human hands) is used to describe special acts of divine work in the world. Jesus himself seems to imply this type of divine handiwork as he anticipated the resurrection of his temple-body after his Passion (e.g., John 2:18–22).[26] Jesus' opponents also used this reference to divine "hands" in their attempt to accuse him of blasphemy (e.g.,

Mark 14:58). This charge of blasphemy arose even when the audience misunderstood the referent of his own body. What else could it mean for Jesus to claim that he could raise up a temple in three days except that he was claiming the ability to utilize "divine" hands? For comparison, the apostle Paul uses phrases that attribute divine "hands" to the special works of God when describing the future resurrected bodies of God's people (2 Cor. 5:1) and of the work of regeneration in the human heart (Col. 2:11).

The term "temple Christology" is well known within the arena of biblical studies (New Testament studies or Johannine studies) because it covers a domain of references used by Jesus himself to describe his death and resurrection. Besides John, the New Testament uses temple imagery in different ways, as one might compare Acts (3:1), 1 Corinthians (6:19), Hebrews (8:5), and Revelation (11:19). This project crosses disciplinary boundaries as it utilizes "temple Christology" as a dogmatic term and applies it to Jesus' incarnation. Jesus' identity as a temple is extrapolated backward from his life and post-resurrection state to his birth. Because Jesus' identity never changed, he was just as much a Messiah-temple during his earthly ministry and resurrected state as he was at his conception. Once this paradigm is in place, the incarnation may be understood as an act of divine construction in which God was building his temple.

Jesus' identification of himself as the temple of God functions as the minor premise in the syllogism. One important text that relates the doctrine of the virgin birth to the temple Christology is the explanatory text from the Gospel of John (2:21), in which the Beloved Disciple explains Jesus' teaching about raising up a new temple in three days. Through the clarity brought about by the Passion and the power of Pentecost, it eventually became clear to the disciples that Jesus was not talking about the temple building in Jerusalem, for "he was speaking about the *temple of his body*." In this text from John, the Beloved Disciple offers an interpretive and editorial comment about what Jesus' previous speech meant.[27] The matter of remembering Jesus' words became vitally important not only because of his physical departure during the ascension but because the cross-resurrection event enabled them to understand teachings that were previously opaque to them.

If Jesus is the temple of God, then an important question emerges: *how are temples built?* Of course, this question is not referring to just *any* building that bears the name of "temple," but only to those buildings that were constructed by a divine command from Yahweh. With this restriction in mind, this question draws attention to the pattern of temple building that begins in the opening chapters of the canon with the establishment of the garden-temple in Genesis 1–3.

Just as the temple of the garden was created by the Spirit who brooded over the waters in Genesis, so the Spirit is the agent of creation-construction

in the virginal conception of Jesus. The Spirit who overshadowed Mary is
the third person of the Trinity. The Spirit was written in Hebrew (*ruach*) as a
feminine noun and in Greek (*pneuma*) as neuter. But the grammatical gender
of words does not define the gender of persons.[28] When referring to the Spirit,
John uses the masculine demonstrative pronoun (*ekeinos*) and the masculine
term *paraklētos* (see John 16:7–8 for both terms).[29] The Spirit is the agent
of sanctification throughout the scriptures, and he is also the agent of temple
building throughout the scriptures.[30]

There is a range of examples of temple construction across the canon that
will help the reader of scripture to answer that very important Christological
question: how are temples built? In fact, the biblical writers were keenly interested in the way in which places of worship were constructed. Conceptually,
there are two ways in which all of the cultic places of sacred space for Yahweh
worship were built: "made without hands" or "made with human hands."

There is a wide range of canonical texts that use words and or concepts to
describe that which is "made without human hands." Things that are made
immediately by divine "hands" are heavenly and true. These texts are important because they explicitly connect divine actions in which God acts immediately upon creation, that is, without the instrumental use of means as found
in typical acts of providence. For example, the interpreted vision of King
Nebuchadnezzar in the book of Daniel concludes with a heavenly kingdom
of God as a stone "cut from a mountain by no human hand" (Dan. 2:34, 45).[31]
Here, the use of mountain imagery evokes the common ancient Near Eastern
(ANE) motif of a sacred mountain representing the cosmic dwelling place of
god.[32] Thus, it is not surprising that this mountain is defined by Daniel as the
"kingdom of God," which destroys any opposing idolatrous mountains (Dan.
2:44–45). The "stone" of Daniel 2 is later used by Jesus to describe his rejection and then his victory (Luke 20:17–18 // Matt. 21:42, 44).[33]

The New Testament has several texts that refer to what God has done
without "human hands." The letter to the Hebrews (13:14) states, "For here
we have no lasting city, but we seek the city that is to come." Whitlark comments, "Rome is not the eternal city, but the community looks for a city to
come whose architect and builder is God."[34] The eternal city of the New
Jerusalem in heaven is built directly by God, the "builder." Theologically,
this text draws attention to the fact that God is both builder and temple, the
dweller and the dwelling place.[35] The same idea of divine action via "God's
hands" is present in Paul's description of the Spirit's work in the heart: "In
him also you were circumcised with a circumcision *made without hands*, by
putting off the body of the flesh, by the circumcision of Christ" (Col. 2:11).
The key idea is that those actions which are done by God's own hand(s)
are immediate, eternal, and permanent. But those things achieved through
"human hands" are subject to corruption and impermanence.

The argument that Jesus had to be conceived or constructed by divine hands because of his identity as God's temple follows the typological relationship between places of Yahweh worship across the Christian canon of scripture. According to this view, Jesus is the climax of the progressive storyline of scripture in which God's people constructed special places of worship for God's personal divine presence.[36] These places of worship and their institutions were regulated by divine revelation so that they might successively anticipate the culmination of God dwelling eternally with his people in the person of Christ, the Messiah-temple. The construction of primitive altars by the patriarchs, Israel's tent of meeting, and the Jerusalem temple were all constructed according to the Spirit because they all pointed forward in salvation-history to the final construction of God's temple in the person of Jesus of Nazareth. In other words, the ways in which the temple and its antecedents were physically constructed inform the nature of the construction of Jesus in his miraculous conception.

The argument of this book is in the form of a categorical syllogism. This argument is "categorical" because it deals with the category or class of what constitutes a "temple."[37] First, the major premise is that a true place of Yahweh worship must be constructed directly or immediately by the Holy Spirit. Second, the minor premise of this argument is that Jesus of Nazareth, in his incarnation as the Son of God, is a heavenly temple and a true place of Yahweh worship. Third, the conclusion is that because of Jesus' identity as a temple, he had to be conceived by a virgin, through the direct or immediate action of the Spirit of God. The careful reader will notice a glaring problem with the form of this argument: the terms are not consistent. The nature of this argument utilizes an analogical relationship between the act of constructing a building and the procreation of a person. This analogous relationship requires the terms of the argument to legitimately move from one term to another based on shared ontological characteristics. As this study progresses, it will be evident that the movement between construction and conception is demonstrably valid because of the way that scripture itself connects the terms.

The argument of this study aims to be catholic in its dogmatic formulations while acknowledging its origins in Protestant and Reformed confessionalism. There is also an explicit attempt to not speak *contrary* to the Apostles' Creed, the Nicene Creed, and the Athanasian Creed, even where this study goes *beyond* them. This means that there may be theological steps taken outside the construal of the various divine intentions associated with the virgin birth. In other words, the postulate that the virginal conception of Jesus was an act of divine temple building is not exclusive of other divine intentions in the same act. The incarnation, like the atonement, death, resurrection, and ascension, is an objectively revelatory act and as such expresses a panoply of God's intentions as he works out all things for his own glory.[38]

The Reformed tradition has consistently worked from the presupposition that God had multiple simultaneous intentions working at the same time in the virgin birth. It is this presupposition that provides a path to add yet another act of divine intentionality: *to build Jesus as a temple*.[39] Here, the term "intention" refers to the related terms "purpose," "goal," and "reason." Divine intentions are the grounds for intelligent action as motivated by God's own loving nature, for God is love (1 John 4:8).[40] This definition of "intention" means that God's love expressed itself through multiple purposes, particularly as related to the virgin birth of Jesus.[41]

Some confessions are simply silent on the divine intention(s) for the incarnation, preferring only to affirm and repeat statements reflecting Nicene and Chalcedonian orthodoxy. Such statements might only assert that in the incarnation, the eternal Son of God took upon himself a fully human nature so that he is understood to be fully divine and fully human. Reformed confessional statements about the incarnation typically include affirmations of Chalcedonian theology, which establishes the incarnation as the unmixed and unchangeable union of a divine nature and a human nature. And, some confessions do refer to a purpose for the virgin birth, typically within the context of explaining the divine purpose(s) for the incarnation.

This short survey establishes the point that there are *many* recognized divine intentions dogmatically attributed to the incarnation. This is a significant point to establish because it situates the present attempt to add yet another divine intention to the incarnation: *to build a temple for God's presence*.

This survey must be qualified by the fact that theological treatises do not always distinguish between the "incarnation" and the "virginal conception." For this reason, this present survey considers discussions of both these concepts. There is no attempt to evaluate or critically engage the following views beyond a cursory consideration of their orthodoxy, only to enumerate them. Nor are the following points exclusive to the Protestant and Reformed traditions. It is also noteworthy that the following list is in no particular order or hierarchy.

1. To Establish Divine Sonship. One of the reasons for the virginal conception was that sinful human parents could "not produce an offspring who is God."[42] Because the preexistent and eternal Son of God united himself with a human nature, there is no sense in which the virgin birth was the "efficient cause or source of his deity."[43] The virgin birth served to highlight the fact "that God alone is the Father of Jesus Christ."[44]

2. To Die on the Cross. Jesus' life was for death. This is because his death was a substitutionary sacrifice for the sins of the world.[45] Paul rhetorically asks in Romans 8:32, "He who did not spare his own Son but gave him up for us all, how will he not also with him graciously give us all things?" Christoph Schönborn argues that this text, which includes the concepts of Christ becoming man and dying, "should not be played off one against the other."[46]

3. To Become a Sinless Savior. Augustine of Hippo's doctrine of the virgin birth has dominated the church for at least 1500 years by providing a rationale for its purpose: the sinlessness of Jesus depended on Mary's virginity because it prevented the imputation of Adam's sin and/or guilt.[47] There are several texts that explicitly teach Jesus' sinlessness (2 Cor. 5:21 and Heb. 4:15). Despite Augustine's massive influence, some Protestants since John Calvin (*Inst.* 2.13.4) have argued that Christ's holiness did not depend upon the virgin birth *per se* but upon the work of the Holy Spirit.[48]

4. To Become the Obedient Last Adam. One of the purposes of the virgin birth was to establish Jesus as the last or second Adam.[49] This purpose was central to Anselm's conclusion that the redeemer of humanity had to be of Adam's progeny.[50] Jesus is the only one who shares the same trait with Adam insofar as they are the only two people to have been created directly or without instrumentality. Even Eve was created out of Adam's rib while he slept (Gen. 2:21). Neither Adam nor Israel was successful in carrying out the mantle of dominion. In response, Graham Cole states, "In general terms the incarnation qualified Jesus to be what Adam failed to be and what Israel failed to be: the true image of God walking the earth and exercising dominion."[51]

5. To Become a Son of David. Another one of the purposes of the virgin birth was to establish Jesus as the Messiah of the house of David to fulfill the covenantal promises to David.[52] Jesus was regarded as a son of David by the multitudes that followed him. He was also identified as such by his disciples. For Paul, Jesus' identity was bound up with his connection to King David, for Jesus was "descended from David according to the flesh" (Rom. 1:3).[53]

6. To Become God-With-Us. A contemporary proposal by the late Reformed theologian Robert Reymond begins with Jesus' divinity as identified by John's Gospel (1:14): "the [preexistent] Word became flesh."[54] This is an important presupposition for his argument because he proceeds to conclude that the virgin birth "was the means whereby *God became man.*"[55] Matthew (1:22–23) identifies the virgin birth as the moment when Isaiah (7:14) would be fulfilled because Jesus is Immanuel, or "God with us."

7. To Defeat Demonic Powers. One of the reasons why Jesus became incarnate was to destroy the kingdom, works, and power of the devil or Satan.[56] An important text related to this point is 1 John 3:8 ("The reason the Son of God appeared was to destroy the works of the devil.").

8. To Redeem Those Under the Law. Jesus' incarnation to Mary, a Jew, is a critically important feature.[57] As Paul explains in Galatians (4:4): "God sent his Son, born of a woman, born under the law, *to redeem those under the law.*" Jesus' virgin birth simultaneously revealed him to be God's Son and Mary's.[58] It is through Israel that God redeemed those under the law of Moses given to Israel. And it is also through Israel that God redeemed anyone and everyone who was "enslaved to the elementary principles of the world" (Gal. 4:3).

9. To Reveal Divine Love. Existentially, we live after the Fall, and we know a world full of sin, death, and darkness. But the scriptures reveal that God is love (1 John 4:16). As noted above, the incarnation was a revelatory moment in salvation-history in which God showed humanity himself, though veiled in human flesh. The incarnation is when "God sent his Son" and can thus be considered the very essence of the good news, and in this sending, he gives us what is everything to him in love: his Son.[59]

This brief review demonstrates that Reformed traditions already offer multiple divine purposes for the virgin birth. Technically, this adds nothing to the thesis at hand, but it helps the reader to understand how the proposal stands within the larger context of historical theology. This review is also defensive in nature insomuch as it anticipates the concern with introducing a new constructive theological proposal. But whatever might be considered new is actually an act of renewal and retrieval that stands in line with existing catholic orthodoxy.

To summarize: the presence of multiple divine intentions in the virgin birth is not a novel claim. Herman Bavinck argued that the virgin birth "simultaneously" obtained several results.[60] Reformed theologians such as Robert Reymond have discussed the virgin birth as though there was a dominant or ultimate divine intention.[61] Yet even this acknowledgment of a hierarchy of intentions proves the point: God was accomplishing more than one purpose in and through the virginal conception of Jesus. To be clear, there is no claim here as to which intention is ultimate or penultimate, only that there were multiple divine intentions operative in this event and that it is theologically legitimate to offer yet another one related to Jesus' identity as the temple of God.

This present argument aims to be constructive in nature by offering a fresh-yet-ancient presentation of how the virgin birth should be understood and why it was even required to begin with. It is unfortunate that the doctrine of the virgin birth has remained relatively disconnected from some studies of Christology as found within contemporary systematic theologies.[62] When and where references to the virgin birth do appear, its miraculous nature often dominates the discussion. For this reason, it is important to observe that Jesus' incarnation included other aspects of miraculous personal action, such as the "Son's humble assumption of his human nature" as indicated by Philippians 2.[63] While the miraculous nature of the virgin birth was privileged in traditional Christology, its purpose was not always explained in a robust manner.

The very notion that the virgin birth should be treated as a Christian doctrine draws from the ancient church's confession of this event in documents such as the Apostles' Creed.[64] As such, it became extracted from its literary and canonical context and then attached to the central tenets of the Christian faith. Thus, the church catholic has, for most of its history at least, testified to its worthiness to be proclaimed and taught as a truth which must be believed. The status of the virgin birth as dogma is not contested in the church catholic outside of a historical-critical reading of its history. In other words, the doctrine of the virgin birth is not typically contested on the grounds that it is a Christian doctrine. Rather, it is contested by those who would deny its status as a historical event.

This study works from the conclusion that the virgin birth was a historical event and is a dogma worthy of Christian proclamation. In doing so, it offers a fresh look at this doctrine and its relationship to the Christian canon. This dogmatic argument is based on a synthetic reading of Old Testament and the New Testament texts. Specifically, this study operates within confessional Protestant views of Mary: regarding Jesus' birth as miraculous because of Mary's virginity but not as an immaculate conception in which Mary was free from "all stain of original sin."[65] From the Protestant perspective, Mary herself was fully human and therefore possessed a fallen human nature. She committed sins and her song indicates her own need for a savior: "and my spirit rejoices in God *my* savior" (Luke 1:47).[66]

The constructive goals of this study are focused on establishing new and fresh explanations of scriptural data that are compatible with ideas already latent in historical Christian traditions, confessions, and creeds. The goal is not to construct a new concept of the virgin birth but to construct a thick explanation for its necessity that is rooted in scripture and engages with ecclesiastical traditions.[67] The aim is not innovation per se but a reading of scripture that offers a robust doctrine that can be tested and evaluated.

This study proceeds in three parts. The first part (chapters 1–4) functions as a prolegomena or set of "preliminary words" for the central argument at hand.

It establishes key definitions, explains presuppositions, and answers critical questions about the methodology employed.

The second part (chapters 5–7) utilizes the canon of Christian scripture as the source for a fresh dogmatic explication of the necessity of the virgin birth. It covers the places of Yahweh worship across salvation-history and considers the promises that God will dwell among his people. This provides the basis for the major and minor premises of the categorical syllogism which forms the heart of this argument.

The third part (chapter 8) is the concluding proposition of the syllogism and explains why Jesus had to be born to a virgin. This last chapter offers a theological synthesis of all the preceding argumentation. It returns to the central thesis statement and develops the argument that Jesus had to be conceived directly or immediately by the Spirit because of his identity as a heavenly temple.

NOTES

1. Letham comments that the expression "virgin birth" does not make sense because Jesus was born in a normal human delivery (2019, 481); similarly noted by Wright (1992, 76).

2. Roman Catholic thought has these two phrases meaning different things. The "virgin birth" refers to Mary's body miraculously retaining its immaculate state even during and after birth, while the "virginal conception" refers to Mary's virginity at the Annunciation. For an example, see the discussion of "Mary's motherhood with regard to the Church" in *Catechism of the Catholic Church: Second Edition* (1994, 273–4).

3. Here, I follow Bockmuehl's definition of the "implied reader" of the Christian canon as one who

> has undergone a religious, moral, and intellectual conversion to the gospel of which the documents speak. Regardless of whether the texts instruct, narrate, or reprove, they implicitly assume that the readers share a stance of Christian faith, that they look to the Christian gospel as both formative and normative in their lives, and that they accept a Christian way of thinking about God, the world, and themselves. (2006, 70)

To this, I would add that the implied reader in a post-Pentecost context has the Spirit-empowered capacity to read and believe the scriptures in light of the gospel.

4. Von Campenhausen (2011, 10) summarizes it this way: "Indeed, it [the virgin birth] appears in the New Testament in only two places, namely in the infancy stories of Matthew's and Luke's Gospels; and in the course of development it is at first taken up only on isolated occasions." All English biblical quotations are from the ESV unless otherwise noted.

5. The apocryphal account called the Infancy Gospel of James (the Protoevangelium of James) and the Infancy Gospel of Thomas (not to be confused with the Gospel

of Thomas) are outside the scope of this study and were likely written in the second half of the second century AD. For a recent study of the Infancy Gospel of James, see Zervos 2019, and of other accounts, see Ehrman and Please 2013. It is also worth observing that these non-canonical accounts have never appeared in any church creed or confession.

6. Matthew (1:19–20) explains that the timing of this miraculous event naturally brought consternation upon Joseph, requiring angelic intervention to prevent a divorce.

7. Of course, there are a plethora of authors who view Matthew and Luke as contradictory. For example, von Campenhausen (2011, 10, also 11–12) views the virgin birth in the New Testament as being characterized by "contradiction." For a discussion of objections to the supernatural doctrine of the virgin birth as found in the accounts of Matthew and Luke, see Treier 2016, 216–42.

8. Bray 2012, 563.

9. A point stressed by Reymond in 1998, 548, and by Erickson in 1998, 768.

10. In support of this statement, I would point to the ecclesial creeds and confessions of the church catholic, which have never considered these passages to be contradictory.

11. For a consideration of the way in which Matthew and Luke might parallel the Genesis story of Adam and Eve, see Schenk 2016, 129–31. Additionally, the reference to rebuilding the "fallen tent" of David in Acts (15:16) may be construed as a reference to Jesus' birth. Such a view would identify Jesus as the center of God's eschatological plan to fulfill the Davidic covenant and to unite both Jews and Gentiles through union with himself.

12. The literature on the meaning of the Greek word *parthenos* is substantial and is related to debates about the nature of Isaiah's prophecy. For recent studies, see Gromacki 2002, 93, and Rico and Gentry 2020. The seminal work on the canonical study of Isaiah as Christian scripture is Childs 1979. The recent resource by Lanier (2021, 424) provides historical parallels that use the word *parthenos*, such as the apocryphal *T. Jos* 19.3.

13. Discussions on the messianic nature of Genesis 3:15 are voluminous. For a discussion of the messianic identity of this "Skull-crusher" in Genesis 3:15, see Hamilton 2006, 30–54 and Wenkel 2018, 16. On the identity of the "Serpent" motif in the Old Testament books of 1–2 Samuel, as well as throughout the canon, see Verrett 2020.

14. For a study of the potential origins of Paul's typology in Romans 5, see Wenkel 2020.

15. For recent comments on the diversity of ancient Jewish messianic expectations, especially as they are related to being "in Christ," see Hewitt 2020, 41, and of the broader "matrix" of expectations, see Wenkel 2021a, 163.

16. Behr 2015, 80. C.S. Lewis (2011) offers a foreword with an English translation.

17. Studies of the virgin birth that do not consider the relevance of temple Christology include recent volumes such as Schenk (2016) as well as older monographs from the twentieth century such as von Campenhausen (1954).

18. For example, the author of Hebrews (9:1) defines the tabernacle as an "earthly" place of worship. This "earthly" place of worship is not a "heavenly" place of worship because it was built with human hands.

19. I define "temple" in a theological and somewhat abstract manner: as a designated place of Yahweh worship where his presence could dwell, even if temporarily and contingently, while at the same time anticipating a final climactic temple that would ensure God's presence could dwell permanently among his covenant people as found in Leviticus 26:12; Jeremiah 32:38; Ezekiel 37:27; and 2 Corinthians 6:16.

20. My phraseology here is an expansion of what Leithart (2013, 119) thinks may be possible to ascertain from sanctuary or tabernacle typology.

21. The use of τοῦ σώματος in John 2:21 is an epexegetical genitive that defines "the temple" as none other than Jesus' "body."

22. References to Jesus identifying his resurrected body as a raised temple include Matthew 26:60b–61; Mark 14:57–58; 15:29–30; John 2:18–22.

23. Kerr 2002, 373.

24. McGraw (2012, 24) discusses the importance of using "clearer passages" to interpret more obscure ones within typological studies of the Old Testament.

25. For biblical texts that identify God as "Spirit" and not a corporeal body, see Isaiah 28:5–6; 31:3; 1 Samuel 16:7; 1 Kings 18:27; John 4:24.

26. Cyril of Alexandria (2014, 92) argues that John 2:19 implies that "there were two natures. If a mixture had arisen, then neither would God have remained God nor would the temple be recognized as a temple."

27. The debate over the authorship of the Gospel of John is vast since the text itself does not identify its author. For the conclusion that the author was "a disciple of Jesus but not one of the Twelve," see Bauckham 2007, 37. A recent thesis by Furlong (2020, 173) argues that the author was a disciple of Jesus named John the Elder.

28. For a brief discussion of gender, the Trinity, and language, see Bray 2012, 190–91.

29. Thiselton 2015, 34.

30. See Duby's (2022, 224) engagement with Aquinas' conclusion that the Spirit is "said to confer grace, sanctification, and sonship" (see Luke 1:35; Rom. 1:4; 8:15–16; 1 Cor. 12:4; Gal. 4:6).

31. Additionally, Daniel (8:25) has another reference to a victory that comes about "by no human hand" in his interpretation of the vision from the angel Gabriel.

32. Clements (1965, 3) comments that the ANE religions often had a sacred mountain which was "the symbol, or representation of the cosmos which formed the true abode of the deity whom men worshipped." Miller (1994, 92) points to parallel texts in the Old Testament that are associated with Yahweh and a sacred mountain in Isaiah 2:2 and Micah 4:1.

33. Beale 2004, 152, also 144; Beale 2008, 193.

34. Whitlark 2022, 370.

35. Morales (2012, 1) argues that "dwelling in the divine Presence" is "the kernel of [the Bible's] principal theme."

36. Any references to "scripture" should be understood to refer to the Christian canon of the Old Testament and the New Testament unless the immediate context is more specific.

37. Dodson 2016, 133.

38. Here, I draw from the discussion of redemption and divine revelation by Vos 2003, 6, and Reymond 1998, 408.

39. For a similar line of argumentation, in which there are multiple divine intentions in the atonement, see Hammett 2015, 149.

40. This phrase is a riff on the definition of human "intention" or "reason(s)" as defined by Finnis (1992, 134–35): "giving ground for intelligent action motivated ultimately by a basic human good (more precisely, by the intelligible benefit promised by the instantiation of a basic good)."

41. Athanasius viewed God's love for humanity as central to the motivation for incarnation (Gemeinhardt 2011, 329).

42. Reymond 1998, 550.

43. Reymond 1998, 550.

44. Thiselton 2015, 237.

45. On the substitutionary sacrifice of Jesus' life through his death as an intentional part of the incarnation, see Cole 2013, 122; Oden 1992, 271.

46. Schönborn 2010, 67.

47. Spong 1992, 217. For a discussion of the view that Jesus had to be protected from the concupiscence of sex based on desire, see Shenk 2016, 46.

48. For a historical discussion, see Letham 2019, 488, and Shenk 2016, 56–57. Pannenberg demurs on this point, stating: "Though Jesus was sinless from the beginning of his life, the point of the virgin birth narrative in the New Testament is *not* that it enabled Jesus to begin life sinless or impeccable." For Pannenberg, Jesus' sinlessness "is not an incapability for evil that belongs naturally to his humanity but results only from his entire process of life" (Duby 2022, 299–300).

49. The Confession of the Evangelical Free Church of Geneva, Article V (1848) states:

> We believe that the Word, which was of all eternity with God, and which was God, was made flesh, and that, alone among men, Jesus, a second Adam, born from a virgin by the power of the Most High, has been able to obey God in a perfect way. (Schaff 1882, 782)

50. For a discussion of Anselm's view of the virgin birth, see Shenk 2016, 73.

51. Cole 2013, 122.

52. Bavinck 2006, 289.

53. On Paul and his knowledge of Jesus, see Perrin 2010, 2.

54. Reymond 1998, 552.

55. Reymond 1998, 552.

56. For a discussion of the purpose related to destroying demonic powers, see Cole 2013, 122; Oden 1992, 271. Shenk (2016, 116) suggests the unprovable theory that one of the ways in which Satan was destroyed was through a fully human and fully divine incarnation that concealed God's redemptive plans.

57. For a full discussion of God's intention to redeem those under the law through the incarnation, see Cole 2013, 125–26.

58. Shenk (2016, 136–37) points to more specific ways in which Mary's act of bearing the God-man reversed the status of women in salvation-history and "redeemed women."

59. Schönborn 2010, 68.

60. Bavinck 2006, 290.

61. Reymond (1998, 552) argues that "before everything else" the virginal conception was the means by which "God became man."

62. A point also noted by Erickson (1998, 760).

63. A point made by Duby (2022, 36).

64. On the history of the Apostles' Creed, see Kelly 2006, 101–102.

65. For a Roman Catholic view of the "Immaculate Conception," see Pope Pius IX, *Ineffabilis Deus* (December 8, 1854). Wright (1992, 77) comments that the virginal conception of Jesus should not be "confused with the Roman Catholic doctrine of the 'immaculate conception' of Mary herself. That doctrine states that, when Mary herself was conceived, she was entirely free of original sin."

66. On this point, see Reymond 1998, 550.

67. For the argument that constructive theology should "construct new concepts" of the divine, see Lakeland and Jones 2005, 19–20.

Part I

PROLEGOMENA

Chapter 1

The Virgin Birth and Theological Grammar

One of the questions that the early church had to wrestle with was: "How, then, should we speak of God as born of a woman?"[1] The present study makes no pretense about answering this question in any comprehensive way. It is for good reason that the second-century bishop Ignatius of Antioch identified "the virginity of Mary" as a mystery "wrought in the stillness of God" (*IEph* 19.1). Even of normal human conception, the preacher of Ecclesiastes says, "As you do not know the way the spirit comes to the bones in the womb of a woman with child, so you do not know the work of God who makes everything" (Eccles. 11:5).[2] Such statements only illuminate how difficult it is to engage with questions surrounding the necessity of Jesus' virgin birth in the womb of Mary.

Nevertheless, identifying the centrality of this question for Christian orthodoxy establishes the need to formulate a common set of signs—a shared ecclesiastical language—that would facilitate discussion about potential answers. Answering this question requires a thorough consideration of how theology communicates. This means paying careful attention to how information is encoded, how terms are defined, and how arguments are constructed.[3] This chapter uses the concept of theological grammar to approach these foundational matters.

The notion of theology as "grammar" draws from the Lutheran-Wittgenstein-like metaphor that relates the two. Ludwig Wittgenstein famously wrote that "Grammar tells us what kind of object anything is (Theology as grammar)."[4] When applied to the present study, the notion of theology as "grammar" focuses on both object and event—Jesus and the virgin birth. Ludwig Wittgenstein's diary from February 1937 indicates that at that point he understood this with the following consideration: "Luther had written that theology is the 'grammar of the word of God,' of the holy scripture."[5] Wittgenstein conceptualized the theological task of constructive dogmatics as an act of communicating or "telling." But acts of "telling" require communicative signals which tell the reader what kind of story or prose to expect: for example, genre signifiers such as "long ago . . ." For the purposes of this study, "theological grammar" refers to dogmatic constructions and propositions that are rooted in Christian orthodoxy and tell the reader about the words and works of God. This concept of "theological grammar" becomes a fitting way to describe the set of prolegomena for the categorical syllogism at hand.

This chapter, as well as the three chapters that follow, offers some foundational explanations for the argument about the relationship between a dogmatic consideration of the virgin birth and temple Christology. These chapters establish expectations for the "telling" of the argument at hand as they explain some methodological considerations. Within the present chapter, the following four sections elaborate on: (1) the need for theological grammar, (2) the trajectory beyond creedal orthodoxy, (3) the relationship of the argument to scripture, and then (4) the location of this study in a framework of salvation-history.

THE NEED FOR THEOLOGICAL GRAMMAR

The difficulty of explaining how Jesus, the divine Son of God, was born to a human mother gave birth to centuries of debate. On the one hand, this is inexplicable. On the other hand, the scriptures provide details about it. This tension requires the pursuit of theological grammar or the ability of human language to partially explain such a great mystery. By recounting the doctrinal and theological issues involved, it is evident that the church must pursue a common theological grammar as it seeks to elucidate the truths of scripture, especially the incarnation of the Son of God. This section describes how the virgin birth has always been included in summary statements of the church's orthodox doctrine and dogmas. However, a brief survey will also demonstrate that such *proclamations* have not always been accompanied by *explanations* that might elucidate why Jesus had to be born to the virgin Mary.

Early Creeds and Councils

This section draws attention to two features of theology in the early centuries of the Christian church: (1) the prominence given to the relationship between Mary and Jesus and (2) the inclusion of the virgin birth of Jesus in summary statements of the church's catholic doctrine.

The early ecumenical councils dealt with the nature and status of Mary as they sought to present a unified, logical, and biblical doctrine of Christ and to condemn heresy. Mary's role in relation to Christology and Trinitarian orthodoxy became prominent as the third-century Alexandrian and Antioch schools debated the use of *theotokos* ("God-bearer"). Nestorius (*ca.* AD 386–450) was hesitant to use this term because it seemed to come at the expense of Jesus' humanity. The Alexandrians, such as Cyril (*c.* 375–444), were hesitant to drop the term *theotokos* or accept an alternative such as *christotokos* ("Christ-bearer") for fear of losing Jesus' divinity.[6] Such concerns about Mary were revived during the Reformation, and some Protestants sought to restrict Mary's role to that of "Son-bearer." The importance of the hypostatic union of Jesus' human and divine natures became solidified in the first four ecumenical councils (Nicea in 325, Constantinople I in 381, Ephesus in 431, and Chalcedon in 451).[7] I do not intend to solve any historical debates about Mary's role or title but only to highlight that there is a need for careful theological grammar when dealing with the various aspects of the incarnation.

For the church catholic, the language of the hypostatic union from the Chalcedonian confession offers the best solution to the union of the immutable God with the undiminished human nature in Jesus. This essential and eternal union of the divine Logos with a human nature is "contingent" because "the Logos would still be the second person of the Trinity apart from the incarnation."[8] Chalcedonian language emphasized the indivisibility of the two natures of Christ based on distinction but not separation (*distinctio sed non separatio*).[9] The hypostatic union is to be distinguished but not separated from the related doctrine of the virgin birth. Charles Lee Feinberg succinctly stated, "the hypostatic union is that which was effected and brought into being by the incarnation."[10] Feinberg further explains: "The incarnation and the hypostatic union are coextensive as to time."[11] Thus, there is a logical but not chronological distinction between the incarnation and the hypostatic union.

It is especially noteworthy that every major creed of the early church includes some kind of statement about Jesus being born of the virgin Mary. The act of assumption about the supernatural conception of Jesus is understood to be an act of confession, a recitation of a belief that the church has always held because it is taught in scripture. The doctrine of the virgin birth appears in the Apostles' Creed, establishing it as a truly catholic doctrine, held by all orthodox Christians across church history:

> I believe in Jesus Christ, his only Son, our Lord, *who was conceived by the Holy Spirit and born of the virgin Mary.*[12]

The Apostles' Creed arguably established a strong confessional connection between the virgin birth and Christology, even if the doctrine was left largely unexplained. Even Justin Martyr's (*ca.* AD 100–165) formulation of the virgin birth within his *Dialogue with Trypho* is largely confessional:

> "My friend," said Trypho, "you have proved your point with much force and copious arguments. Now prove to us that He condescended to become man *by a virgin*, in accordance with His Father's will, and to be crucified, and to die; show us, too, that He arose from the dead and ascended into Heaven."[13] (*Dial.* 63)

The theology of the virgin birth of Jesus is echoed in the other major early creeds as well:

> I believe . . . in one Lord Jesus Christ . . . Who, for us men for our salvation, came down from heaven, *and was incarnate by the Holy Spirit of the virgin Mary*, and was made man. (The Nicene Creed)

> We, then, . . . confess . . . one and the same Son, our Lord Jesus Christ . . . begotten before all ages of the Father according to the Godhead, and in these latter days, for us and for our salvation, *born of the Virgin Mary*, the mother of God, according to the Manhood; one and the same Christ, Son, Lord, Only-begotten, to be acknowledged in two natures, inconfusedly, unchangeably, indivisibly, inseparably. (The Symbol of Chalcedon)

The one exception to this pattern is the Athanasian Creed, which does not explicitly refer to the "virgin birth" of Jesus but does affirm his full divinity and full humanity:

> And the catholic faith is this . . . we believe and confess that our Lord Jesus Christ, the Son of God, is God and man. God of the substance of the Father, begotten before the worlds; *and man of substance of His mother*, born in the world. Perfect God and perfect man, of a reasonable soul and human flesh subsisting. (The Athanasian Creed)

The dogma of the virgin birth has been explicated through confessions and the precise use of technical language that preserves Trinitarian orthodoxy. The mode of these types of creedal formulations is synchronic, being primarily systematic, philosophical, or apologetic in nature. This ecclesial and confessional language regarding Mary and the virgin birth is helpful, and the earliest ecumenical councils offer a baseline for Christian unity in the church. However, the church has never recognized these confessions to be the final word on theological formulation. Moreover, these confessional formulations often lack explicit engagement with redemptive-historical categories, such as temple Christology.

The difficulties attending the virgin birth may also have been pushed to the background by the need to consider Jesus' claim to divinity: that he was the "eternal Word of the Father" (e.g., John 1:1). In this vein, Oliver O'Donovan considers the difficulties of the virgin birth to be merely "symptomatic" when compared with the need to consider that God was in Christ, revealing his eternal pre-existence to humanity.[14]

While apologetic presentations of this doctrine have undeniable value for maintaining orthodoxy, the task of Christian dogmatics is to constructively integrate the doctrine into a full-orbed understanding of the whole Bible. Thus, this present study assumes the supernatural account in which a virgin woman became pregnant with Jesus by the Holy Spirit without any sexual activity with a male. This study makes no attempt to function as an apologetic for the virgin birth but rather assumes it as a foundational belief upon which other theological arguments are based. The importance of the apologetic task is not being dismissed altogether. Rather, a presuppositional approach must be used in order to consider the potential reasons for the event that the church catholic confesses.

The important point here is that the earliest Christian creeds and councils identified the doctrine of the virgin birth of Jesus as important, fundamental, or basic for the shared ecclesiastical language of faith. The doctrine of the virgin birth has always been central to the church catholic, even if it was rarely explained *why* it was important or *how* it exactly related to other doctrines.

PROTESTANT AND REFORMED CONFESSIONS

The need for theological grammar and the use of carefully construed language arises from the history of controversy about Mary's role in the incarnation and from the way in which Protestant and later Reformed confessions have *proclaimed* the virgin birth without *explaining* it.

The difficulty with the virgin birth of Jesus is evident by the way that Protestant and Reformed confessional references to the event simply restate the words of scripture, often without further explanation or development. Positively, this draws attention to the ways in which the Reformers of various countries and even generations sought to follow the pattern as found in the Nicene Creed, which simply states that Jesus "was incarnate by the Holy Spirit of the Virgin Mary, and was made man, and was crucified also for us under Pontius Pilate."[15] However, for all of the doctrinal clarity and developments brought about by the Protestant Reformation and post-Reformation eras, this particular doctrine was left largely untouched. The following confessions of the sixteenth century demonstrate this to be the case:

The Protestant Irish Articles of Religion from 1516 (article XXIX) identify Mary's role as the one providing the human nature or "substance" for the joining of Jesus' divine nature with a human nature:

> The Son, which is the Word of the Father, begotten from everlasting of the Father, the true and eternal God—of one substance with the Father—*took man's nature in the womb of the blessed Virgin, of her substance*, so that two whole and perfect natures—that is to say, the Godhead and manhood— were inseparably joined in one person, making one Christ very God and very man.[16]

The Tetrapolitan Confession of 1530, from the four cities of Strasburg, Konstanz, Memingen, and Lindau and written by Martin Bucer and Wolfgang Capito, avers in chapter 2 that a Christian is one who:

> believes concerning our Saviour Jesus Christ, *conceived of the Holy Ghost, then born of the Virgin Mary*, and who at length after he had performed the office of preaching the Gospel, having died on the cross.[17]

Next, The First Confession of Basel from 1534, article IV "Concerning Christ, True God and True Man," reads:

> Concerning this Jesus Christ, we believe that *he was conceived by the Holy Spirit, born of the pure, undefiled Virgin Mary*, suffered under Pontius Pilate, was crucified and died for our sins.[18]

Additionally, the Confession of Faith Used in the English Congregation at Geneva, 1556, confesses in article II:

> When the fullness of time was come, He was *conceived by the power of the Holy Ghost, born of the Virgin Mary, according to the flesh*, and preached on earth the Gospel of salvation.[19]

Likewise, the Scots Confession of Faith of 1560, article VI, states:

> When the fulness of time came God sent His Son, his Eternal Wisdom, the substance of His own glory, into this world, *who took the nature of humanity from the substance of a woman, a virgin, by means of the Holy Ghost*.[20]

The pattern of confessing the virgin birth by repeating selections of scripture continued into the post-Reformation era of the seventeenth century. In one example, the early Calvinistic confession of the English Baptists from

1646 (article IX) attributes the incarnation to Mary and the Holy Spirit alone but is content to simply restate the words of scripture in Luke 1:35:

> who also when the fulness of time was come, was made man of a woman, of the Tribe of Judah, of the seed of Abraham and David, to wit, of the virgin Mary, *the Holy Spirit coming down upon her, the power of the Most High overshadowing her;* and He was also tempted as we are, yet without sin.[21]

The Westminster Confession of Faith, as drawn up by the Westminster Assembly in 1646, chapter VIII, article 2, also draws from the standard set of source texts of Luke 1:27, 31, 35 and Galatians 4:4:

> when the fulness of time was come, take upon him man's nature, with all the essential properties and common infirmities thereof, yet without sin; *being conceived by the power of the Holy Ghost, in the womb of the Virgin Mary*, of her substance.[22]

The London Baptist Confession of 1689, which drew influence from the Westminster Confession of Faith, follows the same pattern in article VII:

> being *conceived by the Holy Spirit in the Womb of the Virgin Mary, the Holy Spirit coming down upon her, and the power of the most High overshadowing her*, and so was made of a Woman, of the Tribe of Judah, of the Seed of Abraham, and David according to the Scriptures.[23]

There is a range of Protestant confessions, including radical Reformers such as Baptists, which are content to simply restate the words of scripture when describing the virgin birth of Jesus. The best term to describe the approach of gathering together various biblical texts from Luke and Galatians might be "composite citations," as the confessional articles reflect a collection of organized scriptural information.[24] The broad Reformation tradition generally did not develop or explain the doctrine of the virgin birth beyond that which is found in the Apostles' Creed.

This brief survey of prominent confessions draws attention to the way in which they simply used scripture to define and explain the virgin birth apart from explanation. There is an important sense in which scripture must be used to define and interpret scripture. The danger lies in using scripture simplistically or thinly so that prooftexts are used where there could be more robust explanation. The case against the virgin birth and its proclamation in church history here must not be overstated. Many lengthy Protestant confessions, such as the Anglican Thirty-Nine Articles, locate the virgin birth within a larger series of "narrative movements" about Christ, including his incarnation, life, suffering, crucifixion, death, resurrection, and ascension.[25] Such an approach gives context and balance to summaries of the life of Christ meant for ecclesiastical confession. At the same time, there is warrant for pursuing a more robust doctrine of the virgin birth.

MODERNIST AND CONTEMPORARY CONTROVERSIES

The belief in the supernatural virgin birth became a linchpin issue of the Fundamentalist–Modernist controversies of the early nineteenth century. In the midst of the nineteenth century modernist controversies over the historicity of the virgin birth, apologists defended the doctrine as being confessed by the church at large since the second century.[26] But the move to affirm the supernatural character of the incarnation and agree with the creeds and confessions of the church catholic did not always result in doctrinal explication.[27] The result is that the doctrine of the virgin birth is sometimes viewed as unnecessary, isolated, and idiosyncratic.

It is strange that a doctrine that has been repeated so often throughout the creeds of the church since at least the second century should sometimes be considered *not* a "matter of great importance."[28] Along this trajectory, Kyle Roberts argues that the virgin birth is not essential but even detrimental to the Christian faith. He argues, "The resurrection represents the culmination of the incarnation, while the virgin birth stands outside of and runs against its logic. In an ultimate sense, the virgin birth offers neither hope nor healing. The resurrection offers both."[29]

The view that the virgin birth is rather inconsequential may be held by confessional theologians who still find little exegetical data to support the doctrine. For example, Millard Erickson argues that "A close reading will find nothing in Paul's writings or speeches that deals directly with the question of the virgin birth."[30] Erickson dismisses the reference to Jesus being "born" in Galatians 4:4 as based on arguments that "do not carry much weight."[31]

Because of views such as these, Christoph Schönborn laments that modern theology regards "the Incarnation as just a secondary statement."[32] His lamentation serves as a direct response to views such as those found in Kyle Roberts. Together with Schönborn, this present study affirms that Christmas must stand on the same ground as Easter. As Schönborn states of Christmas and Easter: "Yet in fact the two belong together, each unthinkable without the other. Both are central for Christology, as for theology in general, like the two focal points of an ellipse."[33]

The catholic and confessional view of the virgin birth continues to be assailed by those who privilege Enlightenment claims about the impossibility of such miracles. For example, a contemporary attack upon the historicity of the virgin birth postulates that the confessional view of the historical and miraculous virgin birth is effectively a gnostic view of Jesus. This view argues that:

> The assumption that Jesus's origin had to have been supernatural betrays a fundamental suspicion that human nature was beneath God's dignity. Jesus simply had to come from God and not from or through the indignity of natural, human procreation.[34]

However, the suggestion that the virgin birth is gnostic and therefore undermines Jesus' real humanity is at odds with Paul's view of Jesus' identity as the Last Adam (1 Cor. 15:22), among others. Such an argument against the virgin birth also relegates all of the scriptures that refer to it as gnostic, including the whole of 1 Corinthians, Matthew, and Luke. If these scriptures are theologically and historically unsound regarding Jesus' birth, then there cannot be a stable concept of canonical Christian orthodoxy.[35]

At this point, it is helpful to consider John Webster's "diagnosis" of problems with the concept of divine revelation and Christian history.[36] He points out that pre-critical or pre-modern theology was essentially confessional in the sense that it was concerned with proclaiming God's character, purposes, and requirements to humanity. As such, it did not typically answer questions about claims to knowledge or the justification of knowledge. With the rise of the modern period and the Enlightenment, theology was assigned "a job in apologetics."[37] In a nutshell, theology moved from "assumption to argument."[38]

John Webster's sweeping assessment of 2000 years of historical theology is surely vulnerable to the rejoinder that it is too neat and tidy. However, his thesis fits well with the doctrine of the virgin birth, which was often and loudly proclaimed in ecclesiastical settings and writ large in confessions such as the Apostles' Creed, all the while being largely unexplained. It is also noteworthy that the liturgical use of creedal proclamation and catechesis is itself a reflection of a kind of experiential and implicit argument: only those things which are necessary for faith are given such a priority. Yet it is true that when the virgin birth was set forth in doctrinal summaries such as confessional statements, it was mostly done with the same words of scripture without any further explanation.

The history of the Christian church, with its various creeds and confessions of faith, has always attested to the truth of the virgin birth of Jesus. This doctrine has a strong catholic history of *proclamation* but is not typically offered with robust accompanying *explanation*. Whatever explanation might be offered must engage with the information that scripture does provide and with the long history of difficulty surrounding the relationship between Mary and Jesus. Thus, a word of qualification is in order: the pursuit of doctrinal development through new dogmatic formulations does not necessitate the relativizing of the fundamental Christian doctrines.[39] The church must confess the virgin birth even as it confesses Easter but such confessional proclamation must not come at the expense of explication. The act of constructive systematic theology as found in this present study attempts to fill some of this gap by explaining what the Bible means when it describes this miraculous event.[40]

With respect to the doctrine of the virgin birth, it has always been proclaimed by the church catholic, even if it has not been explained. This lacuna means there is room to go *beyond* the church's creeds and confessions, without going *against* them. Previous engagements with the doctrine of the virgin birth have also centered on attempts to answer critical questions, such as Anselm of Canterbury's famous work *Cur Deus Homo* (Latin for "*Why a God Man?*"). There are more questions to pose, and these often provide different angles on centuries-old debates.[41] This present study suggests that the following question provides such purchase: why did Jesus-the-temple need to have a virgin mother? Centuries of debate about these types of questions draw attention to the need for precise grammar in order to communicate clearly and effectively. The salient point here is that church history indicates that there is room for fresh and constructive integration between the doctrine of the virgin birth and temple Christology.

DOGMATICS AND THE GRAMMAR OF THE CREEDS

Christian dogmatics that aims at being useful for the church catholic must reflect the collective voice of the church through careful attendance to her creeds. Following this framework, this study assumes a supernatural perspective of the virgin birth throughout.[42] The use of creeds and confessions in this study is understood to be liberating rather than restraining. This means that the theological reasoning of this study attempts to go *beyond* the Nicene-Chalcedonian creeds but not *against* them. The Reformed Protestant use of the analogy of faith (*analogia fidei* or *analogia Scripturae*) means that interpreters should avoid reading a biblical text "in such a way that it contradicts the received body of doctrine that has been derived from scripture," especially as it relates to the Apostles' Creed, the Nicene Creed, and the Athanasius Creed.[43]

This is not a rejection of the Protestant principle of *sola Scriptura* but an affirmation that the Bible should not be interpreted in a historical vacuum.[44] The selection of clearer passages of scripture is used to interpret the typological significance of passages that are more obscure. By beginning with a consideration of clear textual units within the Christian canon, this chapter applies the principle of theological interpretation in which scripture is interpreted with scripture.[45]

When the Apostle Paul wrote to the church at Corinth (1 Cor. 4:6): "do not go beyond what is written," he was referring to scripture and not the church's confessions. However, a true confession will simply and clearly restate what the scriptures already say or draw out the important elements which are of "good and necessary consequence."[46] While acknowledging that heresy is the "itch for something new," it is also true that our understanding of the virgin birth may still be enriched by further integration of church dogma with biblical theology.[47] We must go beyond what the church has written in the confessions as we seek to conceptualize ("faith seeking understanding") what God has written in the canon.[48]

Using the language of Christian creeds and confessions, even post-Reformation ones, reflects the fact that all theology is contextual in nature, revealing the texts and traditions within one's domain.[49] The use of confessional grammar makes these contexts explicit and accessible to others, thus avoiding radical subjectivity. An additional benefit is that the use of historical confessions roots theology in the life and work of the church over the centuries, helping it to avoid faddishness and folly.

The use of creeds in Christian dogmatics must also be sectarian to some extent because they make explicit refutations and exclusions, both implicitly and explicitly. For example, in the case of non-confessional Modernists, the "virgin birth" was likely an attempt to provide affirmation to a young woman who was seduced or raped in order to preserve her social status because the child was illegitimate.[50] A creedal or confessional approach to the virgin birth excludes a priori such possibilities.

The consistent reference to the virgin birth in Reformed confessions reflects the fact that this event is clearly taught in scripture. Nor is it subject to the claim that it is a doctrine based on a unique and debated passage which is difficult to understand. The clarity with which this event is described in scripture presents it as a touchpoint for faith and obedience. The doctrine of the virgin birth stands in tension because of its role in ancient and catholic doctrine that was regularly confessed and because it does not play a prima facie role in New Testament theology—if one were to assess it only on the basis of explicit repetition.[51] It is true that this event is not mentioned by Paul as essential to the Gospel in 1 Corinthians 15:1–6, but this does not mean the virgin birth may be dismissed without serious implications.

For the church catholic, the act of denying the virgin birth places one outside of the normative boundaries of the ancient Apostles' and Nicene-Chalcedonian creeds.[52] This is significant because the ancient creeds, as well as modern confessions, simply restate the words of scripture in the form of a composite citation. In other words, the intentional denial of the historicity of the virgin birth *is* the denial of the trustworthiness of scripture regarding the account of Jesus' birth.[53] Intentional denial (not ignorance) of the historicity of the virgin birth relates to the discipleship of the risen Lord Jesus because it would untether belief from the scriptures as confessed by the church catholic.

With this background in mind, the present study seeks to go *beyond*, but not *against*, the Apostles' Creed and the Nicene-Chalcedonian confessions. It does so with the aim of being confessional in the sense of offering faithful proclamation *and* of being explicatory as it seeks to ground its theology in reasoned articulations about divine revelation.

DOGMATICS AND THE GRAMMAR OF SCRIPTURE

Christian dogmatics must continually return to, listen to, and follow the grammar of scripture. The image of the spiral so frequently used in hermeneutics can also be utilized by systematic theology as it pursues this type of speaking.[54] This spiral-like movement ideally moves through scripture, history, reason, confessional theology, ecclesial proclamation, and back to scripture again. Constructive work in theology must build on the scriptures and not on human reason alone. The power of the Holy Spirit is required to accurately understand and apply the scriptures and to avoid a vicious circle of interpretation that is never open to being challenged by the scripture itself.[55] The task of constructive dogmatics must use the language of scripture when and where it is possible so that the church might learn to speak its own language clearly.

While some have construed the proto-Trinitarian language of the scriptures to be the "raw data" with which the church has developed the doctrine of the Trinity, there is an alternative perspective. Scott Swain succinctly states, "The relationship between the Trinity in the Bible and the Trinity in the creeds is similar to the relationship between a fluent speaker of a language and the theoretical grammar of that language."[56] Swain draws on the works of Richard B. Hays and Oswald Bayer, who urge the church to see the Bible's language as God's self-disclosure and not merely as the "raw data" that the creeds and confessions have built upon.[57] Swain concludes that such an encouragement directs the church to avoid the conclusion that the confessions are an "improvement" on the language of scripture and that the church must "*follow* the divine Word."[58] This study agrees with this sentiment and offers an additional point: the integration of themes such as temple Christology with the doctrine of the virgin birth can hopefully enrich the church's orthodoxy.

Following the divine Word means following the contours of salvation-history as they ebb and flow through the canon of scripture according to creation, the Fall, redemption, and consummation.[59] This present study seeks to offer such a diachronically sensitive integration by considering how the virgin birth relates to themes and structural ideas from scripture as they are located in the storyline of scripture. The Old Testament and the New Testament form a unified canon that shares thematic and theological unity. Thus, the Old Testament "is not simply *background* to the gospel; it is part of the very fabric" of the New Testament's presentation of Jesus as Israel's messiah.[60] This mode of presentation is not *synchronic* but *diachronic*, as it develops the relationship of key events with other advancements across salvation-history.[61]

This diachronic reading of scripture is also dialectic or conversational in nature as it reads the Old Testament in the light of the New Testament and the New Testament in light of the Old Testament.[62] The entire Old Testament might be likened to a dimly lit room or a reality that remains behind a veil until the death, resurrection, and ascension of Christ is ascertained through the Pentecost power of the Spirit. On the one hand, the Trinity is ontologically present in the Old Testament as it is in the New Testament.[63] The same Triune God is the same throughout the whole canon of scripture. On the other hand, the canon of scripture reflects progressive and escalating revelation that increases in clarity as it moves from type to antitype, from shadow to reality.

Practically speaking, this approach requires reading the Bible forward and backward.[64] The very prologue of Luke's Gospel (1:1) suggests as much when it describes itself as "a narrative of the things that have been accomplished among us."[65] The prologue of the epistle to the Hebrews (1:1) also sets the words of the prophets in dialogue with the final "word" of Jesus.[66] For those who believe Jesus is the messiah (the implied reader of scripture), the multitude of passages about God's redemptive plan and their associations with temples (and places of Yahweh worship) arguably lend themselves to "retrospective messianic interpretations."[67] In other words, Jesus' life, death, and resurrection offer a lens for a coherent explanation of certain patterns, themes, and motifs in scripture. Yet care must be taken to maintain basic grammatical-historical interpretation so that scripture might be read forward as well and avoid eisegesis.

A diachronic reading of the entire canon of Christian scripture enables the reader to consider how Old Testament persons, places, events, and institutions typologically look forward to the fulfillment of God's promises through Christ.[68] The act of drawing theological conclusions from typological relationships across the Christian canon is not merely the employment of a reading strategy but rather it is understood to be an exegetical exercise that draws out relationships that God intended through human authors.

DOGMATICS AND THE GRAMMAR OF SALVATION-HISTORY

The present study seeks to follow the grammar of scripture when attending to the question: how should we speak of God born of a woman? As the previous section explained, this includes the process of the hermeneutical circle and the recognition of typological patterns of meaning across the Christian scriptures that include persons, events, and institutions. As this study continues to consider Jesus-the-temple within a theological framework, this requires a change in grammar that moves from salvation-historical categories for Christology and utilizes them for constructive and dogmatic purposes. Specifically, this present study aims to use the category of "temple Christology" within the theological argument for the necessity of the virgin birth.

This intentional change in grammar is essentially the practice of changing "languages" from biblical studies to systematic theology and is metaphorically analogous to what is typically called "code-switching" in linguistics.[69] This "code-switching" of terms allows this study to move the conversation from the domain of New Testament studies to the domain of Christian dogmatics. Here, code-switching means that terms from one field are being utilized in another related field. Whereas instances of the term "temple Christology" might be expected to be references to Johannine studies (or similar), they refer here to a dogmatic aspect of Christology when contextually appropriate.

The term "temple Christology" is almost exclusively associated with the Gospel of John, as Jesus fulfills the symbolism surrounding the Jewish background of the temple. One could even argue that "temple Christology" is "a central theme in the Fourth Gospel."[70] Beyond the theme of the temple, Tom Thatcher observes that many of John's metaphors, such as Jesus being "the river of life," "the light of the world," "the good shepherd," or the "resurrection and the life," all "explicitly compare Jesus to the beliefs and institutions of Judaism."[71] Thatcher further comments that many analogies between Jesus and the temple are "currently at the forefront of academic debate."[72] What is certain is that New Testament authors such as John viewed Jesus as the fulfillment of Israel's religious institutions and festivals.

Within this perspective are debates about whether the place of the Jerusalem temple has enduring eschatological significance, either in this age or the age to come.[73] Some stress Jesus as *replacing* the temple.[74] After Jesus' exaltation and glorification upon the cross, there "is no substitute for the temple other than Jesus himself."[75] According to this view of "fulfillment Christology" in the Gospel of John, the physical location of Yahweh worship, such as the Tabernacle and the temple, are now inadequate because "Jesus is now the proper focus of worship."[76] Another view has Jesus *fulfilling* the temple in Jerusalem but not replacing it.[77] Middling views are also possible for those who consider Jesus "to be *like* the temple—serving similar religious functions but certainly not all of the Temple's functions."[78]

For the purposes of this present study, the focus is not on ascertaining the possibility of a return to "place" within the framework of various future eschatological stages.[79] Rather, the focus is on the way in which the construction of typologically significant places of worship is fulfilled in Christ but also continues to prophetically function as "shadows" that inform the theology of the virgin birth. The logic of the categorical syllogism and the argument about the necessity of the virgin birth by the divine hand of God are compatible with a range of nuanced views about Jesus' relationship to the Jerusalem temple. Strictly speaking, the argument of this volume would be compatible with any view that sees Jesus as the eternal locus of God's personal presence among his people.

Jesus' identity as a temple is defined in this study as a dogmatic term sensitive to salvation-historical dynamics across the Christian scriptures. Specifically, this involves drawing connections between the use of primitive altars by the patriarchs Abraham, Isaac, and Jacob, as well as the tabernacle and Solomon's temple. This broad relationship between altars, the tabernacle, and the temple is justified on account of at least three facts. First, primitive altars for Yahweh worship provided the occasion for theophanies of God's special presence, often set in relation to a mountain.[80] This includes the particularly noteworthy occasion of Abraham building an altar for Isaac on Mount Moriah in Genesis 22. Even Jacob's stone pillar of remembrance is described as "God's house" (Gen. 28:22, 35:3, 7).[81] Eventually, these theophanies were centralized in Moses' mediation for Israel through the tabernacle and then physically finalized in the temple. Second, the physical site of Abraham's altar on Mount Moriah became the location where Solomon built the temple in Jerusalem (see 2 Chr. 3:1). Even the floor plan of the temple was similar to the tabernacle.[82] Third, the elements of the tabernacle were themselves physically integrated into the building of Solomon's temple.[83] This means that we may justifiably subsume altars and the tabernacle within the larger umbrella of "temple Christology" because these locations of Yahweh worship functioned as antecedents of each other that progressively developed over salvation-history.[84]

The biblical foundations for establishing a dogmatic term of "temple Christology" are found throughout the New Testament. The concept of Jesus' incarnate body being a temple is present, for example, in the Gospel of John (1:14; 2:21), even if it is not greatly developed.[85] A related concept of "temple Christology" is also found in Matthew (Chapters 24–25), who uses Jesus' words and body to contest the fixed sacred and social space of the Jerusalem temple so that it is replaced with the fluid space of Jesus' body.[86] In Acts 3, the Jerusalem temple is shorn of its privileges and claim to Yahweh's sacred space as these are "transferred to the heavenly Christ."[87] The Jerusalem temple only retains its status as a holy place if and when it points to beyond itself to Jesus as Israel's Lord and Savior.[88] Alan Thompson points out "that the only activity Luke records the believers doing in the temple in this context is proclaiming Jesus (Acts 4:2; 5:20, 25, 42)."[89]

The theological terms "temple Christology," "Messiah-temple," or "Jesus-the-temple" are interchangeable and defined throughout this study as: Jesus' fully human body being a place where the fullness of the Godhead dwelt since the incarnation. Furthermore, the concept of temple Christology involves understanding Jesus as the consummation and fulfillment of all earthly altars, temples, and places of worship; for it is in and through Jesus that God is truly worshiped, that sacrifice is offered, and that God is glorified. Temple Christology includes altars and the tabernacle within its scope because of the way that these places, buildings, and institutions progressively revealed God's personal presence and his salvific plans. During Jesus' earthly ministry, this temple-body was spatially located on earth. After his resurrection, his human body is eternally established as the true and living temple of God. After the ascension into heaven, Jesus-the-temple is now at the right hand of God the Father until his Second Coming. This brief, working definition of "temple Christology" offers the basis for further discussion about the relationship between Jesus' identity as the temple and the nature of the virgin birth.

SUMMARY

"How, then, should we speak of God as born of a woman?" This question and its answers may have been addressed by the early Christian councils, but the solutions they provided are by no means exhaustive. The Apostles' Creed indicates that the virgin birth was not an optional doctrine, even if its significance was not fully developed. The confessions of the Protestant Reformation do not show any advancement in articulating the significance of the virgin birth, even while asserting its great importance. This situation has led several contemporary theologians to conclude that the virgin birth is optional or unnecessary for Christian faith. The doctrine of the virgin birth remains disconnected and theologically isolated. This chapter offers a platform for fresh consideration of this doctrine by drawing attention to the need for a theological grammar that draws from exegesis and formulates dogmatic conclusions according to catholic Church confessions. Rather than consider the doctrine of the virgin birth as definitively addressed, the church must continue to ask questions about it and consider answers proposed under the authority of scripture.

NOTES

1. For an introduction to this question and the engagement with it by Christians in the earliest centuries, see Hall 2002, 89.

2. Miller (2010, 181) comments,

No one knows how the enlivening wind or breath [*ruaḥ*] comes to the bones in the mother's womb (Eccles. 11:5 NRSV; cf. 12:7). Likewise, the work of God is mysterious, a term that probably is not meant narrowly here of creation, but generally of the way God operates in the world.

3. Leim (2015, 14) discusses how Matthew's "*theo*logical grammar is radically reshaped by his 'fillial' grammar in which Jesus is the recipient of the worship Israel owed to God" (emphasis his). According to Leim, the way that Israel communicated to God had to be changed in light of Jesus' identity. Leim's use of theological interpretation in Matthew offers a helpful way to define and apply the term "theological grammar" in a dogmatic context.

4. Wittgenstein's (2001, §373) famous statement is widely quoted; for a recent analysis, see Moran 2017, 96.

5. Wittgenstein 1999, 90; the English translation of this excerpt is by Nordmann 2001, 166. For a recent discussion, see Kusch 2011, 46.

6. Cyril of Alexandria, who inherited the tradition of Athanasius, states,

for there was a union of the two natures, and this is why we confess One Christ, One Son, One Lord. According to this understanding of the unconfused union we confess that the holy virgin is the Mother of God [*theotokos*], because God was made flesh and became man, and *from the very moment of conception he united to himself the temple* that was taken from her. (*Acta conc. oec.* 1.1.4.17)

For a translation and discussion, see Wessel 2004, 270. On Cyril's development of Athanasius's theology, see Farag 2020, 60; Farag 2007, 124.

7. Torrance contends that patristic theology used the conception of the hypostatic union to work out the relationship between the transcendence of God and the immanency of the incarnation (1969, 79). For a discussion of Aquinas's approval of the Marian appellation of *theotokos,* see White 2015, 20.

8. DeWeese 2007, 114.

9. MacCulloch 2004, 258.

10. Feinberg 1935, 262.

11. Feinberg 1935, 262.

12. English texts were taken from Brannan 2001.

13. Justin Martyr (trans. Falls) 1948, 247, emphasis mine; also see similar references to the virgin birth in *Apol.* 1.63.

14. O'Donovan 2011, 20.

15. "The Nicene Creed," in Cochrane 2003, 303.

16. "The Irish Articles of Religion (1516)" in Schaff 1882, 3:531.

17. "The Tetrapolitan Confession of 1530," in Cochrane 2003, 56–7.

18. "The First Confession of Basel, 1534," in Cochrane 2003, 92.

19. "The Confession of Faith Used in the English Congregation at Geneva, 1556," in Cochrane 2003, 132.

20. "The Scots Confession, 1560," in Cochrane 2003, 168.

21. From "A Confession of Faith of Seven Congregations or Churches of Christ in London, Which are Commonly (but unjustly) Called Anabaptists: The Second Impression Corrected and Enlarged," (1646). The archaic English phrase "to wit" means "that is, namely."

22. Westminster Assembly (1851, 52).

23. McGlothlin 1911, 240. On the Particular Baptists' use of the WCF, see Bingham 2017, 546–69. On the question of whether the 1689 Baptists sought to deny the WCF doctrine of "good and necessary consequences," see the notes in McGraw 2012, 51–2.

24. Here, I draw from the domain of biblical studies and apply it to historical theology, which defines a "composite citation" as the drawing of "one or more source texts together into a single, composite citation," as found in Adams and Ehorn 2016, 1; also see 2–4.

25. O'Donovan (2011, 21) discusses the "narrative movements" of the one story of Christ in the Thirty-Nine Anglican articles.

26. Randolph (1903, vii) stated, "There is no trace in church history, so far as he is aware, of any believers in the Incarnation who were not also believers in the Virgin-Birth." For similar argumentation, see Machen 1930, 4; Hart (1995) offers a historical analysis of Machen and the crisis he confronted.

27. Belief in the historical truth of the virgin birth has been denied since the early church, but also by modern critics such as Adolf von Harnack (Bavinck 2006, 3:286). A modern example would be Spong (1992, 126). Wegner's (2014, 367) review of Lincoln's (2013) volume on the virgin birth points out that he may be within the "parameters of the Church of England," but he still stands contrary to the Apostles' Creed and the even earlier Old Roman Creed.

28. Erickson (1998, 768) avers, "The absence of any reference to the virgin birth is nonetheless of concern to us, for if it is a matter of great importance, it seems strange that Paul did not make more of it." More recently, Clark and Johnson (2015, 19) offer similar sentiments: "modern Christians view the incarnation with something closer to consternation than wonder, and as a result, they tend to push this grandest of realities from the center to the periphery of their confession."

29. Roberts 2017, 185.

30. Erickson 1998, 768.

31. Erickson 1998, 768; similarly, Lincoln 2013, 21.

32. Schönborn 2010, 65.

33. Schönborn 2010, 65–66.

34. Roberts 2017, 185.

35. Giesler (2004, 529) argues that the denial of the virgin birth "though inconsistent and aberrant, does not jeopardize one's salvation." Giesler (2004, 528) qualifies this statement by explaining that "What is implicitly necessary for salvation is not always explicitly so." Paul's pastoral logic about faith in the resurrection from 1 Corinthians 15:14 arguably applies to the virgin birth and could be packaged like this: And if Christ has not been born to a virgin, then our preaching is in vain, and your faith is in vain.

36. This paragraph draws heavily from the points made by Webster 2019, 119–20.

37. Webster 2019, 120.

38. Webster 2019, 120.

39. Here, I seek to expand Daley's (2018, 4) argument that Roman Catholics should pursue a fresh understanding of long-held doctrines through the "raising of questions and sketching of perspectives" by applying it to all Christians.

40. The very definition of doing systematic theology may be said to be explaining "what the Bible means," according to McGraw 2012, 72.

41. For a recent study of the immaculate conception from a Roman Catholic perspective, see Epsen 2016, 560–74.

42. Spong (1992, 126) reflects a contemporary anti-confessional perspective when he states that Mary likely became pregnant with Jesus by rape or seduction.

43. McGraw 2012, 26. Such sentiments are explicitly found, for example, in The Irish Articles of Religion from 1516, article VII:

> All and every the Articles contained in the Nicene Creed, the Creed of Athanasius, and that which is commonly called the Apostles' Creed, ought firmly to be received and believed, for they may be proved by most certain warrant of holy Scripture. (Schaff 1882, 3:528)

44. For a recent discussion of the Protestant view of the analogy of faith and *sola Scriptura,* see Gaffin 2022, 34–5.

45. On reading scripture in light of scripture as a formal system, see Norris 1997, 149–62. For an argument that this ruled reading of scripture is supported by ancient church orthodoxy, see Goad 2010, 20. McGraw (2012, 24) discusses the importance of using "clearer passages" to interpret more obscure ones within typological studies of the Old Testament.

46. The WCF (article 1.2) states,

> The whole counsel of God concerning all things necessary for His own glory, man's salvation, faith and life, *is either expressly set down in Scripture, or by good and necessary consequence may be deduced from Scripture*: unto which nothing at any time is to be added, whether new revelations of the Spirit or tradition of men. (emphasis mine)

For a discussion and definition, see McGraw 2012, 3.

47. Chadwick 1993, 82.

48. For a similar perspective, which views the formulations of Nicaea and Chalcedon as faithful reflections of the task of "conceptualizing" what Scripture teaches, see Wellum 2020, 72.

49. Crisp (2010, viii) comments, "all theology is contextual in nature."

50. Spong 1992, 128. For the view that Mary was impregnated by a Roman soldier named Panthera, see Lincoln 2013, 154–56.

51. Moltmann (1990, 79) states that the virgin birth "is not one of the pillars that sustains the New Testament faith in Christ;" see the quotation and discussion by Thiselton (2015, 237).

52. This statement could be expanded to include the numerous Protestant and Reformed confessional traditions that refer to the virgin birth. Athanasius also viewed the true church as standing "in the apostolic tradition" (Gemeinhardt 2011, 336).

53. Strong states that the denial of the supernatural virginal conception involves "a denial of the truthfullness of Matthew's and Luke's narratives" (1907, 675).

54. For discussion of the hermeneutical spiral as a portrait of a methodological approach to interpretation, see Osborne 2006, 350–6.

55. John Calvin's doctrine of the internal witness of the Holy Spirit to the authority of scripture (*testimonium Spiritus Sancti interna*) represented "a departure from Rome's doctrine of *testimonium ecclesiae*, which stressed the church's role in defining scripture and giving it its authority" (Wenkel 2011, 98).

56. Swain 2017, 40.

57. Hays 2002, 141; Bayer 2007, 81, 94–96, 125–26, 170.

58. Swain 2017, 40.

59. On these four movements of salvation-history see Wenkel 2012, 78–90; similarly, see the use of this four-part structure as the backbone of the "authoritative structure of the biblical storyline" in Wellum 2016, 111. These four elements were also part of the overarching plot of scripture according to Athanasius (Leithart 2011, 40).

60. Anderson 2017, 99.

61. For a discussion of systematic theology as synchronic in presentation and biblical theology as diachronic in presentation, see Kimble and Spellman 2020, 235.

62. For a view of the Old and New Testament in canonical "conversation," see Anderson 2017, 99.

63. Swain 2021, 129.

64. DeRouchie (2019, 247) explains that a Christian reading of the Old Testament entails reading "the Scripture forward, then backward, and then forward again."

65. Alexander suggests that Luke's use of the word *plērophoreō* in Luke 1:1 encourages "rereading [the text] backwards" (1999, 26).

66. According to Moore (2015, 107), the prologue of Hebrews (1:1) places the speech of the prophets and the divine speech of Jesus in a "hermeneutical circle whereby the OT explains the Christ event, and the Christ event in turn leads to a new understanding of scripture."

67. I am borrowing this phrase from Jipp 2014, 253 n5.

68. Hamilton (2022, 4) explains that the "phrase 'promise-shaped typology' attempts to capture what happens when God makes a promise that results in those who know him interpreting the world in the terms and categories either communicated in the promise or assumed by it."

69. According to Auer and Easton (2010, 88), "metaphorical code-switching" means that where "a code is used out of context, it may evoke aspects of the situation in which it would normally be expected, thus becoming a meaningful metaphor of that situation."

70. Hahn 2008, 107.

71. Thatcher 2007, 178; also see Um 2006, 149, and Gemeinhardt 2011, 297.

72. Thatcher 2007, 178.

73. For the view that Jerusalem has an enduring eschatological significance, see Kinzer 2018.

74. Gawronski (2015, 380) extends John's temple Christology and its "new liturgical sense" to the Letter of Hebrews as well. He finds the Gospel of John "presents Jesus as the very temple, his own body replacing the Jerusalem Temple."

75. For this view, see Köstenberger 2006, 96.

76. Köstenberger 2006, 96.

77. Studies that deny that Jesus "replaces" the temple in Jerusalem include Yee 1989; Coloe 2001; Lieu 1999; Hoskins 2006; and Spaulding 2009.

78. Regev 2019, 221. It is noteworthy that Regev explicitly relates Jesus to the temple rather than the temple to Jesus, thus reversing the locus of divine presence that accords with John's high Christology.

79. Here I refer to a future possibility of a return to the centrality of "place" in the next eschatological age in the sense that the Second Coming of Jesus will be followed by a future state in which person *and* place are eternally united together when the new heaven comes down to a new earth in the eschaton. For biblical texts that refer to new heavens and a new earth as the things above and below are united into one horizon, see Isaiah 66:17, 22; 2 Peter 3:13; Revelation 21:1–2.

80. T. Desmond Alexander (2009, 31) points out the relationship between theophany, the construction of an altar, and the location of a mountain (Gen. 8:20; 12:7–8; 13:4, 8; 22:9; 26:25; 33:20; 35:1, 3, 7).

81. The larger context identifies Jacob's stone of remembrance as indicating that God revealed himself through the dream commonly known as "Jacob's ladder" (Gen. 28:10–22).

82. A point made by Leithart (2013, 122).

83. Chyutin (2006, 78) observes that there are elements of strong continuity between the tabernacle and Solomon's temple if one superimposes "the courts of the Tabernacle onto the podium of Solomon's Temple." For a discussion of some continuities and discontinuities between the tabernacle and Solomon's temple, see Wenkel 2021a, 65–71.

84. Gaffin (2022, 30) explains that "Verbal revelation has its historically progressive character because it is derivative of the historically progressive character that characterizes redemption, the unfolding of the history of redemption."

85. Bockmuehl (2015, 99) states that the "influential language of Christ's body as the new temple" as found in John 1:14 and 2:21 is something that "John himself does not greatly develop."

86. Here I draw extensively from Schreiner 2016, 135.

87. Sleeman 2009, 111.

88. Sleeman (2009, 111) comments that "the Temple must point to him [Jesus]; whether it will function as such remains an open question at this narrative juncture [in Acts 3]."

89. Thompson 2011, 152–53.

Chapter 2

A Map for the Terrain of the Argument

The reader will encounter several methodological challenges on their journey through this study.[1] As a result, this chapter offers a map to guide the reader through the terrain as it seeks to present a compelling case for the necessity of the virgin birth according to temple Christology. This chapter explores the contours, hills, and valleys that must be crossed as the case takes shape. For the sake of clarity, it may help to repeat how the argument of this study proceeds with a categorical syllogism in three parts. The form of reasoning is deductive because it arrives at a necessary conclusion by considering two premises. The first or major premise is that a heavenly temple must be constructed directly by the Spirit. Second, the minor premise of this argument is that Jesus is a heavenly temple. Third, the conclusion is that Jesus had to be conceived of a virgin directly by the Spirit because of his identity as a heavenly temple.

Before presenting the full case for this argument, this chapter deals with preliminary issues under the present section of the book which addresses matters of prolegomena. The first section of this chapter considers the "dance" or hermeneutical spiral of deductive reasoning and inductive analysis. The second section further describes the problem with the categorical syllogism as presented above, relating to the use of the different terms for "construction" and "conception." This is an essential part of the argument because it argues for the ontological relationship between construction and human conception, especially as it relates to Jesus. The third section explains that Jesus' person is a "heavenly temple" and a place of worship. The fourth section locates the metaphysical relationship between construction and the human conception of Jesus within the analogy of faith so that any claims are dependent upon scripture. The fifth and last section explains the Boolean logic at work in the categorical syllogism, which is at the heart of this study.

THE DANCE OF DEDUCTIVE REASONING

Categorical syllogisms are deductive arguments because they always proceed from a set of propositions to a conclusion. Like the form of any deductive argument, the claim comes before the evidence. Arguments like these
may be considered dangerous because of the concern that such theology
may become overly scholastic. Some may even question whether deductive methods are "inherently foreign to the theology of revelation."[2] No
one wants to be guilty of eisegesis that imposes meaning upon the text of
scripture that is not there. But is it true that an inductive study of scripture
is the *only* appropriate method of theology? Must we *exclusively* move from
exegesis to theological conclusions? Is this theoretical approach even possible or desirable?

In response to these questions and the suggestion that deductive arguments
are inherently inappropriate for Christian dogmatics, there are several points
to consider. First, it is not possible to pretend as if we are reading the Bible for
the first time ever and starting all our data collection without any presuppositions. Second, the very claim that a pure act of inductive biblical interpretation is possible is itself simply dubious. It is not possible to approach scripture
as a clean slate that is void of all presuppositions. Third, it is patently not a
virtue to attempt to strip oneself of all church history in an attempt to achieve
a purely inductive study.[3]

The very possibility of a deductive argument being compatible with
Christian dogmatics is due to the perspicuity of certain truths in the canon
of scripture. This means that certain truths are so clear and apparent that a
cursory inductive reading of scripture (even one that does not gather all relevant scriptural data) may offer up certain propositional claims that function
as initial propositions.

One of the benefits of a deductive argument, such as a categorical syllogism, is that it offers clarity of expression and presents itself as open to
analysis. It is for this reason that theologians from Athanasius (*c.* 293–373)
to Girolami Zanchi (1516–1590) used syllogisms to prove that Christ was the
Son of God.[4] Johann Philipp Gabler famously identified systematic theology
as deductive in nature while he proposed the new discipline of biblical theology as being inductive.[5]

The propositions or hypotheses of a deductive argument may be tested
against exegetical evidence.[6] Deductive arguments aid analytic theology
because they make critical propositions explicit and then offer the ability to
see the evidence which might justify or warrant their acceptance. A deductive
argument, such as a categorical syllogism, may be falsified by evidence that
makes either its major premise or its minor premise untrue. Such a condition
would make the entire deductive argument unsound. Moreover, there are

times when deductive assumptions are implicitly built into arguments that are assumed to be entirely inductive.

Another benefit of utilizing deductive argumentation, particularly in the form of a categorical syllogism, is that syllogisms are found in the scripture.[7] The fact that they are found in the New Testament and the Old Testament is only meant to be indicative of a much wider pattern that is outside the scope of this study. Scriptural data demonstrates that categorical syllogisms should not be considered unbiblical or inappropriate for theological method.

Syllogistic reasoning is also a useful tool for capturing the tensions inherent in the metanarrative storyline of the Christian canon. Dru Johnson explains that syllogistic arguments, even in rudimentary forms, "create a tension to be resolved."[8] According to this study, each type of cultic place of Yahweh worship, whether stone or earthen altar, tent, or building, may have been accompanied by God's personal presence, but such theophanies were never sufficient or eternal because they were built by human hands. In other words, the very notion of a temple after the Fall creates a certain tension within the storyline of salvation-history. The entirety of salvation-history is accompanied by tensions that look forward to future events when God will act decisively so that he will finally dwell among his covenant people. This will require a temple made without human hands. For the Christian, Jesus resolves the tensions because he is the fulfillment of all of God's promises, for he is the temple of God made without hands.

In fact, the way in which categorical syllogisms display their inherent logic is especially helpful for presenting constructive dogmatic proposals.[9] The use of philosophical tools within the domain of systematic theology or dogmatics has sometimes been called "analytic theology."[10] The tools of philosophy help to identify things, explore relationships, clarify terminology, and uncover connections that would otherwise be hidden.[11] Analytic theology utilizes logical analysis while working with data drawn from the authoritative source of scripture, for theology begins with divine revelation.[12]

This study aims to avoid the dangers of an *a posteriori* categorical syllogism by locating it within a hermeneutical spiral. This spiral movement or dialectic moves between generalized propositions and exegetical data, as evidenced by the several chapters dedicated to both in their respective sections.[13] The use of syllogistic and deductive reasoning clarifies the theological task and opens the prospect for inductive analysis of the biblical evidence. While it is certainly possible to lean in the direction of either inductive or deductive methodology, it is not possible that either should be wholly separated from the other. This study embraces the tensions of the dance between inductive exegesis and deductive generalizations—a dance which "never ends on this side of glory."[14]

WARRANT FOR CHANGING TERMS

One of the gauntlets through which this syllogism must pass is this: do all of the terms bear the same meaning? If the terms are different, either lexically or conceptually, the entire validity of the argument may be dismissed. Within the philosophy of logic, the term "validity" refers "to the relationship between the premises and does not apply to a single proposition."[15] The matter of validity is critically important because when the premises are true and the form of the argument is valid, then the conclusion is guaranteed to be true.[16] There *must* be an analogy of being or a metaphysical relationship between construction and human conception for this argument to be valid. For this reason, *this section demonstrates that there is a sufficient analogy of being between the terms "constructed" and "conceived" in the categorical syllogism for it to be valid and true.*

This section justifies this change in terms as legitimate on the basis of the Christian canon of scripture. This defense is based on the fact that each of the two terms for "construction" and "conception" within the categorical syllogism is ultimately addressed by exegesis of Jesus' own words in the Gospels.[17] This move between the terms must demonstrate that there is some ontological reality shared by acts of construction and human conception in order for the argument to remain valid.

The problem with the argument as posed above is that it uses different terms in the first premise and in the third premise. Specifically, the categorical syllogism does not meet the prima facie requirements for soundness because the first premise involves the "construction" of a building, and the third premise involves the "conception" of a human being. This problem is not about the actual meaning of what constitutes "construction" or "conception," per se. Rather, one must ask formal and abstract questions about the form of the argument and its use of terms. The basic problem with the categorical syllogism at the heart of this argument is that it does not meet the prima facie requirements for validity because the first premise involves the "construction" of a building, and the third premise involves the "conception" of a human being.

In the case at hand, the very form of the categorical syllogism is being explained and defended because it uses two different terms (whatever they may be) in propositions one and three. Thus, the validity of the core argument must be rigorously explained. In the argument being made about Jesus, one expects that the conclusion would read: "Therefore, Jesus had to be constructed directly by the Spirit of God." However, in this case, such language would arguably be theologically and biblically legitimate, even if it serves as a confusing use of terms in a doctrinally constructive context. There *must* be sufficient warrant to justify the interchangeability of the terms for "construction" and "conception," or the entire argument would be invalid. If the terms are not interchangeable, then it would simply not matter what might be said about the construction of temples, because this would have no bearing on a conclusion about the human conception of Jesus.

One might counter that the argument is invalid because the terms of the conclusion in the categorical syllogism do not formally use the terms of the predicate. According to the rules of logic, this is called the "fallacy of four terms" (*quaternio terminorum*) because a categorical syllogism may only have three terms.[18] From the point of view of information logic, the argument may be initially accused of the fallacy because the term "construction" is not the same as the term "conception."

This problem would not be solved by simply restating the conclusion to read: "Therefore, Jesus had to be constructed directly by the Spirit of God." The reason this will not solve the problem is that the word "construction" is being applied to a building in the first premise and to a person in the conclusion, thus indicating that the term "construction" is being used in an ambiguous or in an equivocal way. The use of ambiguous terms is just as problematic and potentially fallacious, so this would also render the argument informally invalid.[19] The only possible way to accept the premises as originally stated is to view the terms for construction and conception as ontologically related and overlapping enough to sustain the argument.

It is important to define the term "conception" here as the single point in time in which personhood is established. With respect to the creation of any person, God's work must be related to the dichotomous elements of human nature: the material and the immaterial or the "soul" and the "body."[20] According to Psalms 139:13 and Job 31:15, one can conclude that God does something direct or immediate for the immaterial part of every person at conception.[21]

Jesus' fully human conception should also be understood as an act in which all persons of the Trinity had a part. Stephen Duby concludes,

> With regard to the virgin conception in the Synoptic Gospels, although the whole Trinity produces the Son's flesh in the womb of Mary, the conception may be appropriated to the Holy Spirit in a particular respect or for a particular reason.[22]

Similarly, Leithart wrote:

> To be sure, the union of the Logos and flesh is "causally effected by the whole Trinity," the Father sending and the Spirit as the agent of the Son's human conception, yet it still belongs alone to the Son to be incarnate.[23]

As a Last Adam, Jesus' fully human physical body was created immediately and hypostatically joined by the Spirit to the Second Person of the Trinity. The human body is never considered something inherently wicked or negative but only has these characteristics when under the penalty of death for sin.[24] There is a tension that must be maintained here, which is captured by Heinrich Heppe (1820–1879), as he explains:

> Thus Christ's incarnation was at once ordinary and extraordinary: ordinary as regards the material supplied by the V. Mary, extraordinary as regards the formative force added to this material.[25]

With respect to Jesus, the term "conception" always implies fully human personhood and personal identity. Therefore, conception is inextricably linked to the personhood of Jesus so that whatever may be attributed to him at any point during his life may be attributed to him since conception.

The source for the data on the ontological relationship between Christ's conception and his status as the temple of God which was "built" is the scriptures and especially Jesus' own words. The weight given to Jesus' own words does not mean there is a canon within the canon or that one must denigrate the rest of scripture. Rather, the interest in such data is given by the scripture itself as projected by Moses' prophecy about a future prophet: "I will raise up for them a prophet like you from among their brothers. And I will put my words in his mouth, and he shall speak to them all that I command him" (Deut. 18:18). For the Christian reader of the canon, Jesus is the final and authorized prophet of Israel par excellence. Dru Johnson points out that this perspective is reified in the apostolic tradition as "the speech and acts of Jesus attains a status equivalent to divine speech and acts in the Hebrew Bible."[26] The warrant for changing terms between conception and construction is simply based on the exegetical data derived from scripture. The following trio of texts from Matthew, Mark, and Luke offers a data set for this conclusion.

In the Gospel of Matthew, when Jesus was caught plucking ears of corn in the field with his disciples, he was accused of breaking the Sabbath. Part of Jesus' response to the Pharisees included this statement (12:6): "I tell you, something greater than the temple is here" (*legō de hymin hoti tou hierou meizon estin hōde*). David Turner points out that the use of the neuter *meizon* "is used instead of the masculine in order to emphasize the general quality of greatness rather than the specific individual, Jesus."[27] Thus, Jesus is not necessarily calling himself a *something* greater as many English translations suggest but *someone* greater than the temple. One could counter that the point being made is about the temple, not a person per se. But R. T. France highlights the following pattern in Matthew:

> "I tell you, something [*meizon*] greater than the temple is here" (12:6)
> "and behold, something [*meizon*] greater than Jonah is here" (12:41)
> "and behold, something [*meizon*] greater than Solomon is here" (12:42)

Such a pattern demonstrates that the neuter is used even when individuals are in view.[28] Jesus is the "something" that is "here." Thus, the neuter is used when referring to Jesus' fulfillment and authority over any and all aspects of salvation-history, including the role of prophet, priest, and king. While there is a danger of "proving too much" with this text in Matthew, Jesus uses language that creates an ontological overlap between himself and the temple.[29] With respect to the first comparison between Jesus and the temple, the ontological overlap has to do with the dwelling place of God's personal presence. Yet there is discontinuity as well, for Jesus is "greater" than the physical temple building because it was made by human hands.

In the Gospel of Mark (15:38), the theme of Jesus' atonement and the temple intersects when the "curtain of the temple was torn in two, from top to bottom" at Jesus' death.[30] This is a reference to the veil or curtain between the holy place and the most holy place in the temple (Exod. 26:31–33). Because this event happened at the moment of Jesus' death when he cried out and "breathed his last" (15:39), it is associated with God's forsaking of Jesus as an act of atonement. There are myriad of ways in which this event could be considered, and this consideration is limited to the narrow interest in temple Christology. Adam Johnson offers twin theses that capture two key aspects: (1) Jesus Christ is the One who was abandoned and forsaken in the place of the Old Temple and (2) in the place of the old, Jesus was the true Temple.[31] Johnson explains that the torn curtain is an act of destruction upon the temple system and enacts divine abandonment, showing it to be desolate.[32] Whatever wrath God's people deserved was taken out on God's Son, who was the rejected temple, representative temple, and true temple.[33] It is critical to observe that this rending of the curtain happened when Jesus-the-temple was rent. The cross clarifies those who were confused by and even twisted Jesus' own words:

> We heard him say, I will destroy this temple that is made with hands [*cheiropoiēton*], and in three days I will build another, not made with hands [*acheiropoiēton*]. (Mark 14:58, ESV)

The salient point is that the curtain in the temple reveals the identity of Jesus-the-temple. The curtain made with human hands is destroyed even as a resurrected temple would arrive in three days. This single atoning event in the death of Jesus rendered the sacrificial system, the hiddenness of God behind a veil, and its fixed geographical location obsolete.[34] For the purposes of the present argument, it is important to observe that Jesus' status as the "new temple" and "new form of the presence of God" is tied to the physical temple in Jerusalem.[35] For Mark, the torn body of the Lord Jesus in the temple of his body corresponded to the torn veil in the temple building and vice versa.

In the Gospel of Luke, just as Jesus is about to be betrayed, the topic of the temple comes to the foreground. Jesus' short speech to the Jewish leaders who seized him states:

> Have you come out as against a robber, with swords and clubs? When I was with you *day after day in the temple*, you did not lay hands on me. But this is your hour, and the power of darkness. (Luke 22:52–53)

Not only does Luke begin and end with references to the temple building but also directs the reader back to Jesus' association with it just before his death.[36] This reference to the temple is surprising in some sense. Ron Fay argues that this text above "serves as a rhetorical reminder of the importance of Jesus and his connection to it [the temple]."[37] Jesus draws attention to his association with the temple in order to properly frame this event: it is not just about authorities coming to detain an unscrupulous rabbi but rather a cosmic conflict between God's agent and the forces of darkness.[38] God is inextricably aligned with the temple and with Jesus. This relationship with the temple accords with the way in which Luke (2:49) stresses that the temple in Jerusalem was for Jesus, "my father's house." Jesus is associated with the temple as the son of the one who dwelt in the temple. There is a subtle but important point here: Luke's narrative of the virgin birth together with Jesus' status as the Son of God presents him as the temple of God made by God's own hands. The entire Lukan movement of Jesus to Jerusalem may be seen from this perspective: "a momentous journey to claim his right to the father's house."[39] Jesus understood his own vocation in terms of Yahweh visiting his people in person by journeying to Jerusalem. This journey ensured that all the covenantal promises for God's people might be fulfilled in him and by him. N. T. Wright comments that this is "not, then, a matter of an idealized figure but of a story in which YHWH himself, in person, plays the leading role."[40]

In the Gospel of John, we have some of the clearest statements about Jesus' templeness. For John, Jesus is both the tabernacle where the fullness of God's presence dwells (John 14:10) and the temple, where worshipful access to God is found. The cross and the resurrection together demonstrate that Jesus is a temple built by God's own hands:

> So the Jews said to him, "What sign do you show us for doing these things?" Jesus answered them, "Destroy *this temple*, and in three days I will raise it up." The Jews then said, "It has taken forty-six years to build this temple, and will you raise it up in three days?" But he was speaking about the temple of his body. When therefore he was raised from the dead, his disciples remembered

that he had said this, and they believed the Scripture and the word that Jesus had spoken. (John 2:18–22)

This text is important because Jesus explains what *kind* of temple he is: he is the kind of temple that can be destroyed and raised up in three days. After the resurrection and the empowerment of the Spirit, these words became an important memory for the disciples as they gained clarity about what Jesus had said while he was with them.

This section has demonstrated that there is an important conceptual overlap in the New Testament between the construction of a building and human conception. The unified witnesses of Matthew, Mark, Luke, and John not only *associate* Jesus with the temple, but they also *identify* Jesus with the temple. This identification makes it possible to move between conception and construction in terms of the argument. This movement from construction to conception is critical to the argument at hand because the terms of the argument rely upon such a move. The problem with the argument as stated may be resolved by understanding the language of constructing buildings as ontologically analogous to human conception. But if one works within the philosophical framework of the Christian canon, there is no problem with moving between the terms of "construction" and "conception."[41] For this is exactly what Jesus did. By identifying Jesus as the temple of God, there is warrant for understanding the virgin birth (the virginal conception) of Jesus-the-temple as an act of divine construction.

TEMPLE IDENTITY AND ANALOGY

This section demonstrates that Jesus' identity as the temple of God was understood through analogical relationships. For Athanasius, his "analogical vision of reality is of a piece with typological interpretation."[42] This relationship between analogy and typology is important to consider because the minor premise or the middle proposition ("Jesus is a heavenly temple") utilizes an implicit analogy between a person and a place of worship (or building). This proposition entails a move from a building or place to a person. But is this move legitimate or sound? The validity of the argument rests on the validity of the relationship between these two different things, that is, place and person. *The conceptual move from place to person within the categorical syllogism is justifiable because of Jesus' identification of his person as a place of worship.*

While all three propositions in the syllogism refer to the ontological analogy between place and person, the middle premise is the clearest. However, the concepts at work in the middle premise appear to confuse two different metaphysical realities: a person and a place of worship, that is, a temple.

Studies of "place" typically assume a difference between the concepts of person and place. Aristotle defined the concept of "place" as a "bounded container" through analogies that often involved a cup or vessel.[43] A "place" may be defined interchangeably with the terms "spaces" and "habitat."[44] This is an environment in which people live and inhabit in the world. Terms such as these, that transcend metaphors, ideals, as well as human experience, are perhaps the most difficult to define. Despite such difficulties, a "place" is characterized by (1) human experience and (2) boundaries of some sort.[45] According to this typical view, a person is differentiated from place because people inhabit place(s) and may be involved in defining the boundaries of them. Despite this differentiation, the categorical syllogism of this book requires a proposition which is an existential quantifier: Jesus is the heavenly temple of God.

The concept which unites place and person is the concept of God's special covenant presence dwelling (or indwelling) in a particular place. Within salvation-history, person and place overlap when the special presence of God is revealed to persons for the purpose of worship or for special revelation. Jesus' promise unites the concept of "place" with his own eternal personal presence (John 14:3): "I go to prepare a place for you" so "that where I am you may be also."[46] The imagery of person and place is especially important for John's description of the eternal state in the book of Revelation. He explains his vision of the New Jerusalem by stating, "And I saw no temple in the city, for its temple is the Lord God the Almighty and the Lamb" (Rev. 21:22). This passage is considered later in more detail, but at this point, it is only important to point out that Jesus the person takes over the role and function of temple places in the eternal state.

At this point, it is especially important to note that this *analogie entis* of place and person through the concept of dwelling (or indwelling) must be located within the analogy of faith. In other words, the Boolean logic of the categorical syllogism (and its demand for necessity) cannot be separated from the salvation-historical narratives of Christian scripture. It is only within the Christian canon of scripture that a person can be a place of worship. Once the terms of this syllogism are located within such a framework, it is demonstrable that there are no metaphysical contradictions that would render it unsound.

The scriptures themselves identify the common domain shared between persons and places of worship: the dwelling of God's Spirit.[47] This shared domain is evident in Paul's identification of the Church as "God's Temple":

> Do you not know that you are God's temple and that God's Spirit dwells in you? If anyone destroys God's temple, God will destroy him. For God's temple is holy, and you are that temple. (1 Cor. 3:16–17)

According to Paul's admonition to the Corinthian church, they should take care not to destroy "God's temple" through their "fleshly" acts of jealousy, strife, and division (1 Cor. 3:1–4). Within this admonition, Paul appeals to the church with an analogy that is similar to the one being made in the categorical syllogism: "you [the church] are that temple" (1 Cor. 3:17).[48] Paul also identifies the basis for this ontological claim: the indwelling presence of God's Spirit (1 Cor. 3:16).[49] The clarity of this text offers the reader the hermeneutical key to identify other places where the Spirit of God dwells, to identify a place of worship, and to identify people who participate in this reality.

There are several New Testament passages that identify the church as God's temple, building, and dwelling place:

> For we are God's fellow workers. You are God's field, God's building. (1 Cor. 3:9) So then you are no longer strangers and aliens, but you are fellow citizens with the saints and members of the household of God, built on the foundation of the apostles and prophets, Christ Jesus himself being the cornerstone, in whom the whole structure, being joined together, grows into a holy temple in the Lord. In him you also are being built together into a dwelling place for God by the Spirit. (Eph. 2:19–22)

> As you come to him, a living stone rejected by men but in the sight of God chosen and precious, you yourselves like living stones are being built up as a spiritual house, to be a holy priesthood, to offer spiritual sacrifices acceptable to God through Jesus Christ. (1 Pet. 2:4–5)

Peter and Paul's identification of the presence or indwelling of the Holy Spirit as the domain of overlap between the ontological realities of person(s) and temple also enables this study to follow the salvation-historical progression of Yahweh worship across primitive altars, a movable tent, and fixed building(s).

The analogy between construction and conception is a useful way of describing the relationship of causation as it relates to God's creative actions. Theologically defined, the Spirit's begetting of Jesus as the fully human and fully divine Messiah of Israel is analogous to the construction of a building—specifically, a temple that God builds. It is true that neither the church collectively nor individual believers become the "temple of God" through virginal conception. But the identity of the church as the "temple of God" does not undermine our argument because she is still begotten by the Spirit and through union with Christ (Col. 2:11). This is spiritual work done by God's "own hand" or "without human hands" (*acheiropoietos*).

The notion that building or constructing a house is analogous to human conception relies upon the creation narratives in Genesis 1–3. For example, the writer of the epistle to the Hebrews (3:4) argues that "every house [*oikos*] is built by someone, but the builder of all things is God."[50] David DeSilva comments that the author of Hebrews is demonstrating the preeminence of Christ through a series of analogies: Jesus:Moses :: builder:house :: God:universe.[51] This Hellenistic Jewish-Christian document is arguably drawing from the scripturally informed worldview established by the creation narratives in Genesis 1–3 as well as the Greco-Roman truism that "every house is built by someone, since every effect must have a cause."[52] What the author of Hebrews is doing is drawing from the analogous relationship between what humans do when they build a house and what God did when he created the universe. Humans build just as God has built the world.

The Jewish philosopher Mark Glouberman's observations about this analogy between building houses and creating the universe are worth repeating in their entirety (emphasis his):

> What initially comes across as a poor analogy is in actuality an accurate model. The creation story doesn't just correspond to a story of the sort that would be told about the building of a house. It *is* the story of the building of a (kind of) house: an abode for men and women.[53]

The account of the creation of the world according to Genesis 1–3 is the story of building a house with a plan, reflecting a divine design that is in accordance with the needs of its inhabitants. This analogy extends to all things because God—specifically Christ—created all things. For example, Ephesians (3:9) states that God "created all things." The book of Revelation describes a scene in which the "living creatures" give glory and honor to "him who is seated on the throne" (4:9) because "you created all things, and by your will they existed and were created" (4:11). One of the sharpest Christological statements about Jesus and creation appears in Colossians (1:16): "For by him all things were created, in heaven and on earth" and affirms that "all things were created through him and for him." This means that Christ is the one who built the "house" of the world in the divine act of creation out of nothing.

The analogy between builders and events such as human conception is so fitting that Aristotle based his understanding of natural science on this anthropomorphic language.[54] Aristotle's doctrine of the "four causes" is based on an "artisan analogy" and continues to have a prominent role in explaining relationships. For example, when someone is building a house, the

> entire process may be analyzed into the following components: the material which the builder uses (= "material cause"); the idea or plan which the builder eventually realizes (= "formal cause"); the builder's actions which put the

house together (= "efficient cause"); the purpose which the house is meant to serve (= "final cause").[55]

It is noteworthy that Aristotle concludes, "Now surely as in intelligent action, so in nature" (*Phys.* 199a, 10). This is a startling statement because it identifies creation as reflecting intelligence—a creator. Aristotle's insights into what Christians would call "natural law" support the idea that nature, including events such as human conception, is readily explained by the analogy of constructing a building.[56] The overlap between the worldview of Genesis 1–3 and Aristotle should not be entirely surprising. As Dru Johnson explains, "Both Greek and Hebrew literature incorporate reason and revelation as we commonly understand them today."[57]

The Reformed tradition has readily employed the Aristotelian language of causation to explain the virgin birth. Heinrich Heppe is a prime example from the Reformed tradition who applies such language to the conception of Christ. He argues that while the Holy Spirit is the *efficient* cause of the conception, he was not the *material* cause.[58] This means that it was the Spirit's power that was at work but not any divine substance. The material cause—the material that the builder uses—was completely natural and fully human, with an element of mystery notwithstanding. Thus, there was a "double principle" at work in the conception, positing the "active principle" as the Holy Spirit and the "passive principle" as Mary.[59]

The fact that Jesus is God's temple draws us back toward Glouberman's quote cited above. The description of Jesus' virginal conception as an act of constructing a building may initially come across as a rather weak analogy or even invalid. However, once it is clear that Jesus is the temple of God, the divine act of the incarnation must be the act of establishing or constructing this temple. One simply cannot have Jesus' identity as the Messiah-temple without also understanding his incarnation as a temple building event. When scripture is used to interpret scripture, the terms of the categorical syllogism are entirely justified, and even required. The biblical narratives of the virgin birth *are* the story of building a kind of house for God's presence in the world: an abode for the Triune God.[60] This relationship enables the reader of the Christian canon to read backward in order to typologically understand what the construction of God's temple, tabernacle, and altars communicated.

As a place of worship, Jesus' identity as the temple of God must be located between the poles of likeness and totalizing identity. In other words, to say that Jesus is analogous to all other places of Yahweh worship such as altars, tents, and temples is to say that there is an analogous relationship that is the same as the Son is to the Father. This Trinitarian model echoes Athanasius and is derived from the one-ness and many-ness of the Godhead and the Father–Son relationship.[61] The Father and Son are identical in divine essence even though they are different in person, with the Son being the revelation of the Father so closely that the comparative word "as" would fail to fully communicate this reality. Thus, there is a "qualified sense in which the Father is the archetype of which the Son is the image."[62] This Trinitarian model means that the word "as" fails to fully communicate who Jesus is if one were to simply postulate that "Jesus is 'as' the temple of God." Rather, we must state that "Jesus is *the* temple of God" without diminishing his personhood.

ANALOGICAL LANGUAGE WITHIN
THE ANALOGY OF FAITH

The most basic definition of an "analogy" is a comparison of similarities between two things that are mostly different. Because arguments mostly rely upon the meaning of certain words or terms, it is for good reason that philosophical debates are about the "soundness of some analogical argument."[63] Following closely after this, the "analogy of being" refers to the metaphysical or ontological relationship between the terms of the argument—the "beingness" of the things referenced in the argument. Succinctly stated, "Analogical language describes ontological reality."[64] The concept of the "analogy of being" (*analogia entis*) is about metaphysical analogy. The analogy of being may be used *vertically* to describe the different metaphysical realities of God and his creation. It may also be used *horizontally* to describe the relationship between different realities of substance, accidents, and properties. This concept is historically rooted in the thought of Thomas Aquinas (AD 1225–1274), who "described the relationship between God as creator and humans as creatures" as analogous and therefore opened the possibility for natural theology or knowledge of God that may be ascertained by rational and reasonable observation of the world.[65]

The concept of *analogia entis* took on prominence in the discussions between those who supported the idea of natural theology (e.g., Hans Urs von Balthasar) and those who opposed it due to its similarities to Platonism (e.g., Karl Barth).[66] Balthasar captures the problem at hand with this probative question: "How can divine, infinite truth be translated into creaturely, finite truth?"[67] This present study offers a succinct and nuanced answer. There is something about God that cannot be fully captured by human language because of the "inherent inadequacies of all conceptual formulations."[68] Paul likens such inadequacies to "groanings" (Rom. 8:26). In other words, human language has the potential to referentially and truthfully reveal God, although such capacity is limited, especially as it is located in the present eschatological age. This present age is characterized by suffering and vexation. And yet, when God-language is used by God's people, it "enact[s] a relationship with God" which becomes a means of transformation.[69] As Nicholas Healy explains, there is also an eschatological dimension to knowledge of God, for "Thomas [Aquinas] and Balthasar view knowledge of God through the medium of creatures as the beginning *and the end* of human knowing."[70] Despite any shortcomings, the church catholic preaches and groans as it anticipates a day when faith will become sight at Jesus' Second Coming (e.g., John 20:25–29; 1 Cor. 16:22; Luke 21:28).

It is at this point that the proposal of nesting the *analogia entis* within the framework of *analogia fides* becomes so important. According to the contemporary Roman Catholic theologian Thomas Guarino, "the analogy of being must be thought *within* the analogy of faith; the former is simply a child of the Anselmian *fides quaerens intellectum*."[71] Guarino leans in the direction of answering that human language has the capacity to achieve some correspondence between who and what God actually is because this is a reflection of humanity's unique capacity of bearing the divine image (*imago Dei*) as it exercises faith and is the unique agent of God's inspired inscripturated revelation.[72] The nested relationship between these two concepts is important because of the way in which Christ, the God-man, solves all vertically oriented paradoxes of the analogy of being.[73] The "supernatural order of grace" is the realm in which God may be understood to be both Gift and Giver; so that in Christ, there is a nexus of the poles of hiddenness and revelation, transcendence and immanence, infinite and finitude.[74]

Whereas most theologians focus on the role that Christ has as the unique God-man and his role in the *vertical* aspects of the analogous relationship between the poles of God and humanity, it is the *horizontal* aspect that is most important for this present chapter. This is because the soundness of the categorical syllogism at the heart of this study relies upon metaphysical analogies between Christ and objects of this world. The first metaphysical analogy within the argument is found in the explicit uses of different words in the argument. Specifically, the first premise involves the "construction" of a building, and the third premise involves the "conception" of a human being. The second analogy has to do with terms that infer a relationship between two different things. Specifically, the minor premise or the middle proposition ("Jesus is a temple") utilizes an implicit analogy between a "person" and a "place" of worship (or building).

The location of the analogy of being within the framework of the analogy of faith offers a *via media* to avoid the twin perils of God as wholly mysterious and God as wholly familiar. These are, in fact, the two pastoral concerns that go back to the medieval debates about metaphysics between Aquinas' analogical model and Duns Scotus' univocal model. On the one hand, Aquinas postulated that God must be understood as act-of-being (*ipsum esse subsistens*). God is the primary source of beingness and all that is created is an "analogical resemblance to the divine mode of being."[75] This means that God is wholly other and mysterious to us. On the other hand, Duns Scotus proposed God to be "immediately intelligible" according to a metaphysical model in which there is no qualitative difference between God and his creation.[76] The danger with this postulate is that God and his creatures stand "side by side."[77]

According to the present study, natural theology apart from scripture is possible, but it is insufficient for humanity, not only for salvation but for *fully* understanding the world.[78] Thus, the scriptures open up *vertical* aspects so as to truly reveal God and they also help identify *horizontal* aspects so as to more accurately understand creation. The location of the analogy of being within the analogy of faith enables us to negotiate between any Aquinas-like analogies that obscure God and Duns Scotus-like univocal language that domesticates God. Duns Scotus' model of metaphysics is not necessary because the scriptures truly reveal that God is indeed wholly other than humanity. And Aquinas's metaphysical model of analogy may be affirmed in the sense that humanity is indeed made in the image of God. This model is also tempered by scripture which provides what knowledge is necessary for human redemption. There are two concomitant truths that must be held together: persons are made in the *imago Dei* and share an essence with God, yet they are fundamentally different from their creator.

The key to engaging horizontally oriented issues of analogical language is found in locating the analogy of being *within* the framework of the analogy of faith. For example, this explains the analogical connection between temple building and human conception. According to this nested relationship, metaphysical claims that are based on analogies must be found in scripture or be the result of hermeneutics bound by "good and necessary consequence."[79]

The salient point here is that this nested framework establishes *dependency*: metaphysical claims about Christ in relation to the world must be based on scripture. For example, Christ may be said to be "a temple" because such a claim about identity is made in scripture (e.g., John 2:21). This approach to analogies within the categorical syllogism of this study is the same: they are legitimate because they are found within divine revelation—and even taught from the words of Christ. This means that the logic of the argument's categorical syllogism relies on faith and the acceptance of scripture as a legitimate source of knowledge.

BOOLEAN LOGIC AS A THEOLOGICAL TOOL

The core argument of this study proceeds by presenting a categorical syllogism. Such a construction may be considered an analytical theological argument because of the presupposition that there is value in a rigorous and logical presentation. Because this categorical argument makes no attempt to prove the historicity or metaphysical reality of any object, it is Boolean in nature, rather than traditional Aristotelian argumentation. The key idea here is that Aristotelian logic assumes that all the terms in the syllogism refer to actual objects. But Boolean logic does not make this existential assumption and is more suitable for an argument that relies on knowledge claims that are explicitly based on faith and the acceptance of divine revelation, that is, the canon of Christian scripture.

Boolean logic uses three basic conditions: AND, OR, and NOT ("The inclusive OR condition allows for situations where two or more conditions can be true at the same time, but also true individually, that is, one *or* the other").[80] And the heart of Boolean logic is the concept of conditions being true or false.[81] Each of these conditions is used by Paul in the logic of his arguments. Julie Renshaw points out that there are many OR conditions in Christian theology: you either believe in Jesus *or* not; you have faith in God *or* not; and so on.[82] Renshaw also explains how the NOT condition is crucial for understanding 1 Corinthians, where the "Gospel stands in divine antithesis" to human wisdom.[83] There are many instances where Paul makes arguments with Boolean AND conditions. An example of this appears in 1 Corinthians (1:17–31) where God's wisdom and righteousness and sanctification and redemption come to Christians through Jesus.[84] This use of the AND condition is of particular interest because this study argues that one of the many divine intentions in the incarnation of Christ was to build the temple for the dwelling of his presence among the people of God.

The use of Boolean logic in the categorical syllogism means that the argument has no consideration for any claim that it may be falsified by the existential fallacy. Analytic theology utilizes logical analysis while accommodating sets of theological data drawn from authoritative sources, for theology begins with divine revelation (i.e., the scriptures).[85] Thus, the present argument cannot be disregarded as invalid simply because one does not have faith that scripture is a source of knowledge, or that a heavenly temple exists, or that Jesus has risen from the dead, and so on. As with all knowledge, the argument begins with faith—faith that seeks understanding (*fides quaerens intellectum*) according to the canon of Christian scripture.[86] Because existence is not a property of logic, the argument is not subject to the claim of invalidity by those who lack faith.

The use of Boolean logic requires an explanation of the rejection of the claims of logical positivism, which asserts that religious language or theological arguments are meaningless because they are not open to verification by empirical scientific investigation.[87] It is entirely possible to have a categorical syllogism with a valid form and clear propositions be rejected on the basis of an informal critique which is audience-oriented. The audience might reject a valid argument simply because they do not find it relevant, or they might not accept the premises of the content in the propositions.[88] These possibilities are acutely relevant for theological argumentation based on the acceptance of Christian scripture as an authoritative source of divine revelation. The audience simply might not have faith to believe such claims are true. Furthermore, according to the Christian doctrine of God, he is not an object in space and time which can be subjected to scientific investigation, for he is presently known by faith (2 Cor. 5:7). This is qualified by the fact that God will fully reveal himself in Christ so that he will be universally known by "sight" at his Second Coming (1 Tim. 6:15).[89]

The use of Boolean logic is not a rejection of the Trinitarian dogma of one God and three persons. For some have suggested that "theological discourse should resist the 'true/false' dichotomies of Boolean logic."[90] Such an understanding of the Trinity seems to suggest that God's "one-and-many-ness" undermines all logic. But the conclusion that one must resist Boolean logic in order to preserve the Trinity is fallacious because it rests upon a false understanding. The only way in which the Trinity would require a true–false dichotomy to be operative is if God's oneness (his essence) and the persons of the Trinity were the same. But if God's essence is indivisible (as the Athanasian Creed states), and if God's persons are distinct, then one-ness and many-ness do not function as poles on the exact same spectrum and therefore do not represent a dialectical antithesis.

The use of Boolean logic is helpful when formulating an argument that relies upon the canon of Christian scripture as an epistemically critical source of information. The approach taken here utilizes Boolean logic as a *tool* for constructing dogmatic formulations, rather than having logic function as a universal *foundation* for knowledge.[91] For the Protestant, the canon of scripture contains a total of sixty-six books from the Old Testament and New Testament. This claim requires sufficient epistemological warrant and is an act of faith.[92] This act of faith inevitably draws from the Bible itself as the foundation of its justification so that there can be an "accounting" for doctrine that is circular but not viciously so.

The fallacy of circular reasoning is called *petition principii* and assumes the truth of that which one is seeking to prove.[93] But one must always work from certain foundational assumptions of faith as one seeks understanding in any domain. There is some element of circularity in all inquiry and in all interpretation.[94] However, the rigor of the tasks through which faith seeks to understand prevents inquiry from being viciously or tightly circular. According to this model, acts of interpretation must be open to revision as they continually seek to fit with the textual evidence (the data) of scripture.[95] But faith that seeks understanding must also operate from the basis of faith in Christ.

Because scripture always points to Christ by doctrine, command, principle, precedent, or illustration, "Christ is the substance and criterion of right inter-pretation."[96] Faith seeks understanding in ways that can be accounted for but not always proven empirically.[97]

To summarize, the use of Boolean logic is helpful when formulating an argument that accords with the presuppositionalism of faith that confesses the doctrine of the virgin birth as found in the Apostles' Creed and beyond. The ancient creeds from the first three centuries use an element of circular logic in the sense that they simply restate the truths of scripture: the doctrine of the virgin birth is true because scripture says it is true. Whatever may be said of the *form* of this argument, its *content* is not subject to the critique of those who lack faith and reject scripture as a divine source of knowledge. Lastly, the use of Boolean logic is helpful when constructing an argument that makes ontological or metaphysical claims that are based upon an exegetical-dogmatic Christology. In other words, it is God himself who defines reality through the scriptures, including the similarities and/or distance between things—including the relationship between construction and conception.

SUMMARY

This chapter offers a methodological map that enables the reader to proceed through the argumentation ahead. The first section describes the dance of deductive reasoning and then inductive analysis within a hermeneutical spiral. Deductive argumentation is not only helpful in certain instances but it also follows certain patterns of biblical argumentation. The second section shows that changing terminology from that of building to human conception is entirely legitimate because of the way that scripture uses such language. This justifies the move within the categorical syllogism from the term "construction" to "conception." Ultimately, the analogical overlap between the terms "construction" and "conception" is Christocentric because it is dependent upon Jesus himself as revealed in scripture.

The third section on temple identity and analogy demonstrated that the use of the analogy drawn from the act of constructing a house to describe the virgin birth does not constitute a new "Babylonian captivity" of the Word of God to secularism or Hellenistic language.[98] Rather, it is the other way around. The creation itself reveals a "natural law" and these categories reflect the intelligent design of God's universe. In other words, the use of Aristotelian categories is simply a reflection of the ordered world according to Genesis 1–3. The fourth section located analogical language within the analogy of faith. This means that Christ's words in scripture function as the final predicator of analogous relationships. The fifth section described how

Boolean logic functions as a helpful theological tool for analytic reasoning and establishing necessity according to the scriptures.

NOTES

1. Here I borrow the metaphor of "mapping" from Johnson 2021, 116.

2. Berkhof (1938, 56) raises this question about deductive arguments.

3. For a critique of the methodological attempt to read biblical texts apart from their theological *Wirkungsgeschichte,* see Watson 1997, 4.

4. For a discussion of Zanchi and his method, see Rogers and McKim 1979, 157. For a discussion of Athanasius's deductive interpretations of scripture, see Leithart 2011, 39.

5. See Gabler's inaugural lecture at the University of Altdorf on March 30, 1787, "An Oration on the Proper Distinction between Biblical and Dogmatic Theology and the Specific Objective of Each" and the discussion in Gentry and Wellum 2012, 47.

6. Phelan and Reynolds 1996, 155.

7. For example, Beckwith (1986, 429–30) offers a canonical argument for the deity of Christ with the following statements: P1: Yahweh is the only one who participated in creation (Isa. 44:24); P2: Christ is the one who participated in creation (John 1:3, Col. 1:16); C: Therefore, Christ is Yahweh. Similarly, Dodson (2016, 133–4) observes that there are several places in the Old Testament where scriptural history leads the reader to construct categorical syllogisms. For example, when considering the descendants of Levi in Exodus 6:16–20, he concludes: P1: All Levites are among God's chosen people. P2: Gershon is a Levite. C: Therefore, Gershon is among God's chosen people.

8. Johnson 2021, 105.

9. I use the terms "systematic theology" and "dogmatic theology" (or "dogmatics") interchangeably throughout this study without distinction.

10. McCall (2021, 1) defines analytic theology as "very roughly, what happens when philosophers who are interested in doctrine and theologians who think that there is (or might be) value in the appropriate use of philosophical tools get together."

11. Geisler and Feinberg (1980, 67) state, "Philosophy's job is to define philosophic and scientific terms, and clarify the language of ideas."

12. On this description of analytic theology, see Wood 2021, 51. Kerr (2011, 343) also acknowledges that classically speaking, the Trinity has "been regarded as entirely a matter of divine revelation."

13. Horton (2002, 283 n.56) describes Geerhardus Vos's Dutch Reformed theology as holding together "in a genuine dialectic, the exegetical-concrete-temporal grounding of dogmatics with the systematic and more deductive development."

14. Horton 2003, 15.

15. Dodson 2016, 133.

16. Geisler and Feinberg 1980, 68.

17. Given the fact that Jesus may have spoken both Greek and Aramaic, it seems best to take a case-by-case approach to the issue. There are times when the biblical

text refers to Jesus' exact words (*ipsissima verba*) and other times when it refers to the gist or summary of his words as a reproduction of his voice (*ipsissima vox*). See Porter 1993, 199–235.

18. Walton 1996, 15.

19. Martin (2021, 35–6) defines the "ambiguity fallacy" as employing "unclear or equivocal terms or propositions."

20. Here, I assume a dichotomous anthropology of constituent elements of human nature, including the material and the immaterial. Reymond (1998, 423) argues that all of the Reformation creeds adopt the dichotomous view of humanity, for example, WCF 32.1.

21. Here I agree with Augustine (*Ret.* 1.3; cf. *De grat.* 60.244) that it is not possible to make dogmatic statements about the theories of Creationism, Propagation, or Traducianism.

22. Duby 2022, 224.

23. Leithart 2011, 60

24. Against the Marcionites, the Manicheans, and the Platonists, Athanasius held that the body itself is not negative (Gemeinhardt 2011, 328).

25. Heppe 2007, 425.

26. Johnson 2021, 48.

27. Turner 2008, 310; also noted by Mounce 2011, 112.

28. France 2007, 460–1.

29. Nolland (2005, 484) warns that the danger in Matt 12:6 "is of proving too much." This danger is present because of the shocking nature of Jesus' teaching here and the Christological possibilities opened up by such a comparison between himself and the temple. For the view that this text is not a Christological comparison with the temple at all and that the real issue is "mercy," see Luz 2001, 181–2. For the view that Jesus' community is that which is greater, see Harrington 2007, 172.

30. Parallel texts to the curtain of the temple being torn in two are found in Matthew 27:51 and Luke 23:45. For a comprehensive study of Matthew's account of the torn veil, see Gurtner 2007.

31. Johnson 2011, 225–37.

32. Johnson 2011, 232.

33. Johnson 2011, 232.

34. Hurtado (2011, 268) comments on Mark 15:38 that the tearing of the temple curtain "seems to mean that Jesus' death provides the basis for a new access to God, a new 'temple'." Strauss (2014, 705) points out that, for Mark, the tearing of the curtain may have aspects of judgment *and* gracious revelation working at the same time. It was both a symbol of the temple's destruction and a "revelation of Jesus' identity and the significance of his death."

35. Johnson 2011, 232.

36. Lanier 2014, 434.

37. Fay 2006, 258.

38. Here I draw from the exposition of Parsons 2015, 323.

39. Fay 2006, 256 n9, citing McNicol 1998, 32.

40. Wright 2002, 55.

41. For an exhaustive defense of the Christian canon as a philosophical source of metaphysics, and so on, see Johnson 2021.

42. Leithart 2011, 43.

43. Inge 2003, 4.

44. For the interchangeable use of these terms, see Inge 2003, 3.

45. The two components of this definition draw from Inge 2003, 1–5.

46. Hjalmarson (2015, 18–19).

47. Regev comments, "Paul specifies the common domain shared by the community and the Temple: God's Spirit resides in both" (2019, 57).

48. In 1 Corinthians 3:17, the relative pronoun *hostis* in the phrase "*hoitines este hymeis*" refers back to "*ho naos*" in the previous phrase "*ho gar naos tou theou hagios estin.*"

49. Recent studies on Paul, resurrection, and the human body include Tappenden 2016, McGlothlin 2018, and Chang 2021.

50. Calaway (2013, 103) comments on Hebrews 3:4 thus

the text shifts to God as the builder of all. The house represents all creation . . . To move from God's house, with reference to the sanctuary, to "all things" is readily understandable since the sanctuary itself already represented the cosmos.

51. deSilva 2000, 137.

52. deSilva 2000, 137.

53. Glouberman 2012, 59.

54. The points made in this paragraph rely on Itkonen 2005, 177.

55. Itkonen 2005, 177.

56. Schnabel (2019, 225–6) observes that

The Stoics divide theology into three parts (*theologica tripartita*): the mythical discourse about the gods of the poets, the political reference to the gods in the civic cults, and the "natural theology" that aligns the discourse about the gods with nature. (Varro, *Antiquitates rerum divinarum* fr. 6–12)

Here Schnabel refers to the works of the Roman historian Marcus Terentius Varro entitled *Antiquitates rerum humanarum et divinarum* (*Antiquities of Human and Divine Things*). For a recent discussion of this source for philosophy and religion, see Rüpke 2014, 246–68.

57. Johnson 2021, 25.

58. Heppe 2007, 423.

59. Heppe 2007, 423.

60. As noted earlier, the passage from Matthew 1:22–23 is especially important because it identifies the virgin birth as the fulfillment of Isaiah's (7:14) prophecy that a son would be born and be called "Immanuel" or "God with us."

61. The relationship between the Father and the Son was "almost always at the forefront of his Trinitarian-theological considerations" (Gemeinhardt 2011, 297).

62. Leithart 2011, 44.

63. Davies 1985, 1.

64. Tyler 2020, 226.

65. McKim 2014, 11. So also Balthasar, according to Healy 2005, 23.

66. Johnson challenges this classical view of Karl Barth and his rejection of the Aquinas tradition on the *analogia entis* or "analogy of being" (2011). For Barth's rejection of natural theology, see *Church Dogmatics*, II.1 (1957, 170). Also see the related volume by the German Jesuit theologian Przywara (2014).

67. von Balthasar 2000, 17.

68. Guarino 2005, 239.

69. Ticciati 2013, 2–3.

70. Healy 2005, 19, emphasis his.

71. Guarino 2005, 233.

72. With respect to scripture and metaphysical theology, Guarino (2005, 247) states:

The message of Scripture and Christian doctrine is unmistakable in this regard: God has revealed himself uniquely in the history of Israel; Jesus of Nazareth is the Logos incarnate, consubstantial with the Father; the Holy Spirit, worshiped together with the Father and the Son, sanctifies us and leads the church into the fullness of truth.

73. von Balthasar (2004, 2:81) comments:

Perhaps no example shows so clearly as do Jesus' practically oriented parables (along with their exigencies and consequences) how divine logic can and will express itself in human logic on the basis of an *analogia linguae* [analogy of language] and, ultimately—in spite of all objections—an *analogia entis*, fulfilled in Christ, who is God and man in one person.

74. Here I attempt to expand upon what Guarino (2005, 239) means when he explains: "In his dialogue with Barth, Balthasar's entire point has been that a defense of the analogy of being can only take place within the analogy of faith, that is, *within the one supernatural order of grace.*"

75. Barron 2016, 13.

76. Barron 2016, 13.

77. Barron 2016, 14.

78. For the definition of "natural theology" starting with faith seeking understanding, see the comments by McGrath in Dew and Campbell 2024, 9.

79. See WCF (article 1.2) and my discussion in chapter 1.

80. This definition of the inclusive OR condition comes from Renshaw 2003, 184.

81. Brown 2003, 2.

82. Renshaw 2003, 184.

83. Renshaw points to 1 Corinthians 1:19 as a prime example of a NOT condition: "I will destroy the wisdom of the wise, and the discernment of the discerning I will thwart."

84. Renshaw 2003, 180.

85. For a discussion on the relationship between analytic theology and its authoritative source, see Wood 2021, 51. McCall (2021, 4) relates analytic theology to the theological interpretation of the Bible as God's authoritative "word for faith and life."

86. In addition to Anselm, here I am drawing from the Augustinian tradition of "faith seeking understanding" as found in *In Ps.* CXVIII; *Ep.* CXX, CXXXVII, CXX; also see Augustine, *Tractates on the Gospel of John 28–54* (trans. Rettig 1993, 18).

87. For a definition of "logical positivism" as being synonymous with "logical empiricism," see Richardson and Uebel (2007, I).

88. These informal critiques of the content of logically valid arguments come from Martin 2021, 35–36.

89. For a brief discussion of the transformation of the invisibility of God in Second Temple Judaism and the revelation of God in Christ by sight at his Second Coming, see Wenkel 2017, 206–7.

90. Kerr (2011, 344) reviews this concept in his survey of contemporary literature on Trinitarian theology and analytic philosophy.

91. Here I follow Cotnoir (2019, 509), who argues along a similar line of thought when he states, "Theologians should, I argue, think of logical methods as a set of *tools* for constructing (closed) theories, and not think of logic as a universal *foundation* for all possible theories" (emphasis his).

92. The nature of the epistemological warrant or justification for holding to the canon of the New Testament is explored by Kruger 2012, 20–21.

93. Dodson 2016, 135.

94. Leithart (2011, 53) observes that within Athanasius, "There is a circularity, as we have seen, but for Athanasius this is the inevitable circularity of biblical interpretation."

95. This follows Cotnoir's (2019, 510) definition of an anti-exceptionalist understanding of logic, which means that "logic is subject to revision on the basis of abductive considerations like simplicity, explanatory power, unification, fruitfullness, non-ad-hocness, and fit with evidence."

96. Leithart (2011, 53) explains, "Athanasius's biblical work is, throughout, a theological hermeneutics. Christ is both the substance of Scripture and the criterion of right interpretation."

97. For a discussion of "accounting for our knowledge of canon," see Kruger 2012, 21.

98. Adolf Von Harnack argued that the ancient church was in bondage to Hellenism and subject to "acute Hellenization" as it produced doctrines such as the Nicene and Chalcedonian formulations of the Trinity. For a discussion of the Orthodox Christian doctrine of God and of the Logos as being based on "a strong Platonic element," see von Harnack 1898, 4:6.

Chapter 3

The Virgin Birth Concealed and Revealed

This chapter advances the discussion by locating the salvation-historical mystery of the virgin birth within the two poles of divine concealment and revelation. One of the most difficult aspects of the Christian canon is relating the Old Testament to the New Testament. This chapter makes no pretense that it will solve the entanglements. However, the exegetical-dogmatic nature of the argument at hand draws from both the Old and New Testaments. Accordingly, this chapter sketches out a perspective that will help the reader to understand how exegetical evidence is being adduced as typological relationships are established between the Old and New Testaments. The virgin birth (virginal conception), when defined as the visitation of God in human form through the virgin Mary, must be located within a certain tension of divine concealment and revelation. This is an aspect of the slightly broader concept of the incarnation: the visitation of a God-man, who is God in human form. This chapter locates the mystery of the virgin birth within the two poles of divine concealment and revelation. When the Christian scriptures are read forward and backward, it is apparent that the virgin birth fits with what God had revealed and that it accords with the expectations established by the prophets.

THE CATEGORY OF TEMPLE BUILDING

The present argument is proffered to the reader in the form of a categorical syllogism. It is called a *categorical* syllogism because it is an argument about categories or classes of things and how they relate to each other. Both the major premise and the minor premise of this argument are about the category of temples or legitimate places of Yahweh worship in the scriptures.[1] The argument presses the point that Jesus' incarnation was a divine act of temple building and that such an act could only be accomplished directly by the Holy Spirit. That is how heavenly temples of God are built.

This argument relies upon the category or class of "temple" and its function throughout the canon of scripture. The category of temple building is intentionally designed to reflect Jesus' own identity as the "temple of God" (e.g., Matt. 12:6). And Jesus' identity as the temple of God is organically related to the motif of God's dwelling place, which are places where his special divine glory is temporarily located. This type of reading relates things such as altars, tents, and temples within a certain class and develops their relationship within salvation-history. The reader will want to consider the following constellation of points about the definition of typology and use of this hermeneutic.

First, typology is based on a canon-wide understanding of eschatological advancement toward a Christ-centered climax. Escalation often moves through type and antitype relationships between persons, places, and events. The concept of advancement is important because some patterns are escalated as they are filled up and partially fulfilled until the final and greatest comes along. This is why Paul could write that the "fullness of time" had come when God sent his Son (Gal. 4:4). The emphasis here is on promise and fulfillment.[2] These patterns are informed by and interpreted by scripture. This worldview of escalating patterns applies to the past, present, and future and is based on the core contribution of apocalyptic discourse: moving back the curtains in front of human history to reveal the spiritual realities and divine purposes going on behind the actions of people, institutions, and events.

Second, following typological relationships demands exegesis—it must be concerned with a grammatical and historical reading of scripture.[3] Typology is used to determine the meaning of Old Testament texts because it reads them prophetically and forward-looking in their canonical context, reflecting the human *and* divine authorship of scripture. Even though God intended for Old Testament texts to point forward in salvation-history, that does not mean that humans always saw this or understood this was the case.[4] However, the presence of a typological pattern does not change the meaning of texts or the human author's intention in writing them. What this does mean is that the meaning of a given text may only be apparent when it is placed in the canon of scripture and considered theologically. Although R. T. France eschews an emphasis on the original meaning of texts, I would agree that typology depends "on a theological *hindsight* informed by commitment to Christ as the climax of God's work of salvation."[5]

Third, typology is not eisegesis nor allegory. Although typology may be abused, it must be understood as an integral aspect of grammatical-historical interpretation as utilized by Christ and the apostles. In some cases, the human authors of scripture understood these wider relationships.[6] In the case of the virgin birth, this means that the exegetical-dogmatic conclusions are subjectively read through the eyes of faith in the object of the resurrected Christ but are also objectively established historical and canonical connections.[7] The various criteria for these typological connections include patterns, promise–fulfillment, repetition, reuse of key terms, reuse of sequences in describing events, and similarities with covenantal and salvation-historical significance.[8]

Fourth, a typological paradigm for hermeneutical relationships binds a canon-wide approach to interpretation with historical precedents. This means that there is some convergence between a "reader hermeneutic" that considers the whole canon of scripture and a "text author" hermeneutic that is grammatical and historical in nature. The canonical nature of this study allows us to pursue this question: what is the theological drama toward which the temple was pointing, whether the author was *fully* cognizant of this or not?[9] As others have noted, the term "incarnation" is a "term seeking a definition" because it explicitly reads the Old Testament through a post-Pentecost Christian lens.[10] But the implied reader of the Christian canon cannot pluck out their eye, so to speak, and read the Old Testament as though Jesus has not risen from the dead.[11] There must be some overlap between reader-response criticism and grammatical-historical exegesis as the Spirit-empowered disciple of Jesus reads the canon forward and backward in light of the cross. This statement must be qualified with the disclaimer that whatever spiritual empowerment is required on the part of the reader, it does not entitle the reader to eisegesis. Perhaps typology could be labeled as "exposition," when applied to the Old Testament because it *develops* the content of the canon in consideration of progressive revelation that climaxes in Christ. The salient point is that a typological reading of scripture is not merely a hermeneutical strategy, even if it relies upon an implied readership, but is an act of exegesis.

Fifth, a typological reading of Jesus' virgin birth is based on the way in which Jesus' death and resurrection were interpreted by the apostles and the early church. The reference to building and rebuilding this temple of Jesus' body through resurrection in "three days" or on the "third day" was eventually interpreted by Paul as an event that was based on "the scriptures":

> For I delivered to you as of first importance what I also received: that Christ died for our sins in accordance with the Scriptures, that he was buried, that he was raised *on the third day in accordance with the Scriptures*, and that he appeared to Cephas, then to the twelve. Then he appeared to more than five hundred brothers at one time, most of whom are still alive, though some have fallen asleep. Then he appeared to James, then to all the apostles. Last of all, as to one untimely born, he appeared also to me. For I am the least of the apostles, unworthy to be called an apostle, because I persecuted the church of God. But by the grace of God I am what I am, and his grace toward me was not in vain. On the contrary, I worked harder than any of them, though it was not I, but the

grace of God that is with me. Whether then it was I or they, so we preach and so you believed. (1 Cor. 15:3–11)

This focus on Jesus' resurrection on the "third day in accordance with the Scriptures" (1 Cor. 15:4) is paralleled by the previous line that "Christ died for our sins in accordance with the Scriptures" (1 Cor. 15:3). The entirety of Jesus' Passion was a fulfillment of the scriptures, and this included the timeline of events. However, as others have observed, the problem is that there is "no direct verbal prophecy in the ancient Scriptures which predicted such a thing."[12] This quotation from 1 Corinthians was not only Paul's view but likely reflected a "creedal-type formula used by early believers."[13] This means that Paul and the early church understood Jesus' teaching about the rebuilding of his temple-body in three days and understood to follow the prophetic pattern of typology in the scriptures.[14]

Sixth, a typological reading of Jesus' virgin birth is based on the way in which Jesus' death and resurrection were interpreted by Jesus. Events in scripture, such as the salvation of Jonah (1:17) from the belly of the great fish after three days, must have been understood to be figural in the sense that they anticipated an even greater event. Jesus himself teaches such a typological hermeneutic when he stated:

> For just as Jonah was three days and three nights in the belly of the great fish, so will the Son of Man be three days and three nights in the heart of the earth. (Matt. 12:40)

As noted above, it is not immediately apparent that Jonah's presence in the great fish for three days has any significance. However, when this instance is placed within the context of the entire Old Testament canon, a pattern emerges that makes it more significant. Beyond this reference to Jonah, the canonical pattern of "three days" includes the restoration of Isaac from sacrifice on the "third day," as Isaac was as good as dead (Gen. 22:1–24, esp. 22:4). Other texts, such as Hosea 6:2, refer to a person being "raised up" on the third day, but it is not directly cited by any New Testament writer as being part of the third-day prophetic motif.[15] However, within the Old Testament canonical pattern of "three days," the presence of this *Stichwort* provides criteria for including it within the scriptures as it anticipates the "third day" resurrection of Christ.[16]

Seventh, a typological reading of the virgin birth accords with the larger literary and theological pattern of building God's house. Israel's story is the story of God's plan to permanently dwell among his people even after the Fall and even in the face of Israel's perpetual stiff-necked unbelief. On this point, Peter Leithart's analysis of Yahweh's reference to Moses and Samuel in the book of Jeremiah is worth quoting in whole:

Jeremiah is set "over the nations" in order to "pluck up, break down, destroy, and overthrow, and also to plant and build" (1:5, 10). "Pluck up" and "plant" are words from gardening. Israel is pictured as a garden or a vineyard that the Lord has planted in the land (cf. Psalms 80; Isaiah 5), hoping she will produce fruit for His delight. Judah has no fruit, so the Lord is threatening to uproot her (2:21; cf. Ezekiel 19:12). Later in Jeremiah's prophecy, the Lord promises to replant a remnant of the people in the land. Looked at one way, Judah's history is about land. Judah is planted, plucked up, and planted again. The words "tear down" and "built" are associated with building. Here, Judah is being pictured as God's house or God's city. The Lord built her up, but He is now coming to tear her down. Later, the Lord says, He will rebuild her. Looked at this way, Israel's history is a story of the building of God's house.[17]

The breadth of this summary statement is apparent as it crosses biblical books and genres. This is a sweeping calculus of the way that God was at work among his people: he was tearing down and building up in anticipation of a final "building" in which God's presence could dwell permanently among his people. Even those who followed Yahweh in faith and obedience were called "the remnant of the house of Israel" (Isa. 46:3). As Leithart points out above, the ministry of Israel's prophets included the call to anticipate a future day when the "house" of God would be firmly and eternally planted.

Eighth, a typological reading of Jesus' virgin birth is based on the way in which Jesus' death and resurrection were interpreted by early church theologians such as Athanasius. The search for typological connections across the Christian scriptures related to the virgin birth of Jesus-the-temple is based on the historical precedent of the church fathers such as Athanasius, the bishop of Alexandria (*c.* AD 294–373).[18] Peter Leithart explains that typology-oriented exegesis characterized the pre-creedal church's attempts to provide "raw materials" for developing and defining Trinitarian theology.[19] This was so prevalent that Leithart comments, "Before the creeds, typology controlled Christology."[20] This means that biblical language (imagery, metaphors, analogies, etc.) was used to define biblical doctrines. This pattern of drawing from the language of scripture and its typological relationships continued even after the Nicene council.[21] Peter Leithart observes that there are four examples of this paradigm at work in Athanasius: "(1) the Son is the 'radiance' of the Father's glory in Hebrews 1:3, (2) the Father is the 'fountain of living waters' in Jeremiah 2:13, (3) the Son is son to the Father as evidenced by many passages, and (4) the Son is the Word and Wisdom of the Father (John 1:1–3; Prov. 8)."[22] Significantly, Athanasius (*C. Ar.* 2.22.74) also includes the Jerusalem temple as a "particularly fitting model of incarnation."[23] Thus, while Jesus is Son, Radiance, Stream, Word, and Wisdom, he is also Temple.[24] Most importantly, for the purposes of this study, Jesus is *also* the Tabernacle and Altar because they are also dwelling places of God's

presence, even if temporarily so. While neither Leithart nor Athanasius fully
develops the typological significance of the act of *building* the temple (or its
related antecedents), this broader pattern establishes the historical precedent
for such an endeavor.

To summarize this section: this typological reading of the interpretation
of Jesus' death and resurrection was the approach of Jesus, Paul, and early
church theologians such as Athanasius. There are two important points which
follow. First, the soundness of this typological method enables the reader
of scripture to consider texts that the New Testament writers did not cite
but which may have typological import. The possibility of such import also
extends to the wider literary contexts of citations found in the New Testament.[25] Second, this approach "should be able to discover types of Christ
which the New Testament writers did not mention."[26] Such discoveries may
be tentative and qualified as not being based on the quotations of the New
Testament writers, even if they are based on the approach of the New Testament writers.

TWO WAYS IN WHICH TEMPLES ARE CONSTRUCTED

There is an important sense in which *all* places of Yahweh worship fall into
one of two categories: either they are (1) made by human hands or (2) made
without human hands.[27] According to this dichotomy, the way in which
things are made determines their nature. The dualistic language of things
"made by human hands" versus "made without human hands" has its origins
in Jewish anti-idol polemic. The adjective *cheiropoiētos* is "never used in a
positive sense in the Septuagint or the New Testament."[28] And in the Hebrew
Bible, the phrase "the work of men's hands" occurs approximately fifty-four
times and almost half "refer to idolatrous works."[29] Things made by human
hands (*cheiropoiētos*) are temporary and ultimately unfit for the divine presence to permanently dwell in. Broadly speaking, references in the canon to
the "works of human hands" are typically negative because such things are
suitable for idolatry.[30] Those things which are made without human hands
(*acheiropoiētos*) have natures that are heavenly, divinely made, eternal, and
unshakable.

Before proceeding, it is important to add an important qualification: the
distinction between things made by human hands and things made without human hands does not imply any denigration of human conception or
the material world. This truth should be evident by the fact that Mary and
Jesus were fully human in every way. But it is also true that any dualistic
metaphysic of creation may lead to error, and so the point must be made
clear. Again, the point of this argument being made here is not about the

metaphysical substance of what is being created (e.g., Jesus' human nature) but about how the instrumental power of the Holy Spirit was operative as the incarnation took place.

Stephen's speech before his martyrdom in Acts provides important material for the argument that the earliest Christian disciples understood Jesus in relation to his identity as a Messiah-temple. Stephen's speech is especially important because he clearly rejects all human-made places of Yahweh worship as being sufficient to function as a "house" for Yahweh, for they are all temporary and contingent in nature.

Stephen's lengthy speech in Acts 7 addresses three main topics: the land, the law of Moses, and the temple.[31] Each of these topics is addressed because his audience of zealous Jews, both Pharisees and Sadducees, were rejecting Jesus as the messiah and misreading the scriptures. Stephen's argument comes to the following three conclusions.

First, the Jewish possession of the Promised Land must not be equated with God's favor or the guarantee of his personal divine presence. In support of this point, Stephen draws attention to the fact that Abraham did not receive a "foot's length" of the land of promise (Acts 7:5).

Second, the status of being the recipients of special divine revelation in the form of the law of Moses does not guarantee obedience to it or guarantee God's favorable presence. Stephen supports this by pointing out that Israel "refused to obey" Moses, turned to idolatry, and worshiped the golden calf (Acts 7:39–41).

Third, the Jews in Stephen's audience must not assume that the physical presence of a temple building equates to the personal presence of God among his people. This last conclusion should be evident because God does not dwell "in houses made by hands" as indicated by Psalms 11:4 (quoted in Acts 7:49–50).[32]

Stephen explains in his speech before his martyrdom that even though Solomon built a "dwelling place for the God Jacob" and a "house" for Yahweh (Acts 7:46–47), the nature of the temple in Jerusalem must be qualified with this truth:

Yet the Most High does not dwell [*katoikeō*] in houses made by hands [*cheiropoiētos*]. (Acts 7:48a)

Stephen explains the impossibility of such a situation by appealing to Psalms 11:4:

Heaven is my throne, and the earth is my footstool. What kind of house will you build for me, says the Lord, or what is the place of my rest? Did not my hand [*hē cheir*] make all these things? (Acts 7:49–50)

Conceptually, Stephen explains that God cannot dwell in a house that is "handmade."[33] This passage (Acts 7:48–49) is the only place in all of Acts where "house" refers to the temple.[34] But Stephen does not deny that Solomon built Yahweh a "house." In fact, Stephen affirms that Solomon did, in fact, build a "house" for Yahweh. The issue for Stephen is what kind of house it is. Stephen is keen to drive the point that this "house" in Jerusalem was not a permanent house for God's dwelling place among his people. It is critical to note the reason for the Jerusalem temple being a temporary house for God is due to the manner in which it was created: by human hands.

Stephen's theology of the temple building in Jerusalem and its limitations echoes Yahweh's two rhetorical questions to David through the prophet Nathan in 2 Samuel (7:5 and 7:7). The first question is one in which Yahweh asks (2 Sam. 7:5): "Would you build me a house to dwell in?" and in the second question he asks David through Nathan (7:7): "did I speak word . . . saying 'Why have you not built me a house of cedar?'" Those questions indicate that Yahweh never asked for a building to dwell in and that there is a sense in which a physical building is beneath him, for it cannot contain him. Stephen's quotation of Isaiah (66:1–3) alludes to Yahweh's location in heaven and also asks a similar rhetorical question: "what is the house that you would build for me?" (Isa. 66:1 // Acts 7:49).

Alan Thompson connects the dots between the fact that the Jerusalem temple was handmade (made by human hands) and the temptation of idolatry:

> As Stephen draws his history of Israel to a close in verses 48–50 he appears to charge his audience with turning the temple into an idol. The reference to the Most High not living in "handmade" houses (v. 48) repeats the language used of idolatry in verse 41 as the worship of what their "hands had made." The fact that every occurrence of the term *cheiropoiētos* (handmade) in the LXX refers to idols especially strengthens the idea that Stephen is charging his audience with idolatry here.[35]

For Stephen, the inverse is arguably true by implication: Jesus-the-temple was not "made by hands." Jesus is the true temple of God or the Messiah-temple. It is difficult to resist the logical conclusions of Stephen's argument because of his explicit focus on Christ the "Righteous One" (Acts 7:52).[36] According to the theology of Stephen's speech, those who resist this conclusion are resisting the Holy Spirit (Acts 7:51). All other temples and places of Yahweh worship on earth have been handmade. Those who limit God's presence to them commit idolatry. The key point here is that Stephen's Jewish opposition has pursued a temple made by human hands and created an idol out of it. Correspondingly, they are rejecting Jesus the true temple who was made by God's own hands and who is the appropriate object of worship.

The clear witness to Jesus' self-understanding as the temple of God in the Gospel witnesses and in Acts is foundational for an exegetical-dogmatic consideration of the relationship between the temple and Jesus. Jesus' identity as the temple of God is not merely a theological construct deduced by human reason. Rather, this relationship between Israel's institutions of worship and Jesus' identity is inextricably united.

Luke portrays Stephen as an ideal witness to Christ. Theologically, Christ has a temple-nature, or he is a temple-being that is perfectly suited to be a "house" for the divine presence. This stands in contrast to all other salvation-historical antecedents before him. As a perfect martyr, Stephen's face reflects his possession of God's personal presence because he has come to trust in the savior of Israel—Jesus. Stephen achieves what even Moses could not—that is, his face is transformed so as to reflect God's glory and he sees the glory of God and Jesus. Stephen is further proof that the Mosaic era has been surpassed by a new covenant with greater glory.

In the second instance of this terminology in Acts, this dualistic approach to the ways in which temples are constructed is also born out with clarity in Paul's speech at the Aeropagus:

> The God who made the world and everything in it, being Lord of heaven and earth, does not live [*katoikeō*] in temples made by man [*cheiropoiētois*], nor is he served by human hands, as though he needed anything, since he himself gives to all mankind life and breath and everything. (Acts 17:24–25)

The operative verb *katoikeō* here has a semantic range including: (1) "to live," "to dwell," "to reside" and (2) to make "something a habitation or dwelling by being there" as "to inhabit."[37] The logic works this way: any temple made by human hands (*cheiropoiētois*) is unsuitable to be God's dwelling place. Paul's blanket statement is universal and covers both Jewish and Greek places of cultic worship, whatever and wherever it might be. These places of Israel's worship would include primitive altars, Israel's tent of meeting, and the physical temple in Jerusalem.

Jesus' own teaching in Matthew (5:34–35) about oath-taking is important here because he grounds his reasoning for simply using "yes" or "no" in the fact that all of creation is God's. For heaven is God's "throne," the whole earth is but "his footstool," and Jerusalem is "the city of the great King."[38] In this context from Matthew, Jesus forbids four specific vows, toward: (1) heaven, (2) earth, (3) Jerusalem, or (4) one's head/body. The reason is that none of these are truly one's possession because they all belong to God. Therefore, they cannot be offered up as though they could be given if the oath were broken. The key point here is that Stephen's speech and Jesus' teaching in Matthew both agree that the temple-city of Jerusalem is still where God has chosen to reveal his king. Yet, at the same time, the whole earth is still God's "footstool."

The book of Hebrews also refers to the two ways in which a temple (or place of Yahweh worship) could be constructed. The writer of Hebrews pays special attention to the fact that God gave special revelation to Moses regarding the construction of the tabernacle. Bruce observes that "The writer to the Hebrews lays special emphasis on this model, identifying it with the heavenly sanctuary, 'set up not by man but by the Lord' (Heb. 8:2)."[39] For the writer of Hebrews, the priestly work of Christ is in heaven, in "the true tent that the Lord setup, not man" (Heb. 8:2).[40] This concept also appears in the discussion of the tabernacle as an "earthly place of holiness" (9:1) in contrast to Christ's entrance into "holy places not made with hands" (9:24). Again, observe the importance of what *kind* of hands set up the heavenly tent. It is precisely because it was constructed by divine hands and not human hands, that it is the "true" and better tent.[41] The author of Hebrews is interested in this "vertical dualism" that is revealed through redemptive-historical progression in God's plan.[42]

There are several key points to summarize. First, God did not *permanently* dwell in, on, or around any of the earthly places of worship, including Israel's primitive altars, tents, or temples. Second, the reason why God did not permanently dwell in these places is because of the way they were constructed: by human hands. Third, Paul's speech in Acts 17 infers that the final dwelling place of God has been and will be a temple built directly by God's own hand: the nonarchitectural temple of Jesus.

This dichotomous view of the way in which temples were constructed is also evident in the following selection of scriptures from the New Testament:

> We heard him say, I will destroy this temple that is made with hands [*cheiropoiēton*], and in three days I will build another, not made with hands [*acheiropoiēton*]. (Mark 14:58)

> For we know that if the tent that is our earthly home is destroyed, we have a building from God, a house not made with hands [*acheiropoiēton*], eternal in the heavens. (2 Cor. 5:1)

> In him also you were circumcised with a circumcision made without hands [*acheiropoiēton*], by putting off the body of the flesh, by the circumcision of Christ. (Col. 2:11)

The first passage from Mark (14:58) is metaphorically referring to the temple of Jesus' own resurrection body.[43] The second passage in 2 Corinthians (5:1) refers to an eternal and heavenly body created directly by God. The third passage from Colossians (2:11) refers to circumcision as a metaphor for the Spirit-wrought work of inward regeneration. All three of these passages refer to what is done directly by the Holy Spirit: Jesus' resurrection, the eschatological human body, and regeneration. Each of these acts has qualities of the new age (the future and eternal age) which has broken into the present age since Jesus' resurrection. In other words, within the canon of the New Testament, there is nothing natural or of this world, which has been created *acheiropoieta*.

SUMMARY

This chapter explored the nature of typology and the distinction between temples "created by hands" and "not created by hands." The virgin birth was a unique salvation-historical event that is best described as one of the mysteries that was hidden in the Old Testament and then revealed. The virgin birth came about in accordance with what God had promised he would do through the "seed of a woman" and with what God had promised about "dwelling" among his covenant people. Throughout the Old Testament, God repeatedly came to dwell among his covenant people, but the altars, tents, and temples were all temporary because they were made by human hands. All of the theophanies and Christophanies created salvation-historical anticipation that one day God would dwell among his people in an eternal temple—one built by God's own hands.

NOTES

1. The scope of temple building is limited to legitimate temples because there were examples of illegitimate temples. For example, the Samaritan place of worship on Mt. Gerizim would be an example of an illegitimate sanctuary. For a recent discussion of excavations and the possibility that this place utilized an altar versus a walled temple, see Pummer 2016,1–21 and Gensel 2018, 73–93.
2. Caneday 2019, 147.
3. Contra Zacharias 2017, 13 and Baker 1976, 149–150.
4. Carson (2004, 406) explains:

That means that when Paul (or, for that matter, some other New Testament writer) claims that something or other connected with the gospel is the (typological) fulfillment of some old covenant pattern, he may not necessarily be claiming that everyone connected with the old covenant type understood the pattern to be pointing forward, but he is certainly claiming that God himself designed it to be pointing forward.

5. France 2006, 669.
6. Here, I seek to ground the ability to move between the claims of James Hamilton Jr. (2022, 4–5), who thinks that some (later) biblical authors intended to communicate the types found in their texts, and Richard B. Hays (2018, 2), who denies the authors were conscious of any anticipation of Christ. For a discussion of these

respective views, see Hamilton 2022, 4–5. For a discussion of the tensions surrounding human and divine intentions in scripture, see Compton 2008, 23–33.

7. Carson (2004, 404) explains that allegorical interpretation is not grounded in history, whereas typology is "grounded in history and presupposes corresponding events."

8. For a discussion of criteria or micro-level indicators of typology, see Hamilton
2022, 3–5 and of macro-level or "wide-angle literary structures" such as chiasm, see
Hamilton 2022, 331–6.

9. For a helpful discussion of this matter, see Compton 2008, 23–33.

10. Cole 2013, 108 n33, citing Dunn 2009, 37.

11. Cole (2013, 144) rightly states, "we ought not to do Christian theology as
though Christ had never come." Also see the definition of the "implied reader" of
scripture in Bockmuehl (2006, 70).

12. Lunn 2014, 524.

13. Lunn 2014, 523; quoting Ciampa and Rosner 2010, 745–6.

14. For a discussion of Athanasius's reference to the "sign of Jonah" (*C. Ar.* 2.80)
and Trinitarian typology, see Leithart 2011, 43–4.

15. Lunn (2014, 525) states, "It is evident that the use or non-use of an OT text
ought not to be the determining factor as to whether or not it is genuinely messianic."
This means that the reference to the "third day" in Hosea 6:2 should be considered as
part of a larger typological pattern that contributed to the importance of Jonah's stay
in the belly of the great fish for three days.

16. The Gospel of Luke also emphasizes Jesus' resurrection on the "third day"
(9:22; 13:32; 18:33; 24:7, 21, 46); also see references in Acts 10:40 and 1 Cor. 15:4.

17. Leithart 2000, 199–200.

18. For the idiosyncratic view that Athanasius' battle with the Arians in the fourth
century was largely a "polemical construct" designed to support his claims to ecclesiastical power, see Gwynn, 2007, vii; Gwynn, 2012, 9.

19. Leithart 2013, 115.

20. Leithart 2013, 115. Farag (2020, 39) and Leithart (2011, 30, 43) also understand Athanasius to interpret the Old Testament typologically.

21. Leithart 2013, 115.

22. Leithart 2013, 115.

23. Leithart 2013, 116.

24. Athanasius describes the incarnation as a divine "construction project" in his
Orations against the Arians (*C. Ar* 2.22.74). Athanasius uses the language of construction to describe the incarnation of Christ as though it were a house built by a
king in *De Inc.* 9–10. Athanasius uses the language of temple Christology to describe
Jesus' atoning death (*De Inc.* 9) and utilizes temple imagery to describe Jesus' resurrected body and its capacity to offer eternal life (*De Inc.* 31). Lastly, Athanasius
connects Jesus' identity as the temple of God with the concept of God's "dwelling"
place (*De Inc.* 8.3).

25. For the view that when New Testament authors quote the Old Testament, they
are evoking the larger context of the precursor text and inviting the readers to explore
this significance, see Turner 2018, 577–94.

26. Lunn 2014, 526, citing Greidanus 1999, 98 and following Kaiser 1985, 109.

27. Mattson's (2012, 237) summary of Bavinck's theological stance against dualistic anthropologies that set "spirit" and "matter" in opposition to each other is instructive here. For dualisms invariably value one thing and denigrate another.

28. Jipp (2014, 272) comments, "The adjective χειροποίητος [*cheiropoiētos*] is most frequently found in anti-idol polemic and is never used in a positive sense in the LXX or the NT (see, for example, Isa. 2:18; 10:11; 16:12; 19:1; 21:9; 31:7; 46:6; Dan. 5:4, 23; 6:28; Mark 14:58; Acts 7:48; 17:24; Heb. 9:11, 24)"; also see BDAG s.v. χειροποίητος, p. 1083.

29. This analysis of the Hebrew phrase "the work of men's hands" comes from Beale 2008, 192 n19.

30. Keener (2012–2013, 1405) comments on Stephen's reference to "works of their hands" in Acts 7:41 that: "Works of hands" suited idolatry (Deut. 4:28; 27:15; 31:29; 1 Kings 16:7; 2 Kings 19:11; 22:17; 2 Chr. 32:19; 34:25; Isa. 2:8; 37:19; Jer. 1:16; 25:6; 44:8 [51:8 LXX]; Bar. 6:51; Ws. 13:10; Rev. 9:20).

31. For an older study of the tabernacle in Stephen's speech, see Koester 1989, 82–4.

32. Here, I draw from my previous discussion of the theology of Stephen's speech in Wenkel 2018, 114–16.

33. Beale (2008, 190) comments that:

Stephen's terminology that God does not "dwell in temples made by hands" (v. 48) is in line with the rest of the New Testament, where "handmade" refers to the old creation and "made without hands" refers to the new creation, most specifically to the resurrection state as the beginning of the new creation.

34. A point made by Parsons (2008, p. 102).

35. Thompson 2011, 169. Hurtado (2011, 253) associates the Greek word *cheiropoiētos* with the "idols of the gentile nations" so that when the word is applied to the temple, it is "described as a human object that has no more validity than the images of the pagans."

36. For the view that Stephen was not focusing on Christ as a new and mobile place of worship, see Koester 1989, 84–85. But Stephen's vision of Jesus in heaven (Acts 7:55) indicates that Christ is located in heaven—in the place built by God's own hand.

37. BDAG s.v. κατοικέω, p. 534.

38. The origins of this reference to Jerusalem as "the city of the great King" come from Psalm 48:2 (Turner 2008, 173).

39. Bruce 1988, 147.

40. Mackie (2011, 77–117) and Calaway (2013, 108–9) offer a recent discussion of the "true tent" and the heavenly sanctuary in Hebrews.

41. Ellingworth (1993, 401) compares this reference to a "true" thing in heaven (Heb. 9:24) to the Johannine corpus, where "the contrast is less between the heavenly reality and its earthly reflection than simply between true and false, the true God and idols (1 John. 5:20)."

42. Here I attempt to avoid the false dichotomy between "vertical dualism" and "historical progression from promise to fulfillment" as found in Hagner (2011, 117).

43. Beale (2008, 190) finds that Mark 14:58 contains "the abbreviated tradition of which the narrative of Stephen's speech is launched."

Chapter 4

Typology, Anticipation, and Exegesis of Scripture

This chapter considers the possibility that the Old Testament scriptures about temple building anticipate a climactic temple for God's dwelling—a temple that would be made without human hands. Specifically, this is a brief defense of the proposal described in the previous chapter: that typological readings of the Old Testament should be based on exegetical data that are anticipatory and progressively looking forward to fulfillment. This chapter defines typology as exegesis and provides the reader with a sketch of how this approach is related to reading the canon of Christian scripture. Whereas some theologians approach typology strictly as a hermeneutical lens, this study asserts that it is also an exegetical technique.

The very question of whether the virgin birth could have been anticipated by scripture arises from the scripture itself. Just after the Gospel of Matthew narrates the birth of Jesus (Matt. 1:18–25), the reader encounters a pericope that describes the three wise men or magi from the east (Matt. 2:1–12). There are many difficulties attending this section, and historians are not entirely sure where these three men came from.[1] Perhaps the only important fact Matthew wants the reader to know is that they were certainly not Jewish. The most startling thing is that these magi explain their query about the presence of one "born king of the Jews": "For we saw his star when it rose and *have come to worship him*" (Matt. 2:2). It is equally important to observe that Matthew then transitions to Herod the king asking where "the Christ was to be *born*" (Matt. 2:4) and the answer from the chief priests and scribes that it would take place according to the scriptures, specifically as found in the prophet Micah (5:2). The fact that the three magi came to worship a God-baby or God-child who had been "born" implies a divine birth of some kind.

We do not know how these three magi ascertained that this baby was divine, but those seeking to explain the situation to Herod turned to the prophecy related to Bethlehem of Judea in Micah. Matthew's short episode raises the question for the reader: do the scriptures anticipate the arrival of God among his people as a babe? Matthew's theological purposes point to the surprising arrival of these non-Jewish magi *to worship* the baby as they might worship God at the birth of "the Christ."

The questions raised by Matthew 2:1–12 help to sharpen the relationship between typology, anticipation, and exegesis. This is important to consider because it helps to answer the question: does the Old Testament contain an explicit reference to God coming in a personal bodily form as part of the hope of Israel? This chapter also considers these matters from three angles in successive sections. The first section considers the virgin birth as an absolute "novum" or "absolute new reality." The second section evaluates the theory that the virgin birth came about *de novo* or totally unexpected. The third section aims to provide an Augustinian view that captures the tensions of concealment and revelation.

THE VIRGIN BIRTH AS NOVUM

The objection to the exegetical and forward-reading nature of typology is implicit within contemporary Christologies that view the incarnation as an entirely new thing—an absolute "*novum*" or a "new reality."[2]

One of the major proponents of the *novum* view was Karl Barth, who, unlike his father, identified the virgin birth as an event worthy of belief. This position also surprised those who expected him to follow in the rejection of the supernatural that characterized the History of Religions method at the time. However, Barth's view of the virgin birth is that it was a miracle unlike any other and unrelated to any other, for it stood alone as a single "act of God in history."[3]

According to this view, there was nothing, not even a prophecy in scripture, to anticipate the virgin birth because the miracle was the presence of God. This reflects Barth's view in which he rejected all attempts at a "natural theology."[4] For Barth, the virgin birth is only related to what goes forward from it, including the empty tomb. Both miracles of the virgin birth and the empty tomb are "mysteries," with the former being the sole "basis of the mystery at the end."[5] Dustin Resch explains that for Barth, the virgin birth took place in time and history but that it was "grounded" solely in God.[6]

Likewise, for T. F. Torrance, this event was also without precedent in every manner of speaking: "It is a new and unique fact without analogy anywhere in human experience or knowledge."[7] The origins of the incarnation as *novum* lie in theology proper, Christology, and the desire to preserve the radical nature of divine freedom and initiative. It is not surprising that T. F.

Torrance aligns himself with Aquinas's view that God is wholly other and mysterious to us.[8] Torrance states:

> In virtue of the relation of space-time structures to the infinite differentiality of God they are essentially open and not closed to the humble inquirer who accepts and waits upon their rationality, but because of that relation he cannot infer genuinely new knowledge of the world even from what he has already learned and cannot predict *a priori* what he will discover, and only when he does discover what is new can he connect it up with what he has already learned.[9]

Torrance follows up this quote above with the following line: "This applies above all to the knowledge of God in Jesus Christ."[10]

The virgin birth is deeply embedded in Torrance's dialectical theology between the words of scripture and Christ.[11] Like Barth, Torrance wants to identify the virgin birth as an event without precedent, as truly *novum*.[12] For Torrance, the virgin birth presents a "mystery" with a gap that can only be closed by God. Torrance sought to locate the incarnation into a "fallen human nature" so that Christ might "heal it and bend it back to God from within."[13] Andrew Purves explains that both the resurrection of Jesus and the virgin birth in Torrance's thought are a "new kind of historical happening."[14] As such, both events are "new" because they belong to God's new age. His dialectical approach renders the virgin birth as a total mystery because it "bursts through the limitations of time and space" and is not even subject to "cause and effect."[15]

The main problem with this continuous appeal to absolute newness is that the virgin birth becomes fulfillment without promise, climax without anticipation, and knowledge without analog.[16] If the virgin birth was an absolute *novum*, it must remain exegetically disconnected from all typological relationships in the scriptures that might have anticipated it.[17] The doctrine of inspired scripture means that God has already bridged part of the gap between himself and humanity by speaking through his prophets who wrote down his words. It is important to distinguish the idea that the virgin birth should be understood a priori as a supernatural event from the view that it should be understood a priori as unpredictable in any sense.

Positively speaking, there is something Christocentric about the claim that Jesus is the beginning point for knowledge. Thus, the quote from Torrance above means that the revelation of God in Christ is the starting point of all knowledge about God. Yet the difficult question of epistemology remains: how do we know this claim is true? This is a difficult question when ontology always precedes epistemology.[18] For Barth, the Old Testament scriptures cannot be counted because the virgin birth was grounded "solely in God."[19] Furthermore, the question of salvation-historical development arises: how can we follow the storyline of scripture to arrive at the impetus that drove the three magi (Matt. 2:1) to find the child and *worship him* as God?

The *novum* view of the virgin birth draws attention to the fact that it was an act of God. Its absolute newness required that even the three wise magi needed a special sign in the form of a star to guide their journey (Matt. 2:2). While Christ is the supreme revelation of the Triune God, it does not follow that such an event was totally unpredictable a priori in every way if scripture is understood to be the divinely inspired accounts of previous acts of God entering history in ways that created expectations of future developments. The attempt to ground the virgin birth solely in God to the exclusion of scripture is just as naturalistic as denying the event itself.[20] The Christ event, with all that it entailed, was not the *antithesis* of prior human history and experience but the *climax* of gracious events, persons, revelations, and prophecies.

THE VIRGIN BIRTH *DE NOVO*

More recently, Graham Cole has asserted that the incarnation arose in salvation-history as though it were entirely unexpected, as *"de novo."*[21] For Cole, the doctrine of the incarnation is also unique in that it is unlike other Old Testament concepts and themes such as covenant, election, and sacrifice.[22] While the views of Barth, Torrance, and Cole are distinguishable, they are characterized by the same clear and bold claim about the incarnation, which applies to the virgin birth as well: it is an entirely new reality. Positively, the newness of the virgin birth is crucial because Jesus is the Last Adam and, in that sense, God has truly "created humanity afresh for his own personal indwelling."[23] Beyond this affirmation, there are several points to consider about this proposition and those like it that must be addressed before considering how to read the Old Testament typologically.

Those who hold the view that the virgin birth occurred *de novo* do not necessarily mean the entire Old Testament is meaningless. On the contrary, they may offer robust theological accounts of messianic texts. For example, Graham Cole explains that the Old Testament provides background beliefs, data, and ideas that made the incarnation intelligible.[24] As such, Old Testament theophanies with their elements of anthropomorphisms, anthropopathisms, and anthropopraxisms provided the "data-background beliefs that were crucial for the intelligibility of an actual incarnation."[25] There is no disagreement with the assertion that the Old Testament provides intelligibility to the New Testament. The critical question is whether there is any function besides intelligibility and whether there are forward-looking expectations that can be derived exegetically from the Old Testament.[26] In other words, intelligibility is not sufficient to sustain a view of Old Testament exegetical data that can be shown to create forward-looking *and* backward-looking expectations of a God-man.

The postulate that the incarnation or virgin birth is historically *de novo* is a claim about the entire content and nature of divine revelation in the Old Testament. The denial that the event of the virgin birth could be exegetically latent in the typological relationships of the Old Testament is a *claim about the nature of revelation itself.*[27] It is the rejection of the idea that progressive revelation contained ever-more specific information about God's plan of redemption and its climax in Christ. The rejection of forward-looking or anticipatory analogies is the rejection of typological relationships through analogies. It is a theological claim that dismisses the possibility of any antecedent theology which would have created some element of expectation that a God-man would arise in some manner according to Yahweh's promises and the progressive nature of divine revelation.

The view that virgin birth developed *de novo* means that it was totally new and not latent in the Old Testament in some sense. This position also means that the canon can only be read in one direction to understand it: backward.[28] This postulate is a hermeneutical lens that is both universal and negative. It might even be proven true if every single Old Testament text were shown to have no text that anticipated the incarnation through analogies, antecedents, types, prophecies, and so on. Any evidence of the incarnation in the Old Testament is due to Christian eisegesis through the act of reader-response. Those who hold that the virgin birth arose *de novo* must also conclude that the meaning of the Old Testament comes *only* through the lens of the New Testament. If it truly is the case that the incarnation is the one biblical theme "that arises *de novo*," then, "a biblical theology of it can only *start* with the New Testament text."[29] This means that it is not possible to read the canon backward *and* forward. It can only be read backward.[30]

This *de novo* view of scripture and the incarnation (or the virgin birth) is a universal negative claim. Logically, a universal negative is a claim that denies all members of a particular set. In this case, the particular set is the book of natural revelation (the world of human experience) and the book of special revelation (the scriptures). In most cases, it is very difficult to prove a universal negative, especially when the set is not defined.[31] But in this case, if we lay aside Torrance's universal claim about human experience, and if the set is exclusive with respect to the Christian canon of scripture, then the scriptures would need to explicitly state that the incarnation was characterized by the quality of being a new reality that was completely unanticipated.

The burden of proof is upon those who would make such a universal negative claim about the nature of scripture. This is especially true for the claim that the virgin birth (the virginal incarnation) was a new reality and a unique event to the point that it is without analogy, antecedents, types, prefiguration, or prophecies. Such a claim is compounded by the additional claim that the incarnation is a historical event unlike any other in the Old Testament and should be differentiated from patterned salvation-historical themes such as covenant, election, and sacrifice. What is more important is that it would only take one positive piece of exegetical evidence to nullify the universal negative claim in question. Such a piece of positive evidence would have to come from the canon of scripture and demonstrate that there were indeed analogies in salvation-history which anticipated a God-man.

The *de novo* view draws attention to the fact that the virgin birth was so unexpected by Israel that three magi were the ones to take the initiative to search for him (Matt. 2:2). There is no denying that the incarnation was a unique event in history because the scriptures identify Jesus as the only savior, for there is only "one Lord, one faith, one baptism" (Eph. 4:5). And there is no denying that there are some elements of the incarnation of Christ and the virgin birth that are new. But the claim that the incarnation was unprecedented and a historically absolute *novum* is entirely different. How can such a claim be justified? Like any other theological claim, the matter must be solved by exegetical data from the scriptures.

THE VIRGIN BIRTH AS MYSTERION

The central issue at hand is the degree to which the incarnation and virgin birth was a new event in salvation-history. The mysterious and marvelous miracle of the virginal birth at Jesus' incarnation was both surprising and obvious. This is the tension of the revelation of God's mysteries, according to Augustine: In the Old Testament, the New is concealed; in the New the Old is revealed.[32] Despite the enduring importance of Augustine's formula, the difficulties with continuity and discontinuity often deal with more specific questions. In this case, the key question is: was the virgin birth an *absolutely* new event or an event that had some revelatory events that anticipated it? At this juncture, it is important to consider the strongest evidence that could be marshaled in favor of the *novum* view: the Jewish concept and theme of "mystery" (Greek: *mystērion*) in the New Testament.[33] This is a vast topic with many exegetical issues to consider from both the Old Testament and the New Testament.

What *can* be done is to demonstrate that some contemporary scholars have made specific and generalized conclusions that would make it difficult to support the *novum* view from an appeal to "mystery." The point here is simply to raise reasonable doubt about the claim that the entire Old Testament is void of data that anticipated the virgin birth.

First, Jesus held his followers responsible for understanding messianic ideas, concepts, and truths about himself *after the time of* the resurrection (as well as Pentecost).[34] This responsibility is most evident in this scene from the Gospel of Luke as Jesus appeared to the disciples after the resurrection:

> "O foolish ones, and slow of heart to believe all that the prophets have spoken! Was it not necessary that the Christ should suffer these things and enter into his glory?" And beginning with Moses and all the Prophets, he interpreted to them in all the Scriptures the things concerning himself. (Luke 24:25–27)

The key point here is that the perception of messianic truths in the Old Testament is indeed related to one's spiritual disposition. Seeing Christ as the temple-Messiah is just as much about the subjective state of the reader as it is about the objective exegetical data in the text.

Second, there is some conceptual overlap between the "mystery" theme, the Jerusalem temple, and Jesus. This overlap is clear because of the way that Jesus explicitly identified himself as God's temple and the one who was even greater than the temple in Jerusalem (see Matt. 12:6). Beale and Gladd point out that there is a paradoxical relationship in Old Testament prophetic texts about the temple and God's eschatological redemptive plans. Some texts "anticipate the latter-day temple to be a *physical* structure at the arrival of the Messiah and the new creation (e.g., Hag 2:9)."[35] While other prophetic texts "appear to foresee a *nonphysical* eschatological temple of God's revelatory presence (e.g., Jer. 3:16–17; Zech. 1:16–2:13)."[36] Beale and Gladd even conclude that "the Old Testament does have precedents for the end-time temple being nonarchitectural," opening up the possibility that this could be a person.[37] With respect to the Gospel of John, which has some of the clearest instances of temple Christology, Carson states that the term *mystērion* "sometimes provides fresh revelation that has clearly been hidden in times past, but which is somehow said to be connected to the very scriptures in which it has been hidden (e.g., John 2:19–22)."[38]

Third, there is some scholarship that excludes the broad idea that a "mystery" could be absolutely *de novo*.[39] Carson finds that certain elements "can be simultaneously seen as something that has been (typologically) predicted and now fulfilled, and as something that has been hidden and has now been revealed."[40] Beale and Gladd rightly caution that teasing out the relationships between what was previously a "mystery" and what is now revealed in Christ is difficult. Nevertheless, they conclude, "while such things were mysterious from the Old Testament vantage point, there may nevertheless have been *hints* even about these things."[41] To summarize these points, an appeal to "mystery" is not likely to support the conclusion that the virgin birth was an event that had absolutely no texts in the Old Testament that might create some expectations that a God-man might visit his people.

Fourth, there is anticipatory language in the Old Testament about the "house of God" having "living stones" and this is of special interest to New Testament authors. The concept of Jesus the Messiah-temple, who was built by God's own hand, is operative in the hortatory text of 1 Peter 2:1–8. In this text, Peter enjoins the church to identify itself with Jesus and imitate him.[42] According to this text unit, Jesus is the "living stone" who was "in the sight of God chosen and precious," and so the church is to identify itself as "living stones" who are "being built up as a spiritual house" (2 Pet. 2:4–5). Here, Jesus' appellation as a "living stone" is drawn from a combination citation from LXX Isaiah 8:14 and Psalms 117:22 (MT 118:22).[43] The context from Isaiah is one of God's personal presence representing covenantal *judgment,* and the scene from the Psalms being one of covenantal *blessing* from the "house of the Lord" (LXX Ps. 117:26). From the perspective of 1 Peter 2, Jesus is the typological climax of Old Testament institutions, promises, and prophecies about God's "house," so that now what applied to God's temple in Israel's history applies to the Christian community. The point is that Peter sees the temple as prefiguring the church only *because the temple prefigured Jesus.*[44] Thus, Jesus stands at the center of continuity and discontinuity between Israel and the church, with the simple hermeneutic that he is the temple and those who believe in him and are in union with him share in his identity and participate in his experiences.[45]

According to the view of this present study, the incarnation is *not* any different from the doctrines which have some measure of antecedent theology in the Old Testament. The doctrine of the incarnation stands *alongside* other themes such as justification, covenant, election, and sacrifice.[46] They all share the quality of being anticipated in some manner by the Old Testament, even if seen only as hints, glimmers, or as dimly as through a curtain.

There is a sense in which a visitation of God in human form could have been *expected* because of the scriptural testimonies about God's visitation.[47] The divine anthropomorphisms in the Old Testament support the incarnation because they explain the incarnation and virgin birth. But that is not all; they provided some knowledge through divine revelation that created anticipation of a God-man dwelling among his people. The incarnation was not entirely novel and was not absolutely and completely *de novo.*

The rejection of the virgin birth as a salvation-historical event *de novo* must not be pressed too far so as to lose the fact that the way in which God's promises were fulfilled was not entirely clear, even if there were occasional hints here and there. A superior explanation would be to postulate the virgin birth as a salvation-historical event that occurred as a *mystērion* (mystery) between the tension-filled poles of hiddenness and revelation. This approach has the obvious virtue of using New Testament language to describe a New Testament event. It also maintains that Old Testament authors intentionally and knowingly wrote prophetically.[48] Additionally, the following four points are an attempt to succinctly capture what was hidden and what was revealed, with the understanding that these points are not exhaustive.

The mystery of the virgin birth was revealed through Christ's Passion. At the "fullness of time" (Gal. 4:4), God sent forth his Son into the world at the incarnation. As indicated by the introduction, one of the divine purposes of Jesus' life was his death, resurrection, and then ascension into heaven. This cluster of events provided the disciples with a unique historical lens through which they could finally understand the scriptures, the events they witnessed, and the teachings of Jesus. Additionally, the pouring out of the Spirit upon the disciples at Pentecost in Acts 2 indicates that ideal biblical interpretation by the disciples is done through Spirit-empowered faith. Objectively, the events of Christ's Passion enabled the disciples and even non-disciples to understand who Jesus was.[49] Subjectively, the act of faith enables one to understand that the entirety of the scriptures points to Christ in some manner (Luke 24:25–27; Acts 17:11; 18:24–28).

The mystery of the virgin birth was revealed through the canon. One factor is that the scriptural data required to form the constellation of texts necessary to see this doctrine was only complete with the formation of the canon. The canon offers a theological perspective for understanding typology because the whole is greater than the sum of its parts. The entirety of the canon provides the reader with the entire narrative plot of scripture, and this enables the reader to detect its typological structures.[50] This means that the significance of isolated biblical texts may not have been apparent until placed in the canon of scripture and read in a unified fashion in the context of salvation-history.

The mystery of the virgin birth was hidden in the Old Testament through texts that anticipated a woman giving birth to a redeemer figure. The initial redemptive promise in Genesis (3:15) is based on the "offspring" of the woman. This hope continued through the promise to Abraham of a "seed" and a child of promise that required a partial resurrection of Abraham's dead body.[51] Even the Davidic covenant implies the role of a woman because the promise to David is of an "offspring after you, who shall come from your body" (2 Sam. 7:12). Then, of course, there is the oft-cited and much-debated passage from Isaiah (7:14): "Therefore the Lord himself will give you a sign. Behold, the virgin shall conceive and bear a son, and shall call his name Immanuel."[52] Whether one interprets this passage as a direct prophecy about Jesus or a typological foreshadowing is moot, because either case adds legitimacy to the claim that the Old Testament contains texts that offered hints of the virgin birth event. What is clear is that Matthew (1:23) views this prophetic text in Isaiah as directly relevant to Jesus' identity and his arrival.[53]

The mystery of the virgin birth was hidden in the typological relationships based on the promise of God's dwelling place among his people. God's dwelling place was initially without contention in the Garden of Eden. However, with sin and death entering the world through Adam and Eve, the way into this garden was barred by cherubim angels and a flaming sword (Gen. 3:24). After this, the redemptive arc or metanarrative of the canon is filled with God's covenant promise "to dwell" among his people. God did dwell temporarily and contingently in and around places such as altars, the tabernacle, the temple, and even in mediators such as Moses (e.g., his shining face).[54] There is a sense in which Yahweh did dwell in these places but another sense in which he did not. This tension is explicit within Stephen's speech before his martyrdom. Solomon built Yahweh a "house," but the Most High does not live in houses made by human hands (Acts 7:47–48). Stephen's theology of temples is similar to Paul's, who states: "The God who made the world and everything in it, being Lord of heaven and earth, does not live in temples made by man" (Acts 17:24). The theology of the book of Acts makes it clear that God's dwelling place among his people must take place through a temple that is not made by human hands.

SUMMARY

This chapter reviewed three major approaches to the relationship between the virgin birth and its anticipation in scripture. The view which finds the virgin birth to be an absolute *novum* leaves the event as climax without anticipation. It does not account for the ways in which the three wise men read scripture and sought to find a baby to worship (Matt. 1:2). This was not an event that happened absolutely *de novo* even if the Old Testament did not anticipate the way the event worked out in every aspect. The very nature of divinely inspired scripture makes it possible for there to be forward-looking analogies, antecedents, types, and prophecies related to the virgin birth. This is because typology is inherent in the very *nature* of scriptural revelation. Typology is only a reader-response *method* insomuch as it requires the implied reader to recognize the canon of scripture.[55] There is a legitimate dialectic between reading the biblical backward and forward, due to the development and clarity of progressive revelation. But typology is mostly about the nature of God's gradual revelation that anticipates its climax in Christ through escalating patterns of promise and fulfillment.

NOTES

1. Discussions about the identity of the *magoi* in Matthew 2:1 are numerous and wide-ranging. Mounce (2011, 13) points out that there were negative associations with this word *magoi* (e.g., Acts 13:6) and more neutral assessments by the early

church (e.g., Ignatius of Antioch, *IEph.* 19). Turner (2008, 79) identifies the magi thus: "likely were prominent priestly professionals who studied the stars and discerned the signs of the times. They may have come from Arabia, Babylon, or Persia."

2. Resch 2012, 77, citing Barth CD I/2, 178; on the "new reality," see Torrance 2008, 1.

3. Resch 2012, 77.

4. Jobe's (2019, 243) discussion of Barth's use of "leviathan" language for God's death-oriented act of incarnation carefully seeks to expand the possibilities surrounding Barth and his classical rejection of "natural theology."

5. Schenk (2016, 170) discusses Barth's view of the virgin birth in relation to the "mystery" of the empty tomb as found in CD I/2, 182.

6. Resch 2012, 78.

7. Torrance 2008, 1. Torrance (2008, 3) continues to develop this idea by stating,

> Whatever we do, we must be faithful to the actual facts, and never allow preconceived notions or theories to cut away some of the facts at the start because we cannot understand them in terms of what we already know or hold to be possible.

8. Torrance (1969, 73–5) quotes Aquinas favorably: "Christus qui, secundum quod homo, via est nobis tendendi in Deum" [in as much as Christ is man, he is for us the way by which we strive after God].

9. Torrance 1969, 73.

10. Torrance 1969, 73.

11. Habets (2023, 104) explains that Torrance's hermeneutic presents "a bi-polarity (dialectic) between the words and the Word, the worldly form of revelation and its divine content that renders Scripture a witness to the self-revelation of God."

12. For a historical discussion of Torrance's studies with Karl Barth, see Noble 2023, 8–38.

13. Habets and Stamps 2023, 6.

14. Purves 2020, 281.

15. Purves 2020, 281.

16. While Torrance would affirm that Christ is the climax of history, he would also dialectically affirm that Christ is an absolutely new event or fact.

17. Goroncy's (2013, 818–23) review of Resch (2012) explains how Barth saw the virgin birth as a "theological question" rather than a "critical question" and that because the miracle of the virgin birth was an ontological mystery of God's free grace, the Bible evidences a complete lack of concern with a scientific explanation of it.

18. Goroncy (2013, 818–23) summarizes Barth's view of the virgin birth as ontology preceding epistemology. Further discussions of ontology preceding epistemology may be found in Stanley 2010, 152, and Knight 2013, 127.

19. Resch 2012, 77.

20. For the view that the virgin birth is a sign from the Holy Spirit that enables the church to a priori renounce all naturalistic understandings of it, see Shenk 2016, 172.

21. Cole 2013, 113.

22. Cole (2013, 113) avers, "Thus a biblical theology of incarnation can start only with the New Testament text, unlike other themes such as convent, election and sacrifice, to name just a few."

23. Torrance utilized the patristic distinction between *anhypostasia* (no personal subsistence of the human nature outside the Word of God) and *enhypostasia* (a human nature fully in union with God) with regard to Christ's humanity. Pagán (2023, 55) summarizes Torrance's view this way:

> God did not adopt an already existing human being as his Son, but rather created humanity afresh for his own personal indwelling from the Virgin Mary. Indeed, that is the significance of the virginal conception and virgin birth, as Torrance makes clear. Christ is therefore *sui generis*, not identifiable with any other human being.

24. Cole (2013, 113–14) focuses on the way in which anthropomorphisms (and related texts) were necessary because, without them "there would not have been the possibility of data-background beliefs that were crucial for the intelligibility of an actual incarnation."

25. Cole 2013, 113–14.

26. One might also ask whether extra-biblical texts may be marshaled as evidence of the compatibility of the incarnation of a human God-man within certain sects of Judaism. One such text might be the wisdom poem of Sirach 24, where "Wisdom becomes incarnate" (Skarsaune 2002, 337). Pursuing this inquiry is outside the scope of this study.

27. Here I draw from Caneday (2020, 141), who points out that claims about typology should be about the nature of scripture.

28. This may be similar to Hays' (2014, 2) contention that "Figural reading need not presume that the OT authors—or the characters they narrate—were conscious of predicting or anticipating Christ. Rather, the discernment of a figural correspondence is *necessarily* retrospective rather than prospective" (emphasis mine).

29. Cole 2013, 113, emphasis mine.

30. Carson (2004, 406) explains that typology in the Old Testament reflects the fact that "God himself designed it to be *pointing forward*," emphasis mine.

31. Ducharme (1994, 33) comments, it is "notoriously difficult, if not empirically impossible, to prove a universal negative." This matter of proving universal negatives is discussed by the plethora of works engaging Aristotle (*An. Post.* I.19–21).

32. Augustine famously quipped: "In the Old Testament the New is concealed, in the New the Old is revealed" (Novum Testamentum in Vetere latet, Vetus Testamentum in Novo patet) *Quaest. in Hept.* 2,73: PL 34, 623; cf. DV 16.

33. Resch (2012, 78) explains that Barth made an appeal to the category of "mystery" as Barth sought to identify the virgin birth as the sign of God's divine freedom, immediacy, and action. It is noteworthy that Adolf von Harnack (1851–1930) saw "no need for 'mystery' or a mysterious 'otherness' of the Divine being for the Christian faith" (Marga 2022, 357).

34. Here I draw from the point made by Beale and Gladd 2014, 292.

35. Beale and Gladd 2014, 294.

36. Beale and Gladd 2014, 294.

37. Beale and Gladd 2014, 294.

38. Carson 2004, 424.

39. Isaiah (43:19) utilizes a similar tension when he describes the return from exile as a "new thing" while describing it in categories and language of what God had done from of old. The "new" thing is so radically different that "the former things shall not be remembered" (Isa. 65:17).

40. Carson 2004, 427.

41. Beale and Gladd 2014, 300, emphasis mine.

42. When reading this text as the *imitatio Christi*, the "the story of Jesus, his actions, his perspective on life, and his attitude toward God and human beings become normative for 1 Peter's audience" (Joseph 2012, 90).

43. For the source of the "living stone" being LXX 117:22 and Isaiah 8:14, see Joseph 2012, 89; Sargent (2015, 66–7) offers a literature review on the matter, which also includes Isaiah 28:16.

44. Contra Sargent (2015, 68), who concludes, "there does not appear to be any evidence that Peter sees the Temple as prefiguring the Church."

45. Contra Sargent (2015, 68), who argues

that typological interpretation of the Temple is taking place in 1 Pet. 2:4–10 is to assume a much more sophisticated understanding of scriptural meaning than there is evidence for or is accounted for in the simple determinate hermeneutic of 1 Pet. 1:10–12.

46. For example, Carson (2004, 403) notes that "Paul insists that Scripture (i.e., the God who gave the Scripture) 'foresaw that God would justify the Gentiles by faith' (Gal. 3:8) and justifies this claim by alluding to Gen. 12:3; 18:18; 22:18: 'All nations will be blessed through you.'"

47. Cole (2013, 110–11) quotes Bauckham (1998, 74) with approval (in bold text) as stating of the incarnation: "This could not have been expected, but nor was it uncharacteristic. It is novel but appropriate to the identity of the God of Israel."

48. I agree with Hays that the scriptures must be dialectically read backward and forward. But I reject Hays's (2014, 104) conclusion that Christological meaning is only found retrospectively: "This means that for the Evangelists the 'meaning' of the OT texts was not confined to the human author's original historical setting or to the meaning that could have been grasped by the original readers." I am willing to concede that Old Testament authors of scripture may not have *fully* grasped the meaning of what they wrote.

49. Beale and Gladd (2014, 292) state

the apologetic of the New Testament writers is not only "believe in Christ and you will understand the Bible better," but it also indicates that even non-Christians can perceive from the Scriptures that the Messiah was to die and rise again.

50. Gentry (2017, 90) explains that "the progression of the covenants throughout the narrative plot structure of the Bible creates, controls, and develops the typological structures across the canon of Scripture."

51. For an argument that the resuscitation of Abraham's sexual powers was a portrait of the resurrection from the dead *in nuce,* see Wenkel 2018, 51–66.

52. The literature on the interpretation of Isaiah 7:14 is vast and includes Moyise and Menken 2005, 64–5; Abernethy 2016, 122; Witherington 2017, 70–7; Christophe and Gentry 2020, passim.

53. McFarland (2019, 126) agrees and comments that even though "Jesus takes the new and surprising, but (at least according to the first evangelist) not altogether unanticipated form of God's dwelling with God's people as one of God's people (Matt. 1:23)."

54. For a discussion of Moses's shining face and its function in his face-to-face relationship with Yahweh, see Wenkel 2018, 30–40.

55. Here I seek to make a small qualification to the point that Caneday (2020, 141) makes about typological interpretation as an exegetical method.

Part II

THE ARGUMENT AS CATEGORICAL SYLLOGISM

Chapter 5

Earthly Temples Built
by Human Hands

This chapter begins a new section within the overall structure of this study as the focus turns from prolegomena to an exegetical-dogmatic consideration of temple building. The aim of this chapter is to provide scriptural data that supports the major premise of the argument: all heavenly temples must be constructed directly by the Spirit of God. This chapter seeks to support this point by considering its inverse: *the fact that all earthly temples must be built by human hands.* This chapter offers a typology-based set of data drawn from the building of primitive altars, the tabernacle, and Solomon's temple in Jerusalem. In all of these cases, the way in which they were constructed was by human hands (*cheiropoiēton*). Yet, even where and when these temples of Yahweh worship were built by human hands, they had characteristics that typologically anticipated the future construction of its antitype, which would not be built by human hands (*acheiropoiēton*). Ultimately, those things that are made by human hands are temporary and earthly, and these cannot be a permanent house for God's dwelling, even as they anticipate a house built by God.[1]

Broadly speaking, the successive pattern of temples and their antecedents across salvation-history is but a shadow that anticipates the true temple of God in the person of Jesus. It reflects a canon-wide path of escalation that climaxes in Jesus himself. Designated altars, tents, and temples were places where Yahweh's personal presence *could* dwell, but they were also places where Yahweh *could not* dwell. These temples were not "paradoxical" in the true sense of the word, but they were precursors or shadows that anticipated a consummate reality.[2] The paradox or apparent contradiction here is explained by the fact that the cultic architectural places of Yahweh worship were only temporary, and they were designed to be that way, a fact which is apparent by the way in which they were constructed.

Before turning to an exegetical study of the typological relationship of primitive altars, tents, and temples, it is helpful to recall that the previous chapter established that places of Yahweh's dwelling were either made by human hands or made without human hands. The cultic altars, tents, and temples are considered together here because they are united conceptually by their function as being places for Yahweh worship. They were places where Yahweh's covenantal and personal presence dwelt, even if temporarily and diminutively. And they all pointed forward toward a final place and event when God would dwell forever with his people. This means that human-made altars, tents, and temples can all be considered under the theological umbrella of "temple Christology." All of these places of cultic Yahweh worship are united by the fact that they were temporary places of God's dwelling among his people—this is why I use the term "temple" in the broadest theological sense to refer to antecedent places of Yahweh worship.

This consideration of temples built by human hands uses the term "temple" as a broad and encompassing reference to a cultic dwelling place of God's covenant presence among his people. The following sub-sections do not aim to add any additional scholarship, but they do present a cumulative case about the nature of temple building: *that temples built by human hands anticipate a consummate temple built by the Spirit of God.* These temples from the Old Testament provide an antecedent theology for the argument that Jesus is God's temple and the nature of his incarnation in the virgin birth follows the pattern of the ways in which temples are constructed. The following examples of such temples are considered: (1) the primitive altars of the patriarchs, (2) the tabernacle, (3) Solomon's temple, and (4) the Second Temple.

PRIMITIVE ALTARS

This section begins an exegetical-dogmatic consideration of temple building, which is broadly construed to include cultic places of Yahweh's dwelling, including primitive altars of the patriarchs. This study of the typological function of altars focuses on the way that they anticipated further salvation-historical developments, particularly through the way in which they were built. This section demonstrates that the construction of the primitive altars of the patriarchs was typological: the mode of their construction anticipated an altar made without human hands.

It should be obvious that free-standing altars made of mud or stone are not temple buildings. However, the reason why altars are considered first in this chapter is that they played an important role in anticipating the temple in Jerusalem. Like the temple, these altars were places of worship, sacrifice, and occasionally of divine and human interaction. Again, these places of cultic Yahweh worship must be considered by their place within the canon of scripture and the storyline of salvation-history. In this discussion, primitive altars for Yahweh worship are understood to be salvation-historical antecedents of those divinely ordained features in the Jerusalem temple. This means that the anticipatory function of primitive altars was carried forward as they were physically incorporated into Israel's tabernacle, and eventually, into the temple in Jerusalem.[3]

The use of primitive altars of earth and stone by the patriarchs of Israel is understood to be salvation-historical antecedents of the Jerusalem temple. There were three divinely mandated requirements for primitive altars of Yahweh worship: they must be (1) made of "earth," (2) covered with white plaster, and (3) built with unmanufactured stone.[4] (There are even more requirements for the building of the bronze altar associated with Ezekiel's temple in Ezekiel 43:13–27, but that is excluded on the basis that it is associated with a temple.)

Primitive altars that followed Yahweh's dictates were built in ways that emphasized their creation without typical construction tools. Specifically, the creation of the patriarchal altars for Yahweh worship emphasized the silence regarding their origin—thus establishing their holiness and creating anticipation for a final altar of divine origin—an altar made without hands.

Primitive altars of stone, wood, or earth were likely in use since the offerings of Cain and Abel (Gen. 4), but there are no details in the narrative that explain what these were like. Abel offered up "the firstborn of his flock and of their fat portions" (Gen. 4:4), and this likely involved some platform to burn the sheep and their parts. These altars were sometimes responses of worship to theophanies in which Yahweh appeared or spoke (e.g., Abram "built there an altar to the Lord, who had appeared to him" in Gen. 12:7). Even where God does not appear at the altar in a cultic act of worship, altars were sometimes a response to previous Christophanies or theophanies, for example, Abram's altar in Gen. 11:7. These were locations that marked special moments of communion with God, as exemplified by Abram's act of calling "upon the name of the Lord" (Gen. 13:4).

These altars also served as reminders or testimonies to divine revelation as well as a response to God's promises or commands. Such an action is in view when Noah responded to Yahweh's command to leave the ark and repopulate the earth by building the first altar explicitly mentioned in Genesis.[5] He offered up "some of every clean animal and some of every clean bird and offered burnt offerings" (Gen. 8:20). Primitive altars continue to reflect these emphases and appear throughout the lives of the patriarchs in Genesis, including Abraham (12:7, 8; 13:4; 13:18; 22:9), Isaac (26:25), and Jacob (Gen. 33:20). When Jacob dreamt of the ladder reaching into heaven, he established a stone pillar of remembrance or memorial to indicate that the place he slept was "God's house" (Gen. 28:22, cf. 35:3, 7).[6]

There are eleven explicit references to altars used for Yahweh worship by the patriarchs Abraham, Isaac, and Jacob in Genesis. The first explicit instance is the altar built by Noah in the mountains of Ararat (Gen. 8:20). The second and third instances refer to the altar built by Abraham (Abram) by the oak of Moreh in Shechem (Gen. 12:7, 8). The fourth and fifth instances refer to the place where Abram began to "call upon the name of the Lord" in Hebron (13:4, 18). The sixth instance refers to the altar that would have been used for the offering of Isaac on Mt. Moriah (Gen. 22:9; see James 2:21). The seventh instance is the altar used by Isaac where the Lord appeared to him in Beer-Sheba (Gen. 26:25). The eighth through the eleventh instances are associated with Jacob as he erected an altar in Shechem (Gen. 33:20) and in Bethel (Gen. 35:1, 3, 7). Beyond these, it is also noteworthy that Saul's first altar built for Yahweh was made of a rolled stone (1 Sam. 14:33–35).[7]

Elsewhere, the Pentateuch provides very detailed instructions for the establishment of the tabernacle (Exod. 25–27). There are detailed instructions given for the erection of altars (Exod. 20:22–26). Against the background of these details and specifications, the altars that do appear in the patriarchal narratives are without such descriptions. The key point here is that the Pentateuch encourages the reader to consider their origins and construction. Although the primitive altars used for Yahweh worship were somewhat temporary and even crude, they were still places of holiness that were set apart or sanctified to the Lord for the purpose of cultic worship. Altars were a reflection of personal and corporate worship as evidenced by obedience to divine revelation. For example, the altar built by Joshua after the battle of Ai was a direct response to what was written "in the book of Moses" (Josh. 8:31).[8] The key point is that the focus of the biblical text is on the divine fiat(s) governing their construction.

It is significant for the purpose of this argument that the use of tools upon the stone would "profane" the altar which was established for Yahweh worship. The silence about the reason for this repeated prohibition suggests that it is bound up with the very nature of an altar as a place of sacrifice for Yahweh worship and as a place where God would reveal himself to his people. These man-made altars were shadows of a final altar—a place of sacrifice where God put an end to animal sacrifices and revealed himself fully to his people.

The first time that the biblical narrative offers explicit details about the construction of primitive altars is through Moses to the people of Israel after God had established his covenant with them at Mount Sinai.[9] The laws for Israel about occasional altars of either clay/mud/earth or stone are as follows:

And the LORD said to Moses, "Thus you shall say to the people of Israel: 'You have seen for yourselves that I have talked with you from heaven. You shall not make gods of silver to be with me, nor shall you make for yourselves gods of gold. An *altar of earth* you shall make for me and sacrifice on it your burnt offerings and your peace offerings, your sheep and your oxen. In every place where I cause my name to be remembered I will come to you and bless you. *If you make me an altar of stone, you shall not build it of hewn stones, for if you wield your tool on it you profane it.* And you shall not go up by steps to my altar, that your nakedness be not exposed on it.'" (Exod. 20:22–26)

This is a set of instructions for establishing an altar of earth for sacrifices. By prohibiting hewn stone or tools, this text ensures that the stones used to make altars would not reflect the mediation of human hands, either during their establishment or before. The Hebrew verb for "move" (*nûp*) in Exod. 20:25 "designates an act of chiseling" and the Septuagint renders this as a "hand tool."[10]

This prohibition against building altars of "hewn stone" or wielding a "tool" upon them supports the conclusion made in the section above. This prohibition regarding hewn stones and tools encourages the reader to re-read the patriarchal narratives or to at least reflect upon these earliest places of Yahweh worship. Where the reader expects to find a pattern of texts describing these places as built from natural, unhewn stone or even packed mud, there are no details. The earliest places of Yahweh worship simply appear without any apparent concern for their construction. The silence regarding the building of altars for Yahweh worship in the narratives of the patriarchs Abraham, Isaac, and Jacob is all the more striking in light of the prohibition against using tools.

There is a similar prohibition against using tools to build altars for Yahweh worship on Mount Ebal after Israel crosses the Jordan into the Promised Land:

And when you have crossed over the Jordan, you shall set up these stones, concerning which I command you today, on Mount Ebal, and you shall plaster them with plaster. And there you shall build an altar to the LORD your God, an altar of stones. *You shall wield no iron tool on them*; you shall build an altar to the LORD your God *of uncut stones*. And you shall offer burnt offerings on it to the LORD your God, and you shall sacrifice peace offerings and shall eat there, and you shall rejoice before the LORD your God. (Deut. 27:4–7)

Once Joshua renewed the covenant between the nation of Israel and Yahweh on Mount Ebal, the text describes his faithfullness in following these commandments for worship:

At that time Joshua built an altar to the LORD, the God of Israel, on Mount Ebal, just as Moses the servant of the LORD had commanded the people of Israel, as it is written in the Book of the Law of Moses, "*an altar of uncut stones,*

upon which no man has wielded an iron tool." And they offered on it burnt
offerings to the LORD and sacrificed peace offerings. (Josh. 8:30–31)

The use of an altar at this point is a reflection of the Lord's victory over Ai
through Israel's army and Joshua's command. Joshua's outstretched hand
over the battlefield indicated that the power and success belonged to Yahweh alone (Josh. 8:26). It is important to observe that this text from Joshua
(quoted above) is a direct reference to the Deuteronomic (Deut. 27:1–8)
requirement for worshiping Yahweh when possessing the land across the
Jordan.

The relationship between the use of tools for building stone altars and Yahweh's name may be partially explained in negative terms: the altars were not
to be fashioned by idolatrous craftsmen like the pagan nations around them.
Israel would eventually demonstrate such a penchant for crafting idols when
she came out of Egypt during the golden calf incident (Exod. 32:21–24). It is
purely speculative, but there may be some residual negative association with
the line of Tubal-Cain (son of Lamech), who made metal tools from bronze
and iron (Gen. 4:22). This concern for idolatry is further supported by the
wider context concerning altar building in Deuteronomy 27, where the charge
of Moses and the Levitical priests includes the following:

"Cursed be the man who makes a carved or cast metal image, an abomination
to the Lord, a thing *made by the hands* of a craftsman, and sets it up in secret."
And all the people shall answer and say, "Amen." (Deut. 27:15)

Negatively speaking, the requirement that altars for Yahweh worship be
made without the use of tools was preventative in nature because it moved
the people far away from temptations to make images or idols. Positively, the
act of constructing altars according to the explicit requirements of Yahweh
ensures that they do not reflect the handiwork of a craftsman. In this sense,
they were intentionally designed to reflect the quality of being made "without
human hands."

To summarize, this section provides the exegesis to support the major
premise in the argument: a heavenly temple must be constructed directly by
the Spirit. Specifically, this section argues that the construction of primitive
altars for Yahweh worship was made by human hands, but anticipated an altar
made without human hands. Primitive altars were governed by divine laws
that established them as holy. More importantly, when they were made of
stone, they could only be built without tools or chisels. In this way, the erection of these places of sacrifice anticipated a final altar that would be provided
without human hands. This conclusion is directly tied to the overall argument
of this book because it partially establishes the major premise, which is that

a heavenly place of Yahweh worship must be constructed directly or immediately by the Holy Spirit.

THE TABERNACLE

The main point of this section is that the construction of Israel's tabernacle
anticipated a heavenly place of worship built by the Spirit of God. After Israel
was redeemed from Egypt, the nation was led by Moses, who functioned
as an intermediary and mediator between the people and Yahweh. As the
nation moved about in their journey toward the Promised Land, God dwelt
among them in a special tent, the tabernacle ("tent of meeting" or "tent of the
testimony").[11]

The purpose of the tabernacle was to allow God's presence (God's name)
to dwell among his covenant people (Exod. 25:8).[12] This special tent was
where Yahweh's personal and covenantal presence dwelt among the people.
The repeated details given about the furniture inside point to the reality that
this was God's house.[13] The divine presence was mediated through Moses:

> When Moses entered the tent, the pillar of cloud would descend and stand at the
> entrance of the tent, and the LORD would speak with Moses. And when all the
> people saw the pillar of cloud standing at the entrance of the tent, all the people
> would rise up and worship, each at his tent door. (Exod. 33:9–10)

Even though the tabernacle was a dwelling place for Yahweh built by human
hands, it was constructed according to God's Spirit and thus anticipated a
final dwelling place that was not built by human hands. There are several
features of the tabernacle that are important for this argument.

First, the tabernacle was constructed based on a heavenly template or
blueprint provided by divine revelation. The construction of the tent of meeting was strictly regulated by divine fiat. Daniel Hays comments that "In the
tabernacle story, God speaks often and gives explicit instructions about how
to build and furnish the structure."[14] Likewise, Gary Anderson observes that
"Rules about its assemblage and disassemblage emphasize the holiness of the
inner most part of the structure."[15]

Second, the tabernacle was constructed by craftsmen who were empowered by God's Spirit to "carry out the artistic work needed."[16] This may stand
in contrast to the construction of Solomon's temple, which utilized workers
based on their skill, because the text does not explicitly indicate that they
were chosen or empowered by the Spirit of God. However, the description of
the workers as being "filled" evokes the description of those filled with the
Spirit of God. The tabernacle was indeed created by persons filled with the
Holy Spirit and wisdom.

Third, the tabernacle cannot be separated from Moses, the journey to the Promised Land, and the anticipation of Yahweh's permanent dwelling place with his covenant people. The tabernacle cannot be separated from Moses and his intercessory ministry for the nation. As Moses engaged with Yahweh, he became a temporary tabernacle himself as he temporarily reflected God's glory, resulting in a glowing face that terrified the people.[17] Leithart explains the connection between Moses' glowing face and the function of the tabernacle as the dwelling place of Yahweh:

> The fact that Moses sees and begins to reflect the glory of Yahweh is a pledge that Yahweh will remain in the midst of Israel and go with them to the land; Moses' experience is the "firstfruits" of the experience that Israel will have when Yahweh descends to take up residence in the tent.[18]

The connection between Moses and the construction of the tabernacle was so important that Philo called upon his reader to consider how an inquiry into the former would lead to the conclusion that Moses was an exalted "divine man" (*Ant.* 3.180).

Fourth, the construction of the tabernacle was built upon a divinely revealed template or model from heaven. Moses twice states that he was commanded by God to make the tent based on a heavenly pattern:

> And let them make me a sanctuary, that I may dwell in their midst. Exactly as I show you concerning the pattern of the tabernacle, and of all its furniture, so you shall make it. (Exod. 25:8–9)

> And see that you make them after the pattern for them, which is being shown you on the mountain. (Exod. 25:40)

These texts offer strong evidence for the view that there are two ways to create a temple: by the hand of men or by the hand of God. Here, the nature of the tabernacle is undoubtedly built by Moses and those under his authority. Those who built it were given skill, ability, intelligence, and wisdom from the Holy Spirit (Exod. 31:3; 35:1). Yet, it has a special anticipatory nature because it was built according to heavenly dimensions and a heavenly model.[19] The heavenly basis for the earthly tabernacle is repeated several times in the Old Testament.[20]

In conclusion, the tabernacle stands midway in salvation-history between the primitive altars of the patriarchs and the stunning beauty of Solomon's temple in Jerusalem. It was constructed by human hands but occupies a special role because it was based upon a heavenly model that was revealed to Moses. The tabernacle was an earthly and temporary place of worship, yet it pointed to a heavenly reality of something made by God's own hand.

When the tabernacle was built by Moses for the cultic worship of Israel, it was designed based on a heavenly model. Whatever was built by the hands of Moses was a replication of a design that had heavenly origins. In this manner, the tabernacle was evidently a temporary feature of salvation-history and anticipated a time when God's people would have direct access to the heavenly realities of God's dwelling place in the heavens. Again, the interpreter must be careful to avoid the false dichotomy of choosing between historical significance or redemptive-historical purposes in the text.[21]

SOLOMON'S TEMPLE

This section continues to examine data that supports the major premise of the categorical syllogism: that a heavenly temple must be constructed directly or immediately by God. The construction of heavenly temples is directly addressed in the next chapter, while this present chapter considers the data from temples made by human hands. *As with altars and tents, the way in which Solomon's temple was constructed anticipated a climactic temple made without human hands.* There were characteristics of Solomon's temple that communicated it had some heavenly or eternal qualities. It was the place of Yahweh's own choosing.[22] And it eventually was identified as the center of the cosmos, the navel of the earth.[23] Despite these eternal qualities, it was still a temple made by human hands.

The main purpose of the Jerusalem temple was to be a "house" for Yahweh's personal presence among his covenant people. The temple was the "gate" of heaven in God's city of Jerusalem, as indicated by the angelic cherubim above the ark of the covenant.[24] There is a sense in which there was no static architectural temple in Jerusalem because it was always subject to Israel's own spiritual condition.[25] Even though Solomon's temple was beautiful, its function as the dwelling place of Yahweh among his covenant people was contingent upon the Mosaic covenant and its stipulations. Israel's history was one of failure and disobedience.[26] Yahweh's personal presence was never unconditionally guaranteed and is explicitly contingent upon obedience (1 Kings 6:11–13). Moreover, David's request to build a "house" for Yahweh out of cedar was rejected on the basis that such a creation of human hands could never be a dwelling place for God (2 Sam. 7:4, 7).[27] God's dwelling place on earth must be built by God himself, not by human hands.

Even the cultic system of animal sacrifices in Solomon's temple was never designed to be permanent. The temple was the only designated place for the slaughter, roasting, and eating of animals.[28] The entire affair was designed around the shedding of blood. The Talmud describes the Sons of Aaron having blood up to their ankles.[29] The blood of the sacrifices was to be "poured out on the altar of the Lord your God" (Deut. 12:27). Within Leviticus, there are five different types of sacrifices (burnt, cereal, peace, purification, and reparation).[30] The penalty for "high-handed sin" was to be cut off from the people (Num. 15:30). The entire system awaited a better and final sacrifice that would deal with all sin in every form.

The actual construction of Solomon's temple indicated that it anticipated something eternal and made without human hands. The scriptures draw attention to the means by which the temple was built as they describe David's disqualification for the task. Yahweh revealed to David that he could not use his hands to build the temple in Jerusalem because they were "bloody hands." This fact is repeated throughout the historical books:

> But the word of the LORD came to me, saying, "You have shed much blood and have waged great wars. You shall not build a house to my name, because you have shed so much blood before me on the earth." (1 Chr. 22:8)

> "You may not build a house for my name for you are a man of war and have shed blood." (1 Chr. 28:3).

> "Nevertheless, it is not you who shall build the house, but your son who shall be born to you shall build the house for my name." (2 Chr. 6:9)

> And Solomon sent word to Hiram, "You know that David my father could not build a house for the name of the LORD his God because of the warfare with which his enemies surrounded him, until the LORD put them under the soles of his feet." (1 Kings 5:2–3)

Yahweh gave King David the desire to build the temple, but he could not carry out the task. There was a sense in which God required "clean" hands, and only Solomon could fulfill this role. This division of labor between David and Solomon draws attention to the fact that even temples built by human "hands" had to reflect the holiness of Yahweh's own "hands."

Even though the temple of Solomon was built by human hands, it was constructed according to the directions of the Spirit of Yahweh. After a summary of all of David's plans that he gave to Solomon, the Chronicler states:

> All this he made clear to me in writing from the hand of the LORD, all the work to be done according to the plan. (1 Chr. 28:19)

The "hand" of the Lord built the temple through the instrument of David and Solomon's human hands. Again, Yahweh gave King David the *desire* to build the temple and the *plans* to build it, but David could not carry out the task. The temple was built by Solomon's (relatively) clean hands and based on the template given to David by God's Spirit.[31] Together, these aspects of its construction anticipate a final and climactic dwelling place of God among his people, which would not be simply a "footstool" for God.[32]

The dedication of the temple was also anticipatory. Solomon's temple inauguration was based on a seven-day dedication, to which was "added a seven-day feast/banquet (2 Chr. 7:9; 1 Kings 8:65)."[33] The repeated use of the number seven points to the temple as a place of rest modeled after the divine act of rest taken after creating the cosmos in six days (Gen. 1).[34] Thus, Solomon's temple points forward to a place of divine rest.

The anticipatory nature of Solomon's temple is evident in the directions that it should be built according to specifications that included requirements for materials and the related labor. The text of 1 Kings includes the following description:

> When the house was built, it was with stone prepared at the quarry, so that neither hammer nor axe nor any tool of iron was heard in the house while it was being built. (1 Kings 6:7)

The key idea here is that all of the stonework needed to prepare the bricks for use had to be done at the quarry and not on the site of the temple. This is especially surprising because of the great emphasis put on the temple's "complexity and splendor."[35] Even the furniture and vessels were made elsewhere, to keep the place of construction as quiet as possible:

> Now the pots, the shovels, and the basins, all these vessels in the house of the LORD, which Hiram made for King Solomon, were of burnished bronze. In the plain of the Jordan the king cast them, in the clay ground between Succoth and Zarethan. (1 Kings 7:45–46)

The purpose of this (relatively) silent construction site is not specified in 1 Kings and remains elusive to many commentators. Some Sumerian accounts of temple construction also refer to the insistence that the site remain free of noise.[36] But such a parallel with pagan nations makes the sustained use of this feature even more intriguing in Israel. Some simply dismiss 1 Kings 6:7 as an addition to the text by later scribes.[37] Another suggestion is that the prohibition of onsite work was designed to "preserve the pristine quality of the Temple as the center of YHWH's creation."[38] Such a concern would match the perspective that the temple functioned as the center of the universe.[39] However, it is not clear *how* this requirement for silence relates to its cosmological status.

A better approach is to see this requirement for silence as related to the two types of temple construction found throughout the canon (again, "temple" is defined broadly as a place of cultic Yahweh worship). For example, this requirement for pre-cut stone and silence at the job site of the temple creates an element of continuity with the Mosaic laws requiring primitive and occasional altars to be built from natural and unworked stone (Exod. 20:25).[40] Some have speculated that this was simply an act of "reverence."[41] But in the case of the altars and in this case of Solomon's temple, the use of pre-cut stone and silence reflects the anticipatory nature of these places of cultic worship. Thus, the silence at the construction of Solomon's temple is suggestive of a temple like the temple-garden of Eden that was built by God's own hand. The silence expressed the sanctification and holiness of the site because it was being built *as though* it were by God's own hand, even though it was built with human hands.

This perspective that the way in which Solomon's temple was constructed anticipates another future temple is supported and reinforced by Solomon's speech. At first, Solomon seems to indicate that the temple *completely* fulfills the Davidic covenant and is eternal in nature:

> Then Solomon said, "The LORD has said that he would dwell in thick darkness.
> I have indeed built you an exalted house, a place for you to dwell in forever."
> (1 Kings 8:12–13)

There is a sense in which Solomon's temple fulfills the covenant with David—but it is a partial fulfillment. And Solomon's speech toward God offers three reasons: (1) he sits on the throne, (2) he built a house for the name of the Lord, and (3) there is a resting place for the ark of the covenant made between Yahweh and Israel (1 Kings 8:20–21). Even Stephen's speech agrees that this was Yahweh's "house" (Acts 7:47). But this is best understood as inaugurated eschatology (an already/not yet) or even a partial fulfillment. Solomon's mortality meant that this was not the final "house" of Yahweh's name because the covenant with David promised a house and throne that would last "forever" (2 Sam. 7:13/2 Rgns 7:13).

According to the text of 2 Chronicles (2:14), the actual construction of the temple was due to skilled craftsmen such as Huram-abi, who was sent to Solomon by the king of Tire. This man, Huram-abi, was an artisan who was able "to do all sorts of engraving and execute any design."[42] He was able to work with gold, silver, bronze, iron, stone, and wood, as well as colored fabrics and fine linen.[43] This Huram-abi made all sorts of implements for Yahweh worship as well, including pots, shovels, and forks out of burnished bronze.[44] Yet, when Solomon blessed the people before his prayer of dedication after the temple was built, he proclaimed:

> Blessed be the Lord, the God of Israel, who with his hand has fulfilled what he promised with his mouth to David my father. (2 Chr. 6:4)

This particular blessing is important because it attributes the work of skilled artisans as ultimately due to the "hand" of Yahweh. There are also parallels between the description of "Hiram from Tyre" as being "full" of wisdom, understanding, and skill in 1 Kings 7:14 and the Spirit's empowerment of those who built the tabernacle (Exod. 31:3; 35:31). The temple was built by human hands, but in another sense, it was built by the "hand of God." All of the blessings from Hiram in Tire were providentially directed by God so that his promises would be fulfilled. Solomon viewed the human workers as instruments of God.[45] This perspective draws attention to a major point of this section and of the argument at hand: God's dwelling place(s) are built by his own hand.

Solomon's dedication of the temple also identifies the temple as a place that could not function as his dwelling place as he asks the rhetorical question:

> But will God indeed dwell on the earth? Behold, heaven and the highest heaven cannot contain you; how much less this house that I have built! (1 Kings 8:27)

According to Solomon's own words, the temple was not God's dwelling place for it could not contain God.[46] The reason was this: it was constructed by Solomon's own hands—the hands of a mere man. Positively, Solomon identifies "heaven" as the place where God dwells, presumably because it was made by God and not by human hands. Thus, when the people pray toward the temple, Solomon asks God to "listen in heaven your dwelling place" (1 Kings 8:30).[47] This means that Solomon's temple did not fulfill the ideal in which God would finally, fully, and permanently dwell among his people. Solomon's temple was only a temporary, partial, and *imperfect* fulfillment on the typological trajectory of the *perfect* dwelling place promised by God to David.[48]

This section considered how the construction of Solomon's temple—a temple made by human hands—anticipated a final temple beyond it—one not made by human hands. The construction of Solomon's temple was an important step in redemptive history that moved toward the final climactic event when God would once again dwell with his covenant people. But this temple was temporary, and God's presence was contingent upon the nation's fulfillment of the Mosaic covenant. The typological function of the silent construction of Solomon's temple anticipated the eventual building of a "human temple" or nonarchitectural temple. One day, Yahweh would build his "house" for his people without noise—for no tool, hammer, or chisel would be used. The direct and unmediated act of the Holy Spirit upon the physical world is an act of creation "without hands." Negatively stated: a *true* temple of God cannot be made according to the laws and nature of this world. It is important to note that this does not mean a true temple of God cannot be in the world, understood by the world, or accessed by the world—but it cannot be made by what is already created. The creator cannot and will not permanently dwell in a temple that has been created by secondary means, such as human hands.

THE SECOND TEMPLE

The first temple constructed by Solomon was destroyed by the Babylonians when a majority of the Jews were deported to Babylonia in the time known as the exile. When Cyrus II of Persia allowed the exiled Jews to return and rebuild the temple through the leadership of Zerubbabel, this building in Jerusalem is identified as the Second Temple. Later, this temple was expanded and refurbished even further by Herod the Great in 37 BC so that it was known as Herod's temple.[49] This section demonstrates the way in which the Second Temple was constructed anticipated another temple made without human hands.

The first observation about the construction of the Second Temple is that it was achieved through the power of God's Spirit and even partially fulfilled God's promises. Zerubbabel himself was the grandson of King Jehoiachin of Judah and a descendant of David (1 Chr. 3:17).[50] The rebuilding of the temple may be considered a step of inaugurated eschatology or partial fulfillment of the Davidic covenant.

Even providential acts of the people and leadership are explained in terms of divine action. For example, the prophet Haggai (1:14) explains that it was Yahweh who was moving and motivating leaders such as Zerubbabel and the high priest Joshua the son of Jehozadak to work on the "house of the Lord of hosts." The book of Zechariah (4:6) explains the construction of the Second Temple as a work of the Spirit of God: "This is the word of the LORD to Zerubbabel: Not by might, nor by power, but by my Spirit, says the LORD of hosts."[51] Similarly, Haggai (2:4) reveals that God commanded the leadership in Jerusalem to "Work, for I am with you, declares the Lord of hosts."[52]

The second observation about the construction of the Second Temple is that even though it is described as a providential act of God's Spirit, it was still a temple created by human hands. The work of temple building as an act of human hands is especially clear in at least three occasions in the book of Zechariah. First, the prophet Zechariah (4:9) explicitly states, "The hands of Zerubbabel have laid the foundation of this house; his *hands* shall also complete it." Second, Zechariah encourages the people with a word of divine revelation from Yahweh:

Thus says the LORD of hosts: "Let *your hands* be strong, you who in these days have been hearing these words from the mouth of the prophets who were present on the day that the foundation of the house of the LORD of hosts was laid, that the temple might be built." (Zech. 8:9)

Last, Zechariah offers support by reminding Israel that God would save them and that they would be a blessing, and enjoining them to "Fear not, but let *your hands* be strong" (Zech. 8:13). The establishment of the Second Temple was a miracle, yet it was achieved through God's silent or secret hand at work in the providential choices of humans, including the king of Persia. The temple was not a direct creation of God's hand but rather, was the creation of human hands.

The third observation about the Second Temple follows naturally from the point above: the construction of the Second Temple was diminutive and anticipated another temple. Even the book of Ezra laments its stature:

> And all the people shouted with a great shout when they praised the LORD, because the foundation of the house of the LORD was laid. But many of the priests and Levites and heads of fathers' houses, old men who had seen the first house, wept with a loud voice when they saw the foundation of this house being laid, though many shouted aloud for joy, so that the people could not distinguish the sound of the joyful shout from the sound of the people's weeping, for the people shouted with a great shout, and the sound was heard far away. (Ezra 3:11–13)

The construction of the Second Temple was a mixture of joyful shouts and tears because of its very existence but also because of its diminutive status. Mroczek observes that the book of Tobit supports the conclusion that the Second Temple only created anticipation of another final temple, and her analysis is worth quoting in full:

Tobit, in his deathbed speech in Chapter 14, seems ambivalent about the Second Temple, saying only that the people "will rebuild the temple of God, but not like the first one until the period when the times of fulfillment shall come"; the writer looks forward to the real restoration of the city and temple, an end time when "all will return from their exile and will rebuild Jerusalem in splendor; and in it the temple of God will be rebuilt, just as the prophets of Israel have said concerning it" (Tob. 14:5).[53]

Mroczek also highlights the fact that the Enochic *Animal Apocalypse* and the *Damascus Document* from the Dead Sea Scrolls found the Second Temple to be a failure of some kind or at least impure.[54] The diminutive nature of the Second Temple is also highlighted by the fact that God's glory never filled it as it did in Solomon's temple (2 Chr. 7:1). Some view this absence of God's glory in absolute terms, while others view it as an issue of degrees.[55] For example, as Joseph Greene points out, "Many Second Temple Jews believed that God dwelled in the second temple despite the glory cloud not being re-manifested."[56] The fact that Jesus himself cleansed the temple and called it his "Father's house" points to the conclusion that God's glory was indeed resident in the Second Temple in some manner, albeit in a diminished manner.[57] A range of Judaic traditions found the Second Temple to be temporary due to the way in which it was constructed, and some hoped for a new, permanent, and fully glorious temple for God's presence among his covenant people.

SUMMARY

This chapter considered the salvation-historical motif of God dwelling among his people in temporary places of worship, including primitive altars, the tabernacle, and the temple in Jerusalem. Each of these places was temporary in nature and subject to sin, judgment, and destruction. But they all advanced the storyline of redemption by contributing to the anticipation of the fulfillment that God would one day finally dwell among his people forever and eternally.[58] It is especially noteworthy that all of these places of cultic worship are accompanied by special revelations about the way in which they were to be constructed. This is underscored by the way in which the authors of scripture paid careful attention to describe how places of Yahweh were constructed. Those temples built by human hands were providentially guided by God's own hand. For example, the talented artisans who built Solomon's temple were described by the Chronicler (2 Chr. 6:4) as an instrument in the "hand" of Yahweh. All of the places of Yahweh worship that were built by human hands were "earthly" in the sense that they were temporary and contingent even as they anticipated further developments in God's redemptive plan. Even ordained temples for Yahweh worship that were built by human hands were governed by divine revelation so that they anticipated a climactic temple built without human hands.

NOTES

1. Idols, which are the "work of human hands," are lifeless, for they neither see, hear, nor smell, according to Deuteronomy 4:28; Psalms 115:4; 135:15.

2. On typological tensions as an "intolerable paradox," see Carson 2004, 427, and quoted with approval by Beale and Gladd 2014, 299.

3. The anticipatory function of primitive altars was so strong that the recital of related biblical texts replaced the sacrificial cult in synagogue worship (Heger 1999, 366).

4. For a discussion of the continuity between the primitive earthen or unhewn stone altars (e.g., Exod. 20:24) and the altars used in "the place that the Lord will choose" (Deut. 12:27), see Levinson 1997, 37.

5. Longman (2016, 80) comments, "the first explicit mention of an altar is the one Noah builds as he exits the ark in order to offer sacrifices to God."

6. Jacob's stone pillar may be understood as a kind of altar for offering his oath, tithe, and sacrifice of praise rather than a "false image" of Yahweh. The view that this stone was a "memorial stone" (Longman 2016, 362) is not mutually exclusive of this pillar being an "altar" (McKeown, 2008, 141)—a view which is confirmed by Gen 35:5, 7. This is important for this argument here because this altar of Jacob is described with language usually associated with a temple (e.g., the "house of God").

7. Klein (1983, 133) explains that "When the troops sinned by eating meat with blood, Saul took measures to insure ritual purity."

8. This event is arguably the climax of Joshua (Woudstra 1981, 144). For a discussion of the Transjordanian altar in Josh 22:10–34 with references in Josephus (*Ant* 5.100–14) and Pseudo-Philo (LAB 22.1–8) see Begg 1997, 5–19.

9. Heger (1999) offers a historical-critical, rather idiosyncratic, and comprehensive theory of altars and their relationship to Israel's sacrifice.

10. Dozeman 2009, 508.

11. Bruce (1988, 146–7) comments,

It was called the tent of the testimony because it housed the tables of the law, known comprehensively as "the testimony." The ark in which these tables were placed was accordingly called the "ark of the testimony"; the tent, which served as a shrine for the ark, was correspondingly called (among other things) the tent of the testimony. It was no ordinary tent: it was made by the direct command of God, and constructed in every detail according to the model that Moses had been shown on the holy mount.

12. Anderson 2017, 112.

13. Anderson (2017, 103) points out that "the furniture of the temple was treated as quasi-divine in both literary and iconographic sources during the Second Temple period." It was both "dangerous to look at" and paradoxically, "desirable to contemplate."

14. Hays 2016, 85.

15. Anderson 2017, 107.

16. Hays 2016, 86. Hays also points out that the use of Spirit-empowered workers is a point of discontinuity with Solomon's temple, where the workers were not selected or empowered by the Spirit. However, Hiram from Tire was "full of wisdom, understanding, and skill for making any work in bronze" (1 Kings 7:14). Such language is so similar to Exod. 31:3 that it seems suggestive of the Holy Spirit's providential empowerment of those who built Solomon's temple.

17. Wenkel (2018, 39) summarizes Moses' shining face as "the embodiment of YHWH's presence among his people through his federal representative of the covenant as he instructs the nation how to be slaves of the benevolent YHWH. Moses' shining face is so significant that his obituary at the end of Deuteronomy emphasizes his role as one whom God knew face to face (Deut. 34:10)."

18. Leithart 2013, 124.

19. Klawans (2006, 124–25) notes that some rabbinic traditions:

compare the creation of the world with the building of the tabernacle, or view the creation of the world as completed by the construction of the tabernacle, all to the effect of
emphasizing in only a rather general way the cosmic significance of Israel's holy place
of worship.

But Klawans (p. 125) observes that *"Midrash Tadshe* says explicitly that the
tabernacle represents the universe."

20. References in the canon to the heavenly blueprint for the tabernacle include
Exodus 26:30; 27:8; Numbers 8:4.

21. My point here expands upon the argument made by Woudstra (1981, 145),
who finds that a wide range of cultic activities in Israel's history were "meant to
inspire absolute confidence in victory, though they *also* serve other, redemptive-
historical purposes within the present narrative [of Joshua]," (emphasis mine).

22. Deuteronomy (12:5) commands Israel to perform all of its cultic worship at
the place of Yahweh's designation: "But you shall seek the place that the LORD your
God will choose out of all your tribes to put his name and make his habitation there."

23. Klawans (2006, 124) offers a recent discussion of the city of Jerusalem and its
sanctuary as the "navel of the earth."

24. Cohen (1984, 299) identifies the temple as the "gate of heaven." This topic of
gate liturgy is discussed more recently by Morales 2012, 32–50. The importance of
the gates of the city for Christology is also explored by Wenkel (2021a, 137).

25. For a discussion of salvation-historical dynamics with respect to the "city of
David," Jerusalem, and the Temple, see Wenkel 2021a, 98.

26. Hays (2016, 87) points out that Solomon's temple was an extension of the
Mosaic covenant made at Mount Sinai and that "God has no interest in dwelling in
their midst if the people (and the king) do not worship him alone, regardless of how
humanly impressive the dwelling place is." Provan (2012, 66) states that God's dwelling in Solomon's temple "will be on the same condition as before, namely obedience
to the Law."

27. Leithart (2000, 131) comments, "After all the threats to the promise that the
Lord would build His human temple, build David's dynasty, and permit David's son
to build His house, the book of Samuel ends with David buying the threshing floor of
Araunah (2 Sam. 24)."

28. Cohen 1984, 301.

29. *B. Pesahim* 65b as cited by Cohen 1984, 301; the original source may be found
in *The Babylonian Talmud* (ed. Neusner 2011, 4,297).

30. Wenham 1979, 117.

31. Jonker (2013, 161–2) states, "the indication here is that the plans had a divine
origin: all that the Spirit had put in his [David's] mind." Jonker (2013, 165) argues
that the references to the Spirit in 1 Chr. 28:12 would have referred to "Yahweh's
active involvement (i.e., "spirit" with lowercase)." Braun (1986, 275) agrees: "David,
like Bezalel of old (Exod. 31:3; 35:31), is provided by God with plans in detail for all
the temple, its furnishings, and its personnel, that nothing may be left to chance."

32. Here I interpret the reference to the temple of Solomon as the "footstool of our
God" (1 Chr. 28:2) as an indication that it was temporary and not the final dwelling

place of Yahweh among his people. As in Isaiah's (66:1–2) prophecy, the whole earth is likened unto a "footstool" for Yahweh. For Yahweh has created heaven, the earth, and everything by "my hand." It is precisely because Yahweh is the earth's creator that he cannot be completely contained within it. The creator is not subject to his own creation—including temples made by human hands. Abernethy (2016, 109) comments on Isaiah 66:1: "It is true that God may choose to inhabit a temple on earth, but YHWH, the cosmic king, is neither in need of nor confined to a human temple."

33. Walton 2011, 182.

34. For the view that the Genesis account of creation is modeled after the temple-inaugurated account, see Walton 2011, 182.

35. Provan (2012, 73) comments, "This is a building that to the authors is one of famous complexity and splendor—a building designed to impress."

36. "An early Sumerian account of Gudea's building a temple for his god insisted that there be no noise around the area of the temple during the building project" (Matthews, Chavalas, and Walton 2000, 554). Averbeck (2010, 3–35) provides a detailed account of the Gudea Cylinders and their significance for ANE customs regarding temple construction.

37. DeVries (2003, 95) states that 1 Kings 6:7 "is not deuteronomistic, as some have believed, but clearly does not belong to the original document."

38. Barnes 2012, 69.

39. One of the classic passages that points to Jerusalem and the temple as the center of the universe in terms of cosmic geography is Psalms 50:2 ("Out of Zion, the perfection of beauty, God shines forth"). This concept is developed in rabbinical literature, especially Midrash *Tanhuma, Kedoshim* 10 (Levenson 1984, 283). For a recent study of Mount Zion and cosmic mountain ideology, see Morales 2012, 2.

40. Barnes (2012, 69) observes a "clear reflection of the ancient requirement that Israelite altars were to be built of natural, unworked stone (Exod. 20:25)."

41. Provan (2012, 66) observes that in 1 Kings 6:1–13, that "We are assured that the work was carried out with reverence, avoiding the use of iron tools at the temple site (v. 7; cf. Exod. 20:25; Deut. 27:5–6 for the prohibitions that seem to be in mind here)."

42. 2 Chronicles 2:14.

43. For this description of Huram-abi's skills with a wide range of materials, see 2 Chronicles 2:14.

44. Huram-abi's work on implements for Yahweh worship is described in 2 Chronicles 4:16.

45. Selman (1994, 340) concurs as he comments on 2 Chronicles 6:4: "it is as if God's unseen hands were active in all the human hands who contributed to the construction work (cf. 1 Chronicles 29:16)."

46. Fyall (2004, 56) explains the tension around the nature of the temple by finding it to be a place that blended "transcendence and immanence," for this is what "lies at the heart of a true theology of Temple."

47. Provan (2012, 79) observes that in 1 Kings 8:27–30, "As God's eyes are open toward the temple rather than being in it (v. 29), it is sufficient for people to pray toward the temple rather than be physically in it (vv. 29–30; cf. John 4:21–24)."

48. Fyall (2004, 56) argues along these same lines,

> It is difficult to avoid the impression that in Samuel/Kings the Temple, like kingship, is something that God is prepared to accept, rather than being seen as the best. The emphasis in 2 Samuel 7:5–7 is on the best, and that is to become the emphasis of the New Testament when Christ himself embodies the glory of God.

49. The literature on Herod's expansion of the temple is expansive; for introductory issues, see Simkovich 2018, 73, and Shiffman 1991, 145.

50. Zerubbabel is "the son of Pedaiah, while elsewhere (Hag 1:12, 14; 2:2, 23; Ezra 3:2, 8; 5:2; Neh 12:1) he is the son of Shealtiel." Hubbard suggests that this may be due to a Levirate marriage by Pedaiah after Shealtiel's death (1986, 52). Jonker suggests Zerubbabel was simply raised by Pedaiah (2013, 54).

51. Goldingay and Scalise (2012, 225) comment: "To complete his task Zerubbabel had to rely on power from the Lord, not on resources from any human source."

52. Goldingay and Scalise (2012, 162) draw attention to the use of the Hebrew verb for "be strong" (*khazaq*) and its parallel usage in "David's exhortations in Chronicles to Solomon about building the temple (1 Chr. 22:13; 28:10, 20)." This was likely due to the monumental nature of the task but was grounded in Yahweh's own presence with them. This verb is discussed in HALOT s.v. קָזַח p. 302–4.

53. Mroczek 2015, 514.

54. Mroczek 2015, 514.

55. Hays (2016, 167–8) is absolute on the matter: "there is no mention of the return of the presence of God to dwell in the temple. The presence of God does not return to the temple until Jesus Christ walks in through its gates."

56. Green (2018, 780) explains, "This belief could be held because the concept of God's dwelling shifted during the Second Temple period toward less intense ideas of God's accompanying presence while still remaining within the conceptual range of 'tabernacling,'" Greene points to texts such as 2 Maccabees 2:5–18; 14:35–36; Sirach 50:1; 3 Maccabees 2:16 to prove that Second Temple Jews assumed God dwelt in the temple.

57. See Luke 2:49 ("And he [Jesus] said to them, 'Why were you looking for me? Did you not know that I must be in my Father's house?'").

58. Biblical passages that refer to God dwelling eternally among his covenant people include Deuteronomy 33:27; Psalms 23:6; 61:4; 73:26; 125:2; Isaiah 60:20; Ezekiel 43:9; 2 Samuel 7:24; 1 Thessalonians 4:17.

Chapter 6

Heavenly Temples Built
without Hands

This chapter considers biblical texts and ancient sources that draw from the proposition that the nature of a thing is dependent upon the way in which it is constructed. Those things "which are made without hands" have natures that are heavenly, eternal, and unshakable. A heavenly temple has a nature which requires that it be built or constructed in a particular way. This bears directly upon the incarnation of Jesus-the-temple and anticipates the conclusion that Jesus had to be conceived of a virgin directly by the Spirit because of his identity as a heavenly temple. The term "temple" is used here as a broad and encompassing reference to a dwelling place of God's covenant presence among his people. The following sections present canonical data that contributes to the cumulative case about the nature of temple building which supports the major premise of the categorical syllogism. This chapter demonstrates that heavenly temples are those built directly by the Spirit of God. These temples from the Old Testament provide an antecedent theology for the argument that Jesus is God's temple and the nature of his incarnation in the virgin birth follows the pattern of the ways in which heavenly temples are constructed.

The thesis of this chapter and the major premise of the syllogism is one of necessity, but it must be placed within salvation-historical considerations and the canonical context as previously discussed. According to this location, the argument is qualified by the requisite that a temple (or place of worship) is legitimate and ordained as such by God. This means that the phrase "all heavenly temples" in the categorical syllogism is logically universal but also a fixed-set bound by the canon of scripture. This means there is no attempt to make a proposition about any temple that claims to be heavenly by just anyone at any point in time. Rather, the universal claim about heavenly temples is about all temples ordained by God and recorded in the canon.

Given this framework, this chapter offers a typological argument for the nature of heavenly temple construction based on the nature of the construction of places of Yahweh worship across the canon of scripture.[1] There are two criteria by which a temple or place of Yahweh's dwelling can be evaluated: (1) made by human hands as *cheiropoiēton* and (2) made without human hands as *acheiropoiēton*. The previous chapter focused on the former, whereas this chapter focuses on the latter. This typological argument demonstrates that the way in which such places were built anticipates the construction of a heavenly temple built directly by the Spirit of God: the Temple-messiah. (The prolegomena of this study explained foundational ideas for the way in which typology is used throughout this study.)

Each of the sections in this chapter considers the salvation-historical motif of temples built directly by God's own hand (*acheiropoiēton*). These places include the garden-temple of Eden, the house of David, Ezekiel's temple vision, and the New Jerusalem. Each of these places (or projected places) is characterized by the personal presence of Yahweh dwelling among his people. Again, the interpreter must be careful to avoid the false dichotomy of choosing between historical significance or redemptive-historical purposes in the text.[2] Each of these texts functioned historically as an encouragement to faith and obedience, but they also function together as part of a larger typological pattern of temple building. Each of these temples is a place where God would dwell among his people, and each is built directly by God's Spirit. They even overlap with the idea of a person who will sit on the eternal throne of David. This chapter concludes with an excursus on the portrait of the kingdom of God built without human hands in the book of Daniel.

THE GARDEN-TEMPLE OF EDEN

The garden-temple of Eden was not just a garden, it was a heavenly temple created directly by the hand of God. The Garden of Eden was a temple because it was the place where God's personal presence dwelt among his covenant people.[3] There is a sense in which the whole earth is God's temple.[4] If the entire cosmos is configured as a temple in Genesis 1, then the Garden of Eden in Genesis 2–3 functions as a temple-within-a-temple, or, as Michael Morales argues, a holy of holies.[5] There are several points about the Garden of Eden that identify it as a heavenly temple constructed directly by the Spirit of God.

First, there is a lengthy list of qualities of the Garden of Eden in Genesis which have led scholars to conclude that it should be understood as a temple-like place.[6] These qualities are lengthy in number and certain points are debated. Only a few items may be listed here. The entrance to the Garden of

Eden was on the east side, facing the sun. The text of Genesis 3:24 indicates that this entrance was guarded with flaming swords and angelic cherubim to guard the way to the tree of life. The direction of eastward was the direction of the sunrise, the source of light and life-giving provision for a garden sanctuary. The presence of gold and onyx in the garden (Gen. 2:11–12) is echoed in the priestly garments (Exod. 25:7). Additionally, there are parallels between the tree of life and the lampstand in the temple. The wood carvings of fruit and plants in the temple of Solomon were suggestive of a garden.

Second, this temple-garden was created through the Spirit of God. The central role of the Spirit is evident in the *locus classicus* of Gen. 1:2 ("And the Spirit of God was hovering over the face of the waters"). There may be an allusion to God's presence as spirit in the "wind" (*ruah*) as the Lord God walked "in the garden" (Gen. 3:8). God's Spirit not only plants the garden, but he legitimizes it as sacred space when he made his personal presence known (Gen. 3:8). The direct act of God is also apparent in the following text:

> And the LORD God planted a garden in Eden, in the east, and there he put the man whom he had formed. (Gen. 2:8)

It is important to observe that this garden was "in" Eden, so that it is a distinct place within the larger geography.[7] Whereas God constructed or planted the garden-temple, it was to be kept and expanded under Adam's dominion. Adam's role in the garden was that of "keeping" and "guarding" (Gen. 2:15), which are words used to describe the priest's task in the temple.[8] The description of the priests' tasks do not mention "Eden" explicitly, but the lexical parallelisms are strongly evocative of garden-work. Eventually, the act of "planting a garden" became associated with temple construction in Jewish literature such as the Odes of Solomon (38:16–20) and the Qumran Hymn Scroll (1QH 6.15–17).[9]

Third, the identity of the Garden of Eden as a garden-temple directly created by the hand of God is found in other Old Testament references. The identity of the Garden of Eden as a temple is conceptually supported by the following text from Isaiah:

> Thus says the LORD: "Heaven is my throne, and the earth is my footstool; what is the house that you would build for me, and what is the place of my rest? All these things my hand has made, and so all these things came to be, declares the LORD." (Isa. 66:1–2)

John Walton argues that although there "is no explicit mention of a temple per se in the Genesis account," here in Isa. 66:1–2, the idea of "rest" supports a connection between the two.[10] A garden would be a "place of rest" even as a "house" would be. Additionally, this text in Isaiah draws attention to the way in which the "house" would be constructed, for it would done by the hands of men and stand in contrast to the way in which the whole earth was constructed: "All these things my hand has made" (Isa. 66:2a).

The most important problem to address is the "heavenly" quality of the garden-temple of Eden. The answer lies in viewing the Garden of Eden from the two lenses of God's secret will versus God's revealed will.[11] The temple of the Garden of Eden is unique in the sense that all other architectural temples (broadly construed) inherently pointed forward and anticipated further developments in redemptive history. There was nothing *inherent* in the construction of the Garden of Eden that required any further temple for God's presence to dwell with his people.

This does not mean that God's hidden plan did not require the Fall, the redemption of Christ, and the new age. Rather, it means that the garden as revealed did not necessitate anything further. It was the sin of fallen humanity that required the entrance to the garden to be permanently blocked and the provision of a new way for God to dwell with sinful humanity. From the perspective of God's *revealed will* to Adam and Eve, the Garden of Eden would be a permanent place where the Lord would walk with them. But from the perspective of God's *secret will*, the Garden of Eden was temporary, even though it was created directly by the hand of God.

The most important observation to make about the Garden of Eden is that it was a temple sanctuary created *directly* by God's hand—by the Spirit of God.[12] This makes the Garden of Eden a *heavenly* temple because it was planted directly by the Lord. This fact ties the garden-temple of Eden to Israel's tabernacle and the Jerusalem temple. Both the tabernacle and the temple utilized imagery that evoked the garden and thus created anticipation of a final temple created by God's hand that would reestablish the dwelling place of God of among his people forever. Because the Garden of Eden stands at the origins of redemptive history, it is characterized by promise as well as ambiguity. There is no promise of a future garden-temple *per se*, but the events surrounding the fall of Adam and Eve ensured their expulsion from the garden, thus creating salvation-historical tensions that await resolution.[13] The Edenic imagery of the tabernacle and the temple did not only point backward toward the Garden of Eden, but it also pointed forward and created eschatological anticipation for God's new temple, one in which he would dwell among his people forever.

THE HOUSE OF DAVID

The Davidic covenant in 2 Samuel offers further evidence that every "house" for God's dwelling place must be constructed by his own hand. The text of 2

Samuel draws direct connections between the construction of a "house" and the human conception of a messianic king from David's lineage. The Davidic covenant uses the metaphor for building a "house" for Yahweh's dwelling place among his people and enables the Davidic covenantal promises to cover multiple divine intentions. Here we see that the typological relationship between the construction of a building and human conception is rooted in the word choice of the Davidic covenant as found in the Old Testament.[14] The promise of a "house" unites the concept of building a temple with the future appearance of a man who will sit on an eternal throne. *The central point here is that the house of David had to be directly constructed by the hand of God as Yahweh promised to be the one to build a "house" for his dwelling place.*

The best place to start a consideration of the Davidic covenant and the building of a "house" may be the narrative in the book of 2 Samuel (2 Reigns in the Septuagint) about David's desire to build a glorious temple for Yahweh. At this point in time, the ark of the covenant had been brought into the city of David with great rejoicing and dancing (2 Sam. 6:12). And the narrator of 2 Samuel explains that "the Lord had given him [David] rest from all his surrounding enemies" (2 Sam. 7:1). It is within this context that David had the desire to construct a physical building—a temple—for the dwelling of the Lord in the city of David. Then David went to Nathan the prophet and explained that he dwelt in a house of cedar, but the "ark of God dwells in a tent" (2 Sam. 7:2). This is essentially an argument from the lesser to the greater: why should David have a house that is better than the place of Yahweh's presence and the ark of the covenant?

Initially, Nathan affirms David's desire. Who could argue with David's spiritual logic? But after a divine revelation, a prophetic word of the Lord came to Nathan with the rhetorical question for David: "Would you build me a house to dwell in?"[15] After rehearsing the salvation-history of Yahweh's presence among his people, it is evident that the answer for a physical temple is *ultimately* "no." For God's special covenant presence among his people had previously been in tents and movable structures even since he delivered them from Egypt. Where God's covenant people had moved, God had moved with them and dwelt among them.

Although Nathan's prophecy appears to upend the initial approval of David's desire for a physical house for God, it moves toward a new and unexpected direction: the covenantal promise of a "house" from David's offspring. There may be a sense in which Nathan's prophetic word diverts David from his desire to build a physical temple and to focus his attention on the future fulfillment of Yahweh's promises.[16] For the purposes of this study, the most important text is from Nathan's night vision, which reads almost identically in the Hebrew Bible and in the Septuagint:

and the Lord will tell you that you will make a house for him. And it will be if your days are fulfilled and you lie down with your fathers, that I will raise up your offspring after you who shall be from your belly, and I will prepare his kingdom; he shall build me a house for my name, and I will restore his throne forever. (LXX 2 Rgns 7:11b-13, NETS)

This biblical text(s) from 2 Samuel (2 Reigns) provides important points for the present argument.

The expectation of a future Davidic king and Messiah of Israel is related to David's desire to build a temple. But this temple will not be a physical house of cedar as David imagined, at least not completely. Rather, it will ultimately be fulfilled in a temple-person who will be David's progeny. Yahweh's promise through Nathan to David, is that "the Lord will make you a house" and this "house for my name" will be fulfilled when God raises up "your offspring after you, who shall come from your body." In other words, Yahweh will fulfill David's desire not through a house of cedar, at least not completely, but through a person who is his own offspring. God's promise will come about through natural means even while being "raised up" by God.[17] The arrival of David's offspring is likened unto the making of "a house" and this figure will "build a house for my name."[18] The material of God's eternal temple and dwelling place among his people is not cedar, but a human being made in the image of God (*imago Dei*).[19]

The wordplay around the word "house" in Nathan's vision directs the reader to associate physical places of Yahweh's dwelling with a king who will eternally establish the Davidic dynasty. Nathan's vision evokes three different senses of the Hebrew word for "house" (*bayit*).

First, the physical sense of the word *bayit* is apparent when David wanted to build Yahweh a "house" or temple of cedar so that the ark of the covenant would no longer sit in a tent.[20] This is the sense that Yahweh takes issue with when he queries whether a "*bayit* of cedar" is appropriate for his presence to dwell in. This concept of "dwelling" (Hebrew = *yšb*) defines the "*bayit* of Yahweh."

Second, Yahweh then introduces a second sense of the word *bayit* as a dynasty. This second sense is most clear in 2 Samuel 7:11b: "Moreover, the Lord declares to you that the Lord will make you a house [*bayit*]." The inclusion of David's sons in this dynasty is evident by the fact that Yahweh will discipline those of them who commit iniquity.[21]

There is perhaps a third sense of *bayit* in this context, depending on how finely one wants to differentiate the senses.[22] David's desire for a temple will be fulfilled in a *bayit*, which will ultimately be a single person who is the head of the dynasty. This person who will come from his own body will sit on the throne of the Davidic kingdom forever.[23] Prophets such as Isaiah make reference to the Davidic covenant (Isa. 55:3).[24] Jeremiah (23:5) refers to raising up "for David a righteous Branch, and he shall reign as king and deal wisely." Likewise, Zechariah refers to this Davidic promise through references to a "branch." It is especially noteworthy that this Davidic "branch" is not only used in the singular to refer to a single person, but that this person shall "build the temple of the Lord" (Zech. 6:12–13).

The single most important conclusion from this consideration of the Davidic covenant in 2 Samuel is that the Hebrew word for "house" (*bayit*) can refer to (1) a temple building, (2) a dynasty, and possibly, (3) a person.[25] And when these will be built, it will be the Lord God who will be the one to build something/someone eternal: "a house for my name." God's promise of a "house" for David is not an obscure detail, it is a foundational part of the divine promise. This fact supports the interchangeability of the terms for "conception" and "construction" in the syllogistic argument about the virgin birth as an act of temple building.

EZEKIEL'S TEMPLE

The prophetic book of Ezekiel is a book of blessings (hope for the future) and cursings (a covenantal lawsuit from Yahweh against Israel). The first three chapters of Ezekiel open with imagery of Yahweh coming "face to face" (*panim el-panim*) with Israel as God comes among his people, not to dwell among them, but to judge them and purify them with the goal of future restoration from exile.[26] In Ezekiel 40–48, the prophet extends hope for an exiled Israel through the projection of a rebuilt temple that would be even more glorious than the previous one, which was largely destroyed. This is a temple in which God's glory would dwell in the midst of his people Israel "forever" (Ezek. 43:7).[27] Within this entire vision, stretching from Ezekiel 40–48, is the projection of a temple that is often debated, with exegetical details and associated scholarship that is well beyond the scope of this study.[28] Nevertheless, Ezekiel's temple is directly germane to the argument at hand, *because it presents an apocalyptic vision of a heavenly temple that could only be built by God's own hand, that is, by the Spirit of God.*[29]

The nature of Ezekiel's temple vision is characterized by the repetition of the verb "to measure" (Hebrew = *mdd*) and the noun "measurement(s)" (Hebrew = *middâ*). Within the Hebrew text of Ezekiel 40–48, this verb occurs thirty-six times and the related noun occurs twenty-five times with the concept woven throughout.[30] In addition to these, this section utilizes "obscure architectural terms."[31] While Israel is called upon to measure this temple, there is no explicit call to build it. In fact, the Hebrew verb "to build"

(Hebrew = *bnh*) is entirely absent from Ezekiel 40–48. Robert Jenson makes a similar conclusion:

> Ezekiel is instructed simply to report the facts of this accommodation, not to exhort Israel to build it or even to promise that they will be enabled to build it. The building will just be there; by his report to the exiles, Ezekiel is to prepare them for the gift.[32]

The emphasis of the vision is on measuring what has already been built in the sense of considering what is projected by the text. The call to engage in the tasks of measuring, seeing, and then declaring what has been done is reinforced by the angelic being who appears at the outset of the vision with a "measuring reed in his hand" (Ezek. 40:3).[33] While Ezekiel's temple follows a divine pattern, model, or template (Hebrew = *tabnit*) like the tabernacle, this model cannot be wrought by human hands.

The reader gets the distinct impression that they are being called to action: to engage in the architectural work of measuring the building. This call to measure is explicitly integrated into Ezekiel's call for the people to repent of their sins against Yahweh:

> As for you, son of man, describe to the house of Israel the temple, that they may be ashamed of their iniquities; and they shall measure the plan. And if they are ashamed of all that they have done, make known to them the design of the temple, its arrangement, its exits and its entrances, that is, its whole design; and make known to them as well all its statutes and its whole design and all its laws, and write it down in their sight, so that they may observe all its laws and all its statutes and carry them out. This is the law of the temple: the whole territory on the top of the mountain all around shall be most holy. Behold, this is the law of the temple. (Ezek. 43:10–12)

How should the reader interpret this architectural language of measuring and measurements, especially as it relates to repentance? John Taylor overstates the point when he concludes that "if this were an architect's specification we should have expected much more detail about the materials to be used."[34] The problem is that the repetition of this architectural vocabulary is overwhelming. Additionally, Israel was called to respond to the shame of their sins with measuring the plan (Ezek. 43:10). It is not enough to dismiss this literary motif because Ezekiel was a not an architect, but a prophet.[35]

It is especially important to note that the reason why interpreters have dismissed the architectural aspect of this temple vision is because its characteristics make it impossible to build. There are points of continuity with other places of cultic worship in Israel's history, as well as the Ancient Near East, such as its orientation toward the east.[36] But there are additional features to consider. First, the temple must be built on a very high mountain with a city on top of it (Ezek. 40:2).[37] Second, it must be built on a water source so that water flows from a trickle on the south side to a torrent that is impossible to cross (Ezek. 47:1–5).[38] This water makes the dead sea into fresh water (Ezek. 47:8) and gives life wherever it goes (Ezek. 47:9).[39] Third, the boundaries of the tribes and their inheritance of land cannot be fulfilled with the hilly geography of Israel, as it is described in the vision (Ezek. 47:13–23).[40] Fourth, as many commentators point out, the text is actually incomplete in that it does not give a complete set of dimensions for the temple complex and its chambers.[41] The impossibility that this temple can be built by human hands is precisely the point. Such a temple can only be built by God's hands.

The text of Ezekiel does not explicitly indicate who built or would build the temple as projected by the vision. However, it is important to observe that the context of the entire book of Ezekiel points to the Spirit of God. It is the Spirit who entered into the prophet Ezekiel, moved him, and spoke to him.[42] It is the Spirit who had "form of a hand" and took Ezekiel by a lock of his hair as he was lifted up between earth and heaven in his vision (Ezek. 8:3). Ezekiel identifies the Spirit as the one who brought him into the various parts of the temple in the vision as the glory of the Lord filled the temple (Ezek. 43:5). The salient point here is that the theology of the whole book of Ezekiel points to the Spirit of God as the builder of this heavenly temple.

Ezekiel's projection of a new temple (Chapters 40–48) calls God's people to have hope in deliverance and to engage in repentance through anticipating a temple that can only be built by God's own hands. Ezekiel's temple that could not possibly be built without a renewed earth. This view takes the literary motif of architectural measuring seriously. There is a sense in which this text is architectural, but it points to a temple that cannot be built. Faith and repentance in the context of exile begins with anticipating that God can and will do the impossible so that he can dwell among his covenant people. Conceptually, Ezekiel's temple vision is characterized by an overwhelming interest in how it would be built and what its measurements would be. For Ezekiel, the call to such activity can only lead Israel to turn from sin and back to Yahweh, her redeemer and savior. For our purposes, the nature of this temple fits within the wider salvation-historical pattern of dwelling places of God's presence that anticipate a decisive event that will reveal God's final eschatological temple so that his presence can permanently dwell among his people.

THE NEW JERUSALEM TEMPLE-CITY

There is even further data from the canon of scripture to support the major premise that all heavenly temples of God are constructed directly by the Spirit of God. This section briefly considers the temple motif in the book of

Revelation and how it contributes to the distinction between earthly temples made by human hands and divine temples made by divine hands.[43]

One of the most important elements of the climax of temple building in the Christian canon is the merging of heaven and earth at the end of all things.[44] This includes the merger of the earthly "holy city" of Jerusalem with the "New Jerusalem" that comes down from heaven.[45] The following passage is one of the most important texts in this regard:

> Then I saw a new heaven and a new earth, for the first heaven and the first earth had passed away, and the sea was no more. And I saw the holy city, new Jerusalem, coming down out of heaven from God, prepared as a bride adorned for her husband. And I heard a loud voice from the throne saying, "Behold, the dwelling place of God is with man. He will dwell with them, and they will be his people, and God himself will be with them as their God." (Rev. 21:1–3)

It is only with this final merger of heaven and earth with the New Jerusalem on a great, high mountain that God dwells completely and eternally with his covenant people. Now that sin, death, and the powers of darkness have been completely destroyed by Christ, the eternal state commences.[46] This city is characterized by "the glory of God" (21:11).

For the purpose of the argument at hand, it is especially significant that John indicates that the "Spirit" (21:10) is the one who carried him away to the top of the mountain to show him the New Jerusalem. The Spirit is the one who brought John into the visionary state (1:10) and who took him into the wilderness (17:3). To be clear, there is no statement about which person of the Trinity constructed this New Jerusalem, but the Spirit is the one who reveals it.[47] The typological pattern of the Spirit's role in constructing previous temples is suggestive, but only conjecture.

Like the earthly Jerusalem, the New Jerusalem is distinguishable but inseparable from its temple (and its garden).[48] The immediate context of the merger between heaven and earth describes the temple of the city this way:

> And I saw no temple in the city, for its temple is the Lord God the Almighty and the Lamb. And the city has no need of sun or moon to shine on it, for the glory of God gives it light, and its lamp is the Lamb. (Rev. 21:22–23)

The eternal dwelling of God with his people in the New Jerusalem is in and through Christ-the-temple. Jesus is the antitype of all the prior places of worship, whether made by human hand or by God's own hand. For the purposes of this argument, it is clear that the concepts of person and place legitimately overlap because the typological pattern of places of worship (temples) culminates in the person of Jesus. There is "no temple" in the sense that there is a need for an architectural building, for Jesus supersedes and replaces all of the previous person, places, institutes, and shadows of all the past eras of redemptive history.

The nature of the New Jerusalem and its temple is established through a contrast between heaven and earth. This contrast includes the earthly temple and the heavenly temple. The appearance of a "measuring rod like a staff" (Rev. 11:1) evokes the similar imagery of the "measuring reed" used on Ezekiel's temple vision (Ezek. 40–48). In Revelation, John is told to "Rise and measure the temple of God and the altar and those who worship there" (Rev. 11:1).[49] There is a range of views about the exact referent of what is being measured.[50] For the purposes of this study, it is important to observe that this "temple of God" has already been built, it merely needs to be measured. In contrast, the heavenly city of the New Jerusalem is measured with a "rod of gold" (21:15). The best way to understand this act of measurement is based on Ezekiel (Chapters 40–48), where measuring stresses the wonderous nature of God's dwelling place that he himself has built. Like Ezekiel, the call to "measure" is a call to careful contemplation of the mighty works and plan of God so that the implied reader might be enjoined to faithfullness.[51]

The book of Revelation contrasts the heavenly New Jerusalem with the earthly Jerusalem. John urges the reader to consider the "great city" of the earthly Jerusalem symbolically or spiritually (Rev. 11:8), and again, the city cannot be separated from its temple. The fact that this is the city "where their Lord was crucified" confirms that this is an indictment of the earthly Jerusalem. The temple is associated with "earth dwellers" or "those who dwell on earth" (Rev. 11:10). These are not the people of heaven or of God, but they are earthly and will be destroyed with the city (Rev. 10:13). The act of measuring with this rod at least entails an act of evaluation and consideration, even if one views this temple as a physical architectural building.

The book of Revelation views Jesus' presence in the New Jerusalem that descends from heaven as further revelation that expands upon Ezekiel's temple. According to John's vision in the book of Revelation, Ezekiel's temple refers to the new Jerusalem that descends from heaven and merges together with a renewed earth.[52] The point here is not to be exhaustive, but to demonstrate how the New Jerusalem functions as the antitype and fulfillment of the wider canonical pattern of temple building. For example, the rivers of water that flow out of Ezekiel's temple (47:1–11) are now explained to be flowing from "the throne of God and the Lamb (who replace the temple)."[53] There are twelve gates on each side of the New Jerusalem, just like the vision in Ezekiel (48:30–35).[54] Like the garden-temple of Eden and the garden imagery in the tabernacle and Solomon's temple, the New Jerusalem is characterized by gardens (Rev. 21:22; 22:1–5). Daniel Hays draws attention to the fact that, "the story of the Bible starts with God and his people in a garden and ends with God and his people likewise in a garden (actually a garden-city)."[55]

The contrast between the two ways that temples are created forms a "canonical capstone" in Revelation.[56] The earthly temple of God in the earthly Jerusalem reveals itself to be for those who "dwell on the earth;" as an earthly temple it is not completely "of God," for it is that in name only. It is inseparable from the earthly city of Jerusalem which is symbolically "called Sodom and Egypt" (Rev. 11:8). Thus, there are two ways to build a temple, two ways to build a city, and two ways to build its people. Those things that are holy, heavenly, and eternal are built by God's own hand, while those things that are unholy and earthly will be given over to righteous judgment.

SUMMARY

This chapter demonstrates that all heavenly temples of Yahweh must be created directly by the Spirit of God. Evidence for this conclusion was drawn from the fact that all places of Yahweh worship can be divided into two categories: those made by human hands and those made without humans. When the term "temple" is broadly construed, each of these categories supports the major premise of the categorical syllogism. The temples that were "made by human hands" (*cheiropoietos*) were always temporary in nature and anticipated a permanent temple or dwelling place for God's presence among his covenant people. Likewise, all of the temples that were "made without human hands" (*acheiropoietos*), such as the Garden-Temple, the house of David, and Ezekiel's temple all pointed to a future climactic event when God would decisively act to fulfill all of his promises.

The conclusions of this chapter have sought to develop and highlight how the history and theology of primitive altars for Yahweh worship points forward in salvation-history to fulfillment in Jesus. All of the temple-like structures from Abraham to Moses were built in such a way or prophetically described as anticipating a future temple—one made without human hands. Solomon's temple indicates that this future temple will be constructed silently, without construction tools.

The significance of this chapter lies in the identification of the phraseology of being "made without human hands" as a concept for divine acts of construction which establish something eternally true and heavenly. That which is created or constructed without human hands are "new creations," having qualities that are eternal, true, and heavenly. They are to be differentiated from every other material that is used to compose things in the world (gold, silver, bronze, mud, rock, etc.). This chapter establishes keys for a typological reading of other events, institutions, and persons who anticipate other divine acts achieved without human hands. Ultimately, this chapter provides a foundation for understanding the virgin birth of Jesus (the virginal conception) in

Mary's womb as an act of divine construction, achieved by the Holy Spirit without human means.

EXCURSUS: DANIEL'S KINGDOM
BUILT WITHOUT HANDS

The scope of this study and of this chapter in particular has been on temples of Yahweh worship, though the term "temple" is broadly construed so as to encompass primitive altars used by the patriarchs of Israel. These places of Yahweh worship can be divided into two ontological categories: (1) those built immediately by God or without instrumental means are called "made without hands" (*acheiropoietos*) and (2) those which are made normally according to standard practice of human instrumentality are "made with hands" (*cheiropoietos*). In addition to these places of worship, there is an additional item to consider, which is Daniel's interpretation of king Nebuchadnezzar's dream about a stone "cut out by no human hand" which fills "the whole earth" (Dan. 2:34–35).

Daniel interprets this dream for the king and explains the meaning of this stone:

> And in the days of those kings the God of heaven will set up a kingdom that shall never be destroyed, nor shall the kingdom be left to another people. It shall break in pieces all these kingdoms and bring them to an end, and it shall stand forever, just as you saw that a stone was cut from a mountain *by no human hand*, and that it broke in pieces the iron, the bronze, the clay, the silver, and the gold. (Dan. 2:44–45)

The concept of that which is made by human hands or divine hands is central to the dream and its interpretation. The king's dream contains two main features, including a large statue with five different parts and a stone that smashes this statue. Each of the five parts of the stone (iron, clay, bronze, silver, and gold) are the typical materials used to craft idols by human hands.[57] The statue in the king's dream is never explicitly called an idol, but the elements are a typical feature of idols. William Nelson suggests that this "may be a veiled attack on idolatry."[58] This veil is somewhat thin, because the statue is smashed by a rock that was cut out "not by human hands" (Dan. 2:34), indicating that it was destroyed by Yahweh.[59] Additionally, the same Hebrew word *tselem* in Dan. 2:35 is used for the "great image" of the statue that Daniel interprets as being used for the golden idol that received worship (Dan. 3:5). The statue represents both idolatry and the entire course of human history, for apart from God there is no difference.[60] The story of humanity after the Fall is the story of idolatrous worship. Conceptually, there are two kinds of kingdoms in Daniel 2: those made by human hands and those made by divine hands.

Daniel's interpretation of the king's dream adds further features of this "stone" that smashes the statue. Specifically, Daniel explains that this "stone" became "a great mountain" and "filled the whole earth" (Dan. 2:35). As noted previously, the reference to a sacred mountain was a common ANE expression for the cosmic dwelling place of God.[61] Thus, it is not surprising that this mountain is defined as the "kingdom of God" which fills the whole earth and destroys any opposing idolatrous mountains (Dan. 2:44–45). It is especially noteworthy that the extra-canonical text of 4 Ezra 13:3–6 identifies what is cut out of the mountain by no human hand as "the kingdom of the one who comes on the clouds of heaven."[62] This means that the "stone" of Daniel 2 is a divine person, perhaps to be identified with the eternal one who would sit on David's throne (the Son of Man).

Even the patristic writer Justin Martyr views that Daniel's references to the "stone having been cut without hands" is about the human "son of man" that is "evidently not of human offspring" (*Dial.* 76.1).[63] This ancient understanding of the personal nature of what is cut out from the rock is not surprising. If the statute is understood to be a false idol that receives false worship, the text in Daniel 2 may be suggesting that what is cut out of the rock may legitimately receive worship.

While there are several Old Testament texts that refer to Yahweh as being a "rock," (Pss. 94:22; 95:1; 144:1–2) that does not seem to be *exactly* what is going on here.[64] In those texts, Yahweh is simply the "rock." But in Daniel, the "rock" or "stone" that is cut "without human hands" needs some qualification. That is because the "stone" is cut out of a mountain by a divine hand. The stone is not the same divine hand from whence it came. But the stone is the kingdom of God and personal instrument of God's wrath on idolatry. Thus, the stone is divine but differentiated from God in some way. It is almost as though the stone itself is divine but does not encompass all that is divine. The nature of this stone is best understood as a proto-Trinitarian feature where the Father and the Son are distinguishable as persons but are unified in the divine essence.

To summarize, the text of Daniel points to a conclusion which is very similar to the major premise of the argument at hand: *All heavenly kingdoms must be constructed directly by the Spirit.* Given the way that the Davidic covenant in 2 Samuel 7 uses wordplay with the "house" of David to include a temple, a kingly dynasty, and a single person who sits on the throne, it is not surprising that there is overlap in Daniel's prophecy between God's kingdom and that what is "made without human hands." King Nebuchadnezzar's dream and Daniel's interpretation of it contain imagery of a stone-kingdom-cloud-rider which supports the major premise of the categorical syllogism for the following reasons. First, there are two types of kingdoms, just as there are two types of temples: (1) those made by human hands (*cheiropoietos*) and (2) those made directly by God's own hand (*acheiropoietos*). Second, that which is cut from the rock by God's hand is an instrument of God that is personal, heavenly, eternal, and shares in the divine nature. The images of kingdom and divine visitation all seem to merge together and coalesce around the expectation of a single person.

NOTES

1. For a methodological critique of the way in which historical-criticism creates a "canon within the canon" to judge other parts of the Bible, especially with reference to the temple, see Levenson 1984, 278.

2. Woudstra (1981, 145).

3. Here I view Adam and Eve as being in a fundamentally gracious covenant relationship, even though there is a legal principle involved (Green 2014, 165, 170). For an opposing view that denies there was a covenant between God and Adam in the garden of Eden see Bird 2020, 279–80. Adam and Eve's reception of the Gospel (Gen. 3:15) establishes them as God's covenant people.

4. Paul's theology arguably reflects this view when he proclaimed to his gentile audience that "in Him we live and move and have our being" (Acts 17:28). Leithart (2011, 114) explains that according to this verse, Yahweh has formed "the world as a temple to dwell in" and that "creation is in perichoretic relation with the Triune God, indwelling and indwelt by the Creator."

5. Morales 2012, 76–89.

6. Those who view the garden of Eden in Genesis 1–3 as a garden-temple include Beale 2004, 82–83; Alexander 2018, 18; Wenham 1986, 19–25. Block (2013) offers a contrarian opinion; he argues that Eden was a "royal world" rather than a temple space. Block's thesis seems to separate kingship from priesthood in an unnecessary way.

7. Walton 2003, 202.

8. The priest's task in the temple as "to work" and "to keep" is found in Numbers 3:7–8; 8:25–26; 18:5–6; 1 Chronicles 23:32; Ezekiel 44:14. For a discussion of this parallel between Adam's task and the priestly tasks see Beale 2004, 68–69.

9. Beale (2004, 160) argues that these early Jewish texts combine "temple-building language together with that of expanding garden imagery."

10. Walton 2011, 179.

11. See Piper (2000) for an influential article on God's two wills from a Reformed perspective. Heppe (2007, 90) discusses God's "revealed will" and God's "secret will" under the rubric of the attributes of God.

12. Louth (2002, 131) notes that John of Damascus viewed the Garden of Eden as "planted by God's hands."

13. Sin has now separated people from "walking" in the garden with personal presence of the Lord (Gen. 3:8) and from the way to the tree of life (Gen. 3:24).

14. Leithart (2003, 197) explains that "Though the word "covenant" does not appear in the passage, there is ample biblical warrant for saying that this is the announcement of the "Davidic covenant." This is because "The passage itself has all the features of a covenant."

15. The rhetorical question to David is repeated twice, albeit with slightly different wording in 2 Samuel 7:5 and 7:7. The point of Nathan's prophetic word is that Yahweh never asked for a "house of cedar."

16. Eslinger (1994, 29; also 96) focuses his study on the way in which Yahweh's future covenantal promises "divert" David from his temple project.

17. Collins and Collins (2008, 29) draw attention to the way in which 2 Samuel 7:14 places an accent on the human element.

18. See 2 Samuel 7:11, 13.

19. According to Mattson's (2012, 147) study of Herman Bavinck, the *imago Dei* provides the basis for the importance of Adam and Christ as heads of humanity, their final eschatological destiny in the kingdom of God, their status as a holy humanity, and God's glory.

20. 2 Samuel 7:2.

21. 2 Samuel 7:14. For the argument that the beatings that Jesus endured on the cross during his Passion fulfilled this aspect of the Davidic covenant see Wenkel 2017.

22. According to HALOT (s.v. תַּיִב p. 124–25), the semantic range of *bayit* includes: (1) dwelling house, (2) dwelling place, (3) the interior, (4) inmates of a house, family, including dynasty, and (5) a paternal family. It is especially important to note that HALOT (p. 125) includes "head of the dynasty" as a usage reflecting the sense of "inmates of a house, family." For the view that there are only two meanings of "house" in 2 Samuel 7 see Fyall 2004, 56.

23. In 2 Samuel 7:13, the Hebrew pronoun for the person who will build the "house" for Yahweh's name is singular: "*He* shall build a house for my name."

24. For a recent discussion of this text and its messianic nature see Postell 2020, 338.

25. Further support for the notion that a temple-house includes or overlaps with person(s) may be marshaled by pointing to the building of the church as a "temple" in 1 Corinthians 3:16–17 and Ephesians 5:25–27.

26. Ezekiel prophesized, "My dwelling place also will be with them; and I will be their God, and they will be My people" (Ezek. 37:27). For a discussion of God visiting Israel "face to face" see Wenkel 2018, 79–80.

27. Compare with scenes in which God's glory filled the tabernacle (Exod. 40:34–38) and Solomon's temple (1 Kings 8:10–11; 2 Chr. 5:13–14).

28. For discussions of the literary unity of Ezekiel 40–48 see Tuell 2012, 281; Blenkinsopp 1990, 193; Jenson 2009, 299. According to Taylor (1969, 246–7) there are four major interpretive view of Ezekiel's temple: (1) the literal prophetic interpretation, (2) the symbolic Christian view, (3) the direct fulfillment view, and (4) the apocalyptic view, which the author favors.

29. For the descriptor of this temple as "heavenly" see Blenkinsopp 1990, 193 and as "eschatological" see Jenson 2009, 302.

30. My word count is based on the *BHS*.

31. For a discussion of unique and obscure architectural terms in Ezekiel 40–48 see Tuell 2021, 284; Blenkinsopp 1990, 196; Jenson 2009, 301.

32. Jenson 2009, 303.

33. Compare with the references to the "plumb line" for measuring the Second Temple in texts such as Zechariah 4:10.

34. Taylor 1969, 246.

35. Taylor 1969, 246.

36. For a discussion of the historical and theological significance of the temple facing east with Christological implications see Wenkel 2021, 84–91.

37. Those who see the high mountain as impossible to build upon by human means include Taylor 1969, 246 and Blenkinsopp 1990, 198.

38. Commentators who view this water source as non-historical or apocalyptic include Taylor 1969, 246 and Blenkinsopp 1990, 198.

39. Um (2006, 149) comments in his footnotes that the Edenic tradition of a river of life has been merged into Zion theology so that Jerusalem becomes the source of life.

40. For the argument that the divisions of the Promised Land among the tribes of Israel is impossible or utopian in the present earth as portrayed in Ezekiel 47:13–23 see Blenkinsopp 1990, 233; as "theological geography" see Allen 1990, 285.

41. On the incompleteness of the temple dimensions in Ezekiel 40–48 see Tuell 2012, 285; on their feasibility as provided see Blenkinsopp 1990, 198.

42. Ezekiel describes the Spirit entering into him, lifting him up, and speaking to him in Ezekiel 2:2; 3:12, 14, 24; 11:5, 24; 37:1, 14. For a note on how the Septuagint interpreted references to God's Spirit see Allen 1990, 182.

43. The notion of an eschatological temple built by God's own hand is not an exclusively Christian idea, but rather one that organically grows out of the Old Testament. Klawans (2006, 139) points out that rabbinic literature also has the "idea that the eschatological temple has already been constructed, and waits in heaven ready to descend to earth."

44. Osborne (2002, 743) comments, "When the old heaven and earth are destroyed (20:11; 21:1), the 'new heaven and new earth' (21:1) become one."

45. Tabb (2019, 174) observes that elsewhere "in Scripture 'the holy city' denotes Jerusalem (Neh. 11:1, 18; Isa. 48:2; 52:1; Dan. 9:24; Matt. 4:5; 27:53)."

46. Emerson (2016, 5) comments along similar lines: "Jesus Christ took sin, death, and the grave on himself, thus suffering with and for his people on the cross, but he also decisively defeated the enemy in his victorious resurrection."

47. Um (2006, 12–13) discusses how the Spirit according to John is "the revealer" and the "eschatological life-giving power."

48. The New Jerusalem is an eternal "temple / garden" according to Emerson 2016, 27.

49. The inclusion of the altar in this imperative (Rev. 11:1) supports my inclusion of primitive altars as theologically important for the study of places of cultic worship where Yahweh's presence dwelt, even if temporarily.

50. Beale (1999, 557–9) covers five different views of Rev. 11:1–2. Beale's (1999, 558) own view is that "the text figuratively but interprets the outer court as the physical expression of the true, spiritual Israel." Koester (2018, 107) takes a similar view as Beale.

51. Koester's (2018, 107) explanation of the command to measure is very similar to my own:

> even though John was commanded to "measure" the temple, the altar, and the worshipers, the text shows no interest in the physical dimensions of the sanctuary. The importance of the command is in what it signifies: the preservation of true service to God.

52.   Still later, the seer of Patmos, whose debt to Ezekiel is apparent throughout his work, will speak of the new Jerusalem descending from heaven, a city in which there will no longer be need for a temple, since the divine effulgence will penetrate and pervade the entire city and its inhabitants (Rev. 21). (Blenkinsopp 1990, 195)

53. Hays 2016, 177; similarly, Um (2006, 149) comments on the cluster of words including "water, "river," and "life" appear in both Genesis 2, Ezekiel's temple vision, and Revelation 21–22 as they inform Jesus' identity as "living water" in John 4:6–26.

54. Osborne 2002, 750.

55. Hays 2016, 25.

56. Here I borrow the term "canonical capstone" from the title of Tabb (2019).

57. Compare, for example, the mocking of worthless idols made of stone, gold, silver, and metal in Hab 2:18–20.

58. Nelson 2013, 87–88.

59. Note the parallel text explaining divine action in which Daniel interprets the vision of King Belshazzar and explains that one who rises up against the Prince of Princes "shall be broken—but by no human hand" (Dan. 8:25). Widder (2019, 117) points to further parallels to God's hand in Daniel 4:35 and 9:15.

60. For the view that "Nebuchadnezzar's statue symbolized the course of history" see Widder 2016, 52.

61. Clement (1965, 3) comments that the ANE religions often had a sacred mountain which was "the symbol, or representation of the cosmos which formed the true abode of the deity whom men worshipped." Miller (1994, 92) points to parallel texts in the Old Testament that are associated with Yahweh in Isaiah 2:2 and Micah 4:1.

62. This imagery from Daniel likely influenced the text of 4 *Ezra* 13 (2 *Esdras* 13) (Hamilton 2015, 172).

63. The primary source for Justin's *Dial.* is found in Lanier 2021, 628.

64. Widder (2016, 52) observes this connection between Daniel's "stone" and Yahweh as the "Rock."

Chapter 7

Jesus' Identity as the Temple of God

This chapter offers an exegetical-dogmatic consideration of the minor premise within the categorical syllogism at the heart of this study. It defines, defends, and explains the minor premise that *Jesus is a heavenly temple of God.* The proposition as stated in this minor premise functions as an existential quantifier because it establishes an equation between Jesus and his ontological status as a heavenly temple. Within the context of the canon, this postulate reflects the typological relationship between Jesus and the places of worship inherent in the cultic worshipful institutions of the patriarchs and Israel.[1] This relationship is important for the overall argument because Jesus the Messiah-temple is the climax of God's temple-building activities, including altars, the tabernacle, and the temple in Jerusalem. The burden of this chapter is twofold. First, it must demonstrate that Jesus' identity is that of the temple of God. Second, this chapter must provide evidence that Jesus is a *heavenly* temple of God.

This chapter pursues these twin rhetorical aims through a dogmatic-exegetical evaluation of biblical Christology. This chapter aims to establish Jesus' identity as the heavenly temple of God. As an exegetical study, it draws from biblical material, and as a dogmatic study, it does so in order to establish propositions for Christology. N. T. Wright laments that modern systematic theologians have been "implicitly warned off" from using actual biblical material for developing a picture of Jesus' self-understanding.[2] Yet the theological evidence that Jesus' identity includes templeness must draw from scripture. The following sections consider Jesus' activity (words and deeds) and his templeness as actuality.

The rhetorical burden of this chapter is very narrow, and the validity of this minor premise could be demonstrated by simply proof-texting any number of references to Jesus' identity as the temple of God alongside texts that clearly develop his divinity (e.g., Matt. 12:6; Mark 14:58; John 2:19). Of course, there are a variety of ways in which the biblical authors describe Jesus' relationship to the temple in Jerusalem, but his personal identity as the temple of God would not be difficult to theologically demonstrate. However, there is much more to consider, and a robust evaluation of this premise can only strengthen the case of the whole syllogism. This chapter explains that understanding Jesus' templeness (or, his temple qualities) requires a Christological model that takes into account Jesus' activity and actuality. However, this chapter does not explain every angle and aspect of Jesus' identity as the temple of God. While there is no claim that this chapter is exhaustive, it provides *sufficient* warrant to accept the premise that Jesus is a heavenly temple of God.

TEMPLE ACTIVITY FOLLOWS TEMPLE-BEING

This section demonstrates that Jesus' words and deeds reflect his identity as the Messiah-temple of God. According to Jesus' own words, his opponents, and those who remembered him after his ascension, he was himself the definitive temple of God. As noted above, this self-identification as the temple of God bridges the gap between building construction and human conception. More specifically, Jesus' identity as the fully human and fully divine Son of God requires such language. The description of Jesus as the temple is not merely an optional metaphor; rather, it is part of his identity. This means that Jesus cannot be described fully, as the Christian scriptures would portray him, without an account of his templeness.

Any attempt to define Jesus apart from his templeness would be an incomplete account of his identity and personhood. With this temple ontology in place, we turn to the governing rule for the task of constructive dogmatics: *action follows being*.[3] This rule follows Thomas Aquinas' own understanding of the *analogia entis*, which relied on a distinction between *esse* and essence.[4] The former (*esse*) is the act-of-being which is limited because it receives its existence or ("thatness") from an essence ("whatness"). Aquinas' *esse* is an act-of-being which depends on an essence. Aquinas states:

> Every created substance attains likeness to God through the very of being (*per ipsum esse*). . . . Therefore, *esse* itself has this status with respect to all created substances: it is their act.[5]

More specifically, action or *esse* follows being because all individuals are located within God's plan of salvation-history.[6] The identity of persons will determine their actions. This maxim means that any discussion of "God's acts take us back to God's being" as its presupposition.[7] There is a certain circularity here: Jesus' words and deeds reveal his temple-being, while his temple-being is the source of his temple activity. However, this circularity is not vicious because it is accompanied by a plurality of witnesses to his words and deeds, even including false witnesses.

TEMPLE CLAIMS AND TEMPLE ONTOLOGY

The Synoptic Gospels portray Jesus as a Messiah-temple through dialogues that present claims about what kind of hands were used in the act of temple construction. They portray Jesus as being fully human but also being the "temple of God," who shares in the ontological category of things made without human hands.

The scriptures primarily use the category of personal testimony to provide this information about Jesus' identity. This even extends to false witnesses who were trying to destroy Jesus and his ministry at the time. The category of testimony is an epistemological source that belongs next to memory, perception, and reasoning, and so on.[8] Testimony is not only a critical part of human communication, but it plays a vital role in the formation of reasonable or warranted belief.[9] For this reason, the Old Testament requires multiple attestations in legal cases and the New Testament requires the same for ecclesiastical disputes.[10] The effect of multiple witnesses is knowledge that is supported by reasonable belief. The examples here demonstrate that Jesus, and those who followed him, understood that the nature of a temple of God was dependent upon the way in which it was made.

The Gospel of John offers an important source about Jesus' claims to be a temple because it offers an explanation for the source of false testimony. John reveals that Jesus clearly taught that he identified himself as a temple and that he would be raised up in three days:

> So the Jews said to him, "What sign do you show us for doing these things?" Jesus answered them, "Destroy this temple, and in three days I will raise it up." The Jews then said, "It has taken forty-six years to build this temple, and will you raise it up in three days?" But he was speaking about the temple of his body. When therefore he was raised from the dead, his disciples remembered that he had said this, and they believed the Scripture and the word that Jesus had spoken. (John 2:18–22)

The first thing to observe here in John 2 is that his opponents, the Sanhedrin, and the disciples all implicitly understood the distinction being made in this accusation: that the ontological nature of a thing being made *with* human hands is different from that which is made *without* human hands. This explicit reference to the way in which things are made is found in Mark 14:57–58 and implicit in the others. The nature of the charge against Jesus involved the words and/or concept(s) that God might rebuild a temple "made without human hands." The dialogue about this controversy never focuses on whether God could do such a thing or would do such a thing. Rather, the controversy swirled around Jesus' words, which involved himself (in the first-person language) as participating in such an activity. There was plenty of confusion swirling around about what Jesus meant regarding rebuilding a temple in three days.[11] However, the debates, accusations, and plots against Jesus that reference this language of his body being "a temple" built in three days never involve misunderstanding about Jesus—everyone in this historical context knew this language involved a claim to divinity.

Second, the reason why the charges against Jesus were made this way is that they imply or suggest an act of blasphemy on his behalf. If Jesus' opponents could prove that Jesus spoke against the Lord, he could be justifiably put to death. Ideally, this would have been done according to Mosaic law but at this point, it would have required some approval from the Roman government.[12] For example, Leviticus 24:16a states, "Whoever blasphemes the name of the LORD shall surely be put to death. All the congregation shall stone him."[13] This accusation against Jesus had two aspects that related to blasphemy. It charged Jesus with speaking against the temple, which was the house of Yahweh. Speaking against the temple was equated with speaking against God himself. Additionally, the heart of the accusation against Jesus was that he spoke of being able to take actions in himself or through himself that only God (Yahweh) himself could do: build something monumental such as the Jerusalem temple in only three days.

Third, the contrast between that which is "made with hands" (*cheiropoiēton*) and that which is "made without hands" (*acheiropoiēton*) draws from that which "belongs to this age and that which belongs to the age to come."[14] Morna Hooker points out that there were some Jewish expectations that God would rebuild his temple in three days.[15] This distinction is based on an eschatological worldview that distinguishes between "this age" and the "age to come," while allowing room for some overlap.[16] The Jewish opponents of Jesus did not explicitly reject the notion that things which belong to the age to come could break into the present age, but they did reject that such a status belonged to Jesus' person.

Fourth, the reference to the "third day" in the accusations against Jesus and in John's own positive rendition evokes an apocalyptic discourse in which a temple is destroyed but is then raised again by God's divine power. The entire series of events, including Jesus' ministry, suffering, death, resurrection, ascension, and return, must be framed eschatologically. Within this framework, the reference to the temple of Jesus' body being raised on the "third day" evokes a range of possible intertextual references and possibly the entire canonical motif in which persons such as Isaac (Gen. 22:4) and Jonah (1:17) are "as good as dead" but figuratively come back to life on the third day.[17]

In John (2:21), Jesus claims to be greater than the temple because it is he who could be destroyed and then rebuilt in three days—a claim that only makes sense in terms of his identity being the fulfillment or climax of the Jerusalem temple's purpose. While there were multiple purposes or intentions inherent in the Jerusalem temple, its greatest function was to be the place where God's personal presence dwelt among his covenant people. Robert Gromacki comments on this passage:

"The only one who could be superior to the temple was the one who built the temple and filled the temple with the glory of His presence (cf. Heb. 3:3–4)."[18] The false claims about Jesus and his identity as one who was made directly by the hand of God align with his own claim to be greater than the temple:

Or have you not read in the Law how on the Sabbath the priests in the temple profane the Sabbath and are guiltless? *I tell you, something greater than the temple is here.* And if you had known what this means, "I desire mercy, and not sacrifice," you would not have condemned the guiltless. For the Son of Man is lord of the Sabbath. (Matt. 12:5–8)

Here, Jesus claims to be greater than the temple (Matt. 12:6). This claim echoes the theology of the Gospel of John with respect to Jesus' temple-nature. While there were multiple purposes or intentions inherent in the Jerusalem temple, its greatest function was to be the place where God's personal presence dwelt among his covenant people.

TEMPLE CLAIMS AND FALSE WITNESSES

When it comes to the false accusations against Jesus, the authors of scripture reveal that one of the ontological attributes of something made without hands is that it belongs to the age to come because such a thing would have been created directly by God. The Synoptics draw attention to the ironic but false charges made against Jesus. In short, these charges were ironic because Jesus' self-understanding as the temple of God is directly tied to the way in which his own temple-body was rebuilt after three days in his resurrection. The false claims about Jesus and his identity as one who was made directly by the hand of God align with his own claim to be greater than the temple (Matt. 12:6).

The Synoptic accounts from both Mark and Matthew agree that Jesus' opponents sought to charge him with blasphemy (or a related charge) by calling witnesses who would testify that Jesus identified himself with the temple in some manner. In the Gospel of Mark, the false witnesses stated: "We heard him say, 'I will destroy *this temple* that is made with hands, and in three days I will build another, not made with hands'" (Mark 14:58).

This testimony against Jesus was gathered by his Jewish opponents as the chief priests and scribes were seeking to arrest and kill him (Mark 14:1). At this point, Jesus has been betrayed by Judas (Mark 14:10), the Last Supper had been eaten (Mark 14:22–25), and his impending death was prophesied about in terms of Zechariah 13:7 as quoted by Jesus (Mark 14:27): "I will strike the shepherd, and the sheep will be scattered." With his death in view, Mark uses a repetition to create a "witness" motif by using various forms of that word within nine verses: *martyria* ('witness, testimony'; vv. 55, 56, 59); *pseudomartyrein* ('to testify falsely'; vv. 56, 57); *katamartyrein* ('to testify against'; v. 60); *martys* ('a witness'; v. 63)."[19] Mark indicates that despite all of the efforts to find false testimony against Jesus, they did not agree (Mark 14:57). This stands in strong contrast with the Mosaic law's requirements for two corroborating witnesses in capital cases (Num. 35:30; Deut. 17:6; 19:15).[20]

Whereas Mark records that many false witnesses came to testify against Jesus, the only testimony that he quotes is the "false" account that Jesus claimed he would: (1) destroy the Jerusalem temple, and (2) raise up another temple to replace it in three days. Mark's sustained interest in this false claim against Jesus is evident in its quotation by those who passed by Jesus on the cross:

> And those who passed by derided him, wagging their heads and saying, "Aha! You who would destroy the temple and rebuild it in three days, save yourself, and come down from the cross!" (Mark 15:29–30)

Both parts of this false claim against Jesus are ironic when understood through the climax of the Passion and the understanding offered through the outpouring of the Holy Spirit at Pentecost.

The first claim is undoubtedly false, yet it is ironic because Israel's rejection of Jesus led to the divine judgment that would eventually lead to the destruction of the temple.[21] The second false claim about Jesus may have had some reference to his actual teachings that referenced rising after three days (e.g., Mark 9:31; 10:34). This second claim is also ironic because Jesus would eventually die and then rise from the dead after three days, thus revealing himself to be God's true temple. Morna Hooker observes that this mockery of Jesus is used by Mark to "make theological comment on Jesus' death."[22] His death would truly be the destruction of Israel's true temple; and his resurrection would truly be the rebuilding of Israel's true temple in three days.

Matthew also has an account of this incident before the high priest Caiaphas and the Sanhedrin. Matthew explains that the council sought false testimony against Jesus so that they might have cause to put him to death but could not find any (Matt. 26:60a). Matthew's account explains that "though many false witnesses came forward" to testify against Jesus, finally, some witnesses were found who truthfully could recall some of Jesus' controversial teachings:

> At last two came forward and said, "This man said, 'I am able to destroy the temple of God, and to rebuild it in three days.'" (Matt. 26:60b–61)

To this charge, Jesus remained silent. It is noteworthy that Caiaphas queried Jesus: "What is it that these men testify against you?" (Matt. 26:62). In the face of this silence, the high priest pressed the issue: "I adjure you by the living God, tell us if you are the Christ, the Son of God" (Matt. 26:63). To this, Jesus simply states, "You have said so" (Matt. 26:64a). According to Matthew and Mark's portrait of this scene before the Sanhedrin, Jesus' claims to be the "temple" of God were: (1) partially true in some sense, (2) controversial, (3) unclear to his opponents, (4) related to messianic claims, and (5) related to the messianic title "the Son of God."

A canonical reading of Matthew and Mark along with John demonstrates that the false witnesses were simply twisting Jesus' words or adding false statements alongside accurate ones. The texts of Matthew and Mark witness to the fact that Jesus was falsely accused by his opponents of destroying the Jerusalem temple himself. The text of John draws attention to the fact that Jesus taught about the destruction and then construction of his temple-body. The charge of blasphemy by Jesus' opponents accurately captured the essence of his claim to be able to do what only God could do. These gospel texts reflect the true teaching of Jesus about his identity and his abilities—that his temple-body would be destroyed and raised up again in three days. These multiple witnesses substantiate Jesus' heavenly identity as the heavenly temple of God because only a direct act of God could build a temple for his presence in three days. The accusation that Jesus would destroy the temple building endured even after his death, a fact that is evident in the reference to it by the accusations against Stephen in Acts 6:14. Similarly, Paul is falsely accused of defiling the temple by bringing Gentiles into it (Acts 21:28; 24:6).

TEMPLE DEEDS AND TEMPLE ONTOLOGY

This section considers some of the ways in which Jesus' deeds and actions flow from his identity as the temple of God. The following points are not comprehensive but offer substantial exegetical evidence connecting Jesus' actions to his temple identity.

First, Jesus' resurrection was a "sign" to his opponents. A sign was a divine act of acquiescence toward those in Israel who demanded a special event to confirm that God was truly present and truly at work among them.[23] Jesus' signs ensured that their requests were fulfilled but their unbelief grew in culpability because they did not like what God had done.[24] An important question is posed to Jesus after he cleaned out the money-changers from the temple (John 2:18): "What *sign* do you show us for doing these things?" Jesus' answer to them is that the resurrection of his temple-body in three days is the sign that he will provide (John 2:19). Part of the meaning of the resurrection was to offer "proof" to those in Israel who demanded a sign that God was truly dwelling among them in his Son. At this unique transition point in salvation-history, Jesus-the-temple cleanses the architectural temple where God's name dwelt among his people.

Second, the actions surrounding Jesus' resurrection from the dead are described as the raising of a temple. Jesus' resurrection from the dead is an act of God—an event in which the entire Triune God was involved in raising up Jesus as a temple of God. This resurrection from the dead was a thorough-going act of the Trinity, and the New Testament refers to each member of the Triune God in some manner. The Gospel of John (10:18) also refers to the Son of God having the divine right or authority to lay down his life and to "take it up again." Similarly, Paul argues that it was the Spirit who "raised Jesus from the dead" (Rom. 8:11). But Paul also refers to "Jesus Christ and God the Father" who "raised him [Jesus] from the dead" (Gal. 1:1). The text of 1 Peter 1:21 refers to "God, who raised him [Jesus] from the dead." Thus, the witness of the New Testament makes it clear that each person of the Godhead can be said to be responsible for the resurrection.

Third, the actions which Jesus performed in word and deed were an extension of his identity as the temple of God. Whereas the first two points in this section are explicitly drawn from scripture, this third and final point is an inference. However, it is an inference based on Jesus' being and identity as the temple of God. According to the maxim that "action follows being," *everything* about Jesus relates to his identity as the temple of God in some manner. Jesus is the temple where the fullness of the Godhead is dwelling. Jesus' divine personhood never changes and his actions are always consistent with his divine nature. It is especially important that Jesus describes his relationship with the Father in terms of "dwelling":

Do you not believe that I am in the Father and the Father is in me? The words
that I say to you I do not speak on my own authority, but the Father who dwells
[*menōn*] in me does his works. (John 14:10)

The Greek verb *menō* occurs 118x in the New Testament (NA28) and
79x in Ralphs edition of the Septuagint and has a relatively wide semantic
range that includes the idea of permanence with respect to abiding, remaining, continuing, staying, and enduring.[25] It is significant that the same word
is used by the Septuagint (LXX Isa. 8:17) to describe the Lord of hosts "who
dwells [*menō*] on Mount Zion." Again, Jesus is greater than the Jerusalem
temple because the Father and the Spirit dwell in Jesus without qualification
or continency.[26]

Fourth, Jesus' actions of clearing the temple reflect his association with
his "Father's house" (Luke 2:49). This was a sign of Jesus' messianic
authority before the Jewish authorities, but it also drew attention to the
contingent nature of God's dwelling among his people and the purity of the
people. When the Father's house was used as a place for taking advantage
of others for monetary gain, it undermined its divine mandate to be a place
of prayer for people seeking God's presence. Jesus' act of driving away
the merchants was an attempt to restore the temple to its divine mission
and mandate. This is also apparent in John as Jesus cleared the temple by
flipping the tables of the pigeon sellers and proclaimed: "do not make my
Father's house a house of trade" (John 2:16). Later, John writes that the disciples "remembered that it was written, 'Zeal for your house will consume
me'" (John 2:17).[27] Michael Ramsey's interpretation of this verse aptly
states: "Zeal for the house of God will consume Jesus, that is, it will bring
about his death at the hands of the temple authorities."[28]Although there was
no explicit statement that God's glory filled the temple as it did during Solomon's temple, there must have been some diminutive presence. It is difficult
to understand how Jesus could identify the building as his Father's without
God's presence dwelling in it in some manner. There is a sense in which
Jesus associated himself with and even legitimized the Second Temple (or
Herod's Temple).[29]

To summarize this section: the construction of Jesus as a temple in his
incarnation follows and flows from his being—for he is the Son of God.
Jesus' words and deeds reflected his temple-ontology. Jesus' teaching about
the destruction of his body and his future resurrection from the dead was
literal in the sense that his body *is* the temple of God.[30] But it was also a symbolic or metaphorical teaching in the sense that it required an understanding
of the physical temple building in Jerusalem to be interpreted as a sign or
shadow of himself. Like most apocalyptic language, Jesus' teaching was both
literal and metaphorical at the same time.[31] Access to God was to come about

through Jesus via his death and resurrection, not through the cultic temple building of the Mosaic covenant.[32]

JESUS' TEMPLENESS AS ACTUALITY

This section demonstrates that there is a sense in which Jesus, the incarnate Son of God, became a temple of God *and* a sense in which he was the temple of God from his conception in Mary's womb. With respect to the categorical syllogism at hand, the previous section establishes that Jesus is the temple of God, and this section demonstrates that Jesus is the *heavenly* temple of God. These two truths are apparent by any cursory consideration of the events in the Passion narrative and his resurrection. This means that the actualization of Jesus' templeness as part of his identity must take into consideration that his temple-body was constructed during conception, torn down in death, and raised again to a new and eternal temple. The interest in Jesus' identity as it relates to actuality or actualization is based on his humanity and the events of his life, death, resurrection, and ascension. Here, the aim is to consider how Jesus' identity as the temple of God did not change during any of the significant events of his earthly life as indicated by the scriptures.

The following points about Jesus' templeness as actuality are important for the validity of the categorical syllogism at hand because they demonstrate that any actuality, changes, or developments during the events of Jesus' life did not affect his identity as the temple of God. If there was a point in time in which Jesus was not the temple of God, whether at conception, death, resurrection, or any other, then the syllogism would be invalid. But this section demonstrates the opposite is true: there was never a time when Jesus was not the temple of God. This means that the minor premise of the syllogism (Jesus is a heavenly temple) is universally valid and must be accepted as part of the argument.

First, Jesus identified himself as the temple of God during his pre-Passion earthly life. Of special consideration is the following passage where Jesus refers to his present status as a temple:

> So the Jews said to him, "What sign do you show us for doing these things?" Jesus answered them, "Destroy *this temple*, and in three days I will raise it up." The Jews then said, "It has taken forty-six years to build this temple, and will you raise it up in three days?" But he was speaking about the temple of his body. When therefore he was raised from the dead, his disciples remembered that he had said this, and they believed the Scripture and the word that Jesus had spoken. (John 2:18–22)

This text is important because Jesus explains what *kind* of temple he is: he is the kind of temple that can be destroyed and raised up in three days. That was equivalent to saying that he was the heavenly temple of God. This memory was especially important to the earliest disciples because the Spirit-empowered perspective after the resurrection enabled them to understand this enigmatic teaching. But Jesus' resurrection from the dead enabled them to clearly understand that Jesus viewed himself *before* his Passion as the "temple of his body." His temple-body would be destroyed in death. The key point here is that Jesus' own language, especially in the Gospel of John, reflects the tensions surrounding the actuality of his temple-body.

Second, Jesus identified himself as the temple of Israel and the place of Yahweh worship in his resurrected life. For the purposes of the present argument, it is not necessary to determine the exact relationship between Jesus and the Jerusalem temple, whether it is a relationship of replacement or not.[33] It is vital to observe that Jesus is simply concluding that he himself is a temple of God. It is especially significant for the present argument that Jesus refers to his own resurrection as an act of raising a building—specifically, a temple: Jesus answered them, "Destroy this temple, and in three days *I will raise it up*" (John 2:19). This passage from John, as well as 1:14 and 12:41, exemplifies the sense in which Jesus always was the temple of God *and* the sense in which he became the temple of God through the resurrection of the dead. According to John's Gospel as quoted, Jesus is the builder of the new and true temple of his own resurrected body.

Third, the virgin birth through the direct handiwork of God's Spirit ensures that the temple of Jesus' body was always a functioning temple. Broadly speaking, every temple must be "legitimized by the divinity."[34] The presence of God must actually dwell in it. John Walton explains this ancient Near Eastern perspective:

> As is the case in temple construction, the mere completion of the material construction phase does not produce a functioning temple. Only when the functions are identified, the functionaries installed, and the deity has entered the temple does it begin to function.[35]

All of the places of Yahweh worship that were constructed by human hands had periods of time when they were not functioning because God's personal presence was not dwelling in, on, or around them. However, in the case of Jesus, he was God's functioning temple from the very beginning of his conception. The full templeness of Jesus' nature was always operative, but it was veiled in human flesh as he was "born in the likeness of men" (Phil. 2:7). The resurrection demonstrates that Jesus is the legitimate place of God's dwelling among his covenant people. The effect of the resurrection revealed Jesus' true identity as the Son of God to spiritual powers and earthly powers. The effect of the resurrection was cosmic in scope.[36]

Fourth, the virgin birth of Jesus according to the power of the Spirit revealed that Jesus' temple-nature (his templeness) was never contingent as all other temples were. While Yahweh's presence did fill Solomon's temple and then the Second Temple to some extent, his presence was contingent upon Israel's obedience to the covenant stipulations established at Mount Sinai. As a result, Israel's temple(s) had been polluted by sin and God's covenant punishment upon the nation included the withdrawal of his presence at certain times. God had often hidden his face from Israel as he withdrew his personal presence, glory, and power. Jeffrey Jay Niehaus explains:

> The consummate example, then, of temple abandonment is Jesus Christ himself, whose body/temple was forsaken and then destroyed as a divine punishment for sin but restored ultimately to an eternal glory when that punishment had been accomplished.[37]

According to Niehaus, Jesus' Passion includes an aspect of a temple becoming polluted with sin and rejected by God as Jesus the Messiah-temple "became sin" for his people (2 Cor. 5:21).[38]

Fifth, Jesus became the temple of God at his birth. As noted above, there is a sense in which Jesus became the temple of God at his resurrection. Yet this is best understood as the public vindication or public legitimizing of his temple identity. One of the best indicators that Jesus was the temple of God at his birth is found in the Gospel of Matthew, where Isaiah (7:14) is quoted to identify Jesus as "Immanuel," which means "God with us." The continual presence or dwelling of Jesus among his people provides the opening to Matthew as well as its bookend, with the promise "I am with you always, to the end of the age."[39] According to Athanasius, Jesus' baptism was a moment in which the Spirit descended upon him for the purpose of "anointing" (*Discourses* 1.47). The descent of the Spirit at his baptism does not render Jesus' identity before this point in time any different with respect to him being "a human temple, bearing the indwelling Spirit."[40] Jesus did not earn the status of being the "temple" of God, even as he did not earn his status as the Son of Man (or the Son of God for that matter). Augustine quotes the Gospel of John (1:14) "The Word was made flesh *and dwelt [tabernacled] among us*" to negate any assertion that Jesus earned his rank as the Son of God.[41] This line of thinking applies equally to Jesus' identity as the temple of God. The hypostatic union is critically important as it summarizes how Jesus is the eternal and preexistent Word of God who took on a human nature through the virgin birth.

The canon of Christian scripture justifies the terms of the middle premise from the categorical syllogism by demonstrating that it is entirely legitimate for a person to be a place of worship. There is no point in time in which Jesus was not the temple of God. Jesus himself declared that he was the temple of God during his pre-Passion life. He also explained his own resurrected life as a temple which was to be raised up. The act of Jesus' resurrection was a divine act of temple renewal. The fact that the divine Son of God was united to Jesus' human nature in both his pre-Passion earthly life and his resurrected body is the point of continuity which enables us to see his templeness unchanged through stages of actuality. The key difference between Jesus' temple-body of his earthly life and his resurrected body is that of a *public and cosmic legitimization* of his templeness. Jesus' resurrection from the dead has testified to peoples and powers, whether on earth or in heaven, that he is the true eternal temple where the fullness of the Godhead dwells bodily.

SUMMARY

One of the burdens of the argument at hand is to prove the validity of the middle or minor premise (Jesus is a heavenly temple of God). In some sense, this is the easiest premise to establish because warrant to accept it can be provided by simply referring to Jesus' own claims in texts such as John (2:19) or Matthew (12:6). In order to provide this argument with the rigor it deserves, this chapter has sought to demonstrate that the incarnate Son of God, Jesus, always was, is, and will be a heavenly temple of God. Jesus was the temple of God from the moment of his incarnation when the eternal and divine Word of God took on a human nature through the virginal conception in Mary's womb. Jesus became the temple of God at his resurrection in the sense that he was fully and cosmically legitimized. Now that the major premise and the minor premise of the argument are established, the next chapter focuses on the conclusion and the nature of Jesus' temple-conception by the Spirit of God.

NOTES

1. For the typological function of institutions in biblical theology, see Hamilton 2022, 285.

2. Wright 2002, 50.

3. O'Donovan (2019, 82) summarizes John Webster's thoughts when he states, "'Action follows being' is the overarching rule, not only governing the relation of dogmatic and ethical tasks, but also the internal dynamics of each." According to O'Donovan's (p. 81) reading of Webster, an ethical "ought" follows and flows from one's nature.

4. Healy 2005, 25.

5. Aquinas, *Contra gent.* II, ch. 53 as quoted by Healy 2005, 39.

6. In response to this model of ethical ontology as found in John Webster, Alasdair Macintyre (1981, 216) would likely add: "I can only answer the question 'What am I to do?' if I can answer the prior question, 'Of what story or stories do I find myself a part?'"

7. O'Donovan 2019, 82.

8. Coady (1992, 6) laments the attention given to the category of testimony-based epistemology within traditional philosophical studies.

9. Coady 1992, 7.

10. Biblical texts that require two or three witnesses for attestation in the Old Testament see Deuteronomy 17:6; 19:15; Numbers 35:30, and in the New Testament see Matthew 18:16; Luke 10:1; John 8:17; Acts 5:32; 2 Corinthians 13:1–14; 1 Timothy 5:19; Hebrews 10:28; Revelation 11:1–19.

11. Hays (2016, 176) comments that this confusion arose from Jesus using "a complicated double entendre" when he spoke about destroying a temple and raising it in three days.

12. Josephus confirms that the Romans did allow the Jews to execute criminals (*Ant.* 14.9.3) and (*Wars* 6.2.4). For a discussion about the debate over the Sanhedrin's authority, see Vanderkam 2001, 185–6.

13. This death penalty for blasphemy was used maliciously by the wicked Queen Jezebel to steal a vineyard from Naboth during the reign of Ahab (1 Kings 21:10–4).

14. Hooker 1991, 359.

15. Hooker 1991, 359.

16. For a discussion of two-age eschatology in Matthew, see Wenkel 2009, 137–57 and on eschatological discourse within the Gospel of Matthew, see Wenkel 2021b, 259–70.

17. Also note the reference to the appearance of Yahweh who spoke to Moses, saying: "and let them be ready for *the third day*, for on *the third day* the Lord will come down on Mount Sinai in the sight of all the people" (Exod. 19:11, also 19:15, 16). When this passage is read within the typological and canonical pattern suggested, God would provide "new life" to his people by establishing a covenantal relationship with them.

18. Gromacki 2002, 66.

19. Edwards 2002, 441.

20. Edwards 2002, 444.

21. Hooker (1991, 357) sees this claim as "ironic."

22. Hooker 1991, 357.

23. Other examples of Israel asking for a "sign" include Gideon (Judg. 6:36–40) and Samuel (1 Sam. 10:7).

24. Here I draw from the definition provided by Köstenberger (2021, 2), who explains that in the Gospel of John, "Jesus performed seven startling signs (the perfect number). And yet people still would not believe. John's point is that people's unbelief was their own fault." Branch-Trevathan (2020, 134) agrees that Israel's requests for signs are expressions of obstinance.

25. See BDAG s.v. μένω pg. 630–1.

26. An anonymous reviewer pointed out that this continuous indwelling is supported by John's distinctive wording at Jesus' baptism: "I saw the Spirit descend from heaven like a dove, and it remained [*menon*] on him."

27. Commentators regularly discuss the citation of Psalms 69:9 here (Köstenberger 2004, 107).

28. Michael 2011, 51.

29. John's Gospel draws positively from the temple institutions such as festivals so that they function as pointers to Jesus as well as the Father who sent him. This positive view of the Jerusalem temple as an enduring and essential pointer to Jesus is supported by Paul's own participation in the temple rituals of purification at the request of the Jerusalem elders in Acts 21:20–26. Klawans (2006, 244) agrees that "Paul also regarded Jerusalem's sacrificial worship positively."

30. Hamilton (2022, 244) concludes that "As so often in John, Jesus makes a symbolic statement that is initially misinterpreted in a literal direction only to be clarified as the narrative continues." According to my view, this is only partially correct.

31. On apocalyptic language being both "simultaneously literal and figurative" or "metaphorical," see Murphy 2012, 12–13.

32. Murphy (2012, 242) comments that the tearing of the temple curtain in Mark may "symbolize the idea that access to God is no longer through the cultic establishment but through Jesus—his death in particular."

33. Regev (2019, 57) points out that replacement theology is not necessitated by the text of 1 Corinthians 3:16–17 by observing: "the metaphor [of the Church as Temple] does not necessarily imply any antagonism toward the Jerusalem Temple. Paul may merely mean that God's presence resides in the Christian congregation."

34. Nobile 2004, 93.

35. Walton 2011, 183.

36. For a discussion of the cosmic scope of Jesus' resurrection, see Migliore 2004, 196. Even though Heppe (2007, 496) does not use the term "cosmic," he refers to the concept when he states that Christ's exaltation through the resurrection made him "exalted far above all creatures."

37. Niehaus 2008, 134.

38. Niehaus 2008, 134.

39. For this point about God dwelling in Jesus among his people as bookends to Matthew, see Hays 2016, 167.

40. Leithart 2011, 158.

41. Augustine, *On Rebuke and Grace* (11.30), as quoted by Billings (2011, 41), who identifies Augustine's doctrine of the incarnation as a doctrine of grace.

Part III

THEOLOGICAL SYNTHESIS

Chapter 8

Jesus' Temple-Conception by the Spirit

This chapter focuses on the conclusion of the categorical syllogism: *Jesus had to be conceived directly by the Spirit of God.* According to the argument at hand, the virgin birth (virginal conception) was necessary because of Jesus' identity as the temple of God. The necessity of the virgin birth may be proven according to this tri-part argument. First, this study demonstrated that all heavenly temples are constructed directly by the Spirit of God or the "hand of God." Second, this study proved that Jesus is the heavenly temple of God. According to the logic of the categorical syllogism, one *must* conclude that Jesus had to be conceived directly by the Spirit of God.

The result of this argument is the conclusion that Jesus' virgin birth (his virginal conception) at the moment of his incarnation was an act of divine construction. Thus, Jesus' virginal conception was a *temple-conception*. The term *temple-conception* captures the concept of Jesus' virginal conception in Mary's womb as an act of divine temple building.

This identification of the virginal conception as an act of temple building develops and explicates a neglected but important aspect of temple-Christology. The hypostatic union of the Son of God with a human nature was an act of constructing a place of Yahweh worship. In doing so, God built a place where his Triune-being could fully dwell among his people. The concept of sacred space as it relates to altars, tents, and temples culminates in Mary as the mother of Jesus in the incarnation. The conclusion that the virgin birth was necessary because of Jesus' identity as the temple of God is an extension of temple Christology. Jesus was, is, and always has been a *Messiah-temple* who fulfills all of God's promises. This is especially important for all of the divine promises that God would dwell among his people. Jesus' identity as the temple of God in his life and in his resurrection is one of the most clearly attested aspects of his personhood in the four Gospels.

At this point, the concluding proposition may feel repetitive to the careful reader. However, this is only natural for an analytic argument based on a categorical syllogism. This is because a valid categorical syllogism will not introduce any new information in the concluding proposition. For a deductive argument is "sound by virtue of entailment."[1] Everything in the conclusion of a categorical syllogism has already been introduced, even if implicitly, in the two premises. This means that if the first two premises in the syllogism are accepted, then "it is impossible to rationally resist the conclusion."[2] At the highest level, the categorical syllogism is a deductive argument in which the conclusion is *necessarily* true.

The aim of this chapter is not to restate the entire argument but to explain how the conclusion functions as a dogmatic formulation and how it relates to other dimensions of Christian theology. This dogmatic account of Jesus' temple-conception is considered in three sections. The first section examines how Jesus' temple-conception offers *cohesion* to the reader of the canon of Christian scripture, especially when read through the lens of Jesus' death, resurrection, and ascension. The second section considers how Jesus' temple-conception *coheres* with canonical Christian doctrine. This refers to the way in which the central thesis has qualitative attributes of being logical, consistent, and able to be understood. The third section draws from the work of Athanasius of Alexandria to show how this study is corroborated by his biblical and typological approach to dogmatics.

TEMPLE-CONCEPTION AND CANONICAL COHESION

This section demonstrates how Jesus' temple-conception offers *canonical cohesion* to the reader of Christian scripture because of the way the argument holds together with the way that altars, the tabernacle, and the temple are interpreted.

The concept of cohesion is the quality of forming a united whole so that the dogmatic formulations fit with the data of the Old Testament and the New Testament. In this context, cohesion is largely an *effect* of a coherent argument as provided in the form of a categorical syllogism. The presence and value of cohesion are most apparent in light of the problem that the syllogism addresses. Dru Johnson explains that syllogistic arguments "create a tension to be resolved."[3] According to the argument of this study, Jesus resolves the tensions surrounding the fact that Yahweh dwelt in, on, and around places of worship built by human hands. This section explains that there is canonical cohesion through the legitimate places of Yahweh worship across the canon of scripture, including altars, the tabernacle, and the temple.

Jesus is the dwelling place of God and therefore he fulfills all of the previous shadows and types that had God dwelling temporarily among his covenant people. Here, canonical cohesion is demonstrated by showing that the data of the New Testament provides a warrant for using primitive altars, the tabernacle, and the temple in Jerusalem as a source for constructing Christological doctrine. Each of the following sub-sections demonstrates that there is at least one New Testament text that has cohesion with an interpretation of altars, the tabernacle, and the temple as being significant for the development of dogmatic temple Christology.

Cohesion with Primitive Altars

There are several New Testament texts which construe Jesus as the final sacrifice so that the cross becomes the altar upon which the propitiation to God was made through his death.[4] Traditionally, Christology focuses on the ways in which Jesus was the fulfillment of (1) the priest making the offering and (2) the offering itself, for example, the lamb that takes away the sins of the world. But there is also a third aspect of Jesus' person and work: his identity as the altar upon which the offering was made. The primitive altars for Yahweh worship in the Old Testament are significant for this typological understanding of Christology on several accounts.

First, the altars were governed or regulated by divine revelation, particularly as revealed through Moses.[5] They could not be established or used for cultic Yahweh worship according to human reasoning alone. Second, the altars had physical characteristics that signified they were places where God met with humanity in a qualitatively unique manner (e.g., a theophany or a Christophany). Even if these characteristics were arbitrary as "signs," these attributes communicated to the ancient audience that they were not the same altars as those used by other people-groups around them. Third, altars of some kind were integrated into the tabernacle and then later into the Jerusalem temple, thus ensuring some salvation-historical continuity between them.

Lastly, the nature of the primitive religion of the patriarchs was "pre-covenant, pre-tabernacle, and pre-priestly," and thus characterized by direct revelation and direct encounters with Yahweh.[6] This means that his personal presence sometimes dwelt temporarily upon the place where the worship was taking place. This is significant because the fact that altars functioned as temporary places of Yahweh's dwelling makes them function in continuity with the tabernacle and then the temple.

The animal sacrifices upon these altars could never propitiate human sin. For this reason, the New Testament contains texts that encourage the reader to consider Old Testament altars as direct antecedents of Christ himself. Jesus' dialogue in Matthew includes the following questions:

You blind fools! For which is greater, the gold or the temple that has made the gold sacred? And you say, "If anyone swears by the altar, it is nothing, but if anyone swears by the gift that is on the altar, he is bound by his oath." You blind men! For which is greater, the gift or the altar that makes the gift sacred? So whoever swears by the altar swears by it and by everything on it. And whoever swears by the temple swears by it and by him who dwells in it. And whoever swears by heaven swears by the throne of God and by him who sits upon it. (Matt. 23:17–22)

In this context, Jesus' rhetorical questions draw out the concept that the altar is what sanctifies or sets apart the offering unto the Lord. This concept lies behind the nature of Jesus' death and what it accomplished. There is a sense in which Jesus is both the sacrifice on the altar and the altar itself. Thus, Christ is the altar par excellence because it is *through* him that all sacrifices are accepted by God.[7] Jesus is the "gift" being offered on the altar, but He makes it clear that the altar makes the gift sacred. A person would not offer a sacrifice on an altar less dignified than the sacrifice itself. Theologically, that makes Jesus (who sanctifies) both the gift and the altar.

The theological perspective in which Jesus is the salvation-historical *telos* of more than one part of the sacrificial system is especially evident in the Gospel of John, where Jesus states during his high priestly prayer: "And for their sake, I consecrate [*hagiazō*] myself" (John 17:19a). Murray Harris comments, "The officiating priest is simultaneously the sacrificial victim."[8] In the same way that Jesus is both the priest and the sacrifice, he is also the altar.

In summary, Jesus should be understood as the climax of primitive cultic altar building. The entirety of the sacrificial system, both primitive and Mosaic, pointed to Jesus. Matthew's Gospel draws attention to the way in which altars made the gifts upon them sacred. He is the propitiation or sacrifice that was made once and for all upon the cross, *and* he was the altar itself that made the sacrifice acceptable, for he himself was the place of God's dwelling. The silent and tool-less construction of primitive altars finds its canonical climax in the virgin birth because Jesus was established as the divine-human altar that was built without human hands.

Cohesion with the Tabernacle

The pursuit of tabernacle Christology through typology is both ancient and (very recently) modern. Such an approach was utilized by church fathers such as Athanasius, and there is renewed interest in how the Tabernacle and the temple related to first-century Jewish Christology. The recent work that has been done on sanctuary Christology with a view toward dogmatics has been acknowledged as but a "slice" of the possibilities.[9]

It may be easiest to begin with the clarity the New Testament provides about the relationship between the tabernacle and Christology. The lexical choice of the Greek verb *skēnoō* in John 1:14 directs the reader to think about the "tent" (*skēnē*) or tabernacle in which Yahweh would be personally present with Israel. Such language presents Jesus' incarnation as God "tabernacling among us." This is the word associated with the "tent of meeting" that was set up for Yahweh to dwell with his people (Exod. 27:9–19; 37:1–9). The tent of meeting became the template for and perhaps provided the "core" of the more permanent temple building in Jerusalem.[10] According to John's prologue, every aspect of Judaism "becomes a signpost pointing toward Jesus," including "the Temple and its associated ritual and festivals."[11] Daniel Hays comments that "John is not just saying that Jesus is *a* temple or tabernacle but that Jesus is *the* temple."[12]

The Gospel of John joins the incarnation and the temple/tabernacle together but only in a context in which the virgin birth is never explicitly mentioned. Nevertheless, John 2:21 offers a clear starting point for relating the incarnation to tabernacle Christology (again, as a subset of temple Christology) that applies not just to Johannine references but also to any canonical text that deals with the temple and its antecedents.[13] The act of following the divine word and attending to the scripture's own language connects the incarnation and the temple motif.

Within this discourse in 2 Samuel 7, it is Yahweh himself who draws connections between the tent of meeting and the conception of a Jerusalem temple.[14] These connections are best described as typological in nature and progressive as they anticipate the culmination of God dwelling among his people in a Messiah-temple. According to Yahweh's revelation through Nathan, each of these places of Yahweh worship are "dwelling" places of his personal presence: ("I have not lived in a house since the day I brought up the people of Israel from Egypt to this day, but I have been moving about in a tent for my dwelling").[15] Even the Second Temple should be understood to have been a place of Yahweh's personal presence, albeit in a diminutive way and chronologically bound by Jesus' arrival.[16] Eventually, the place of Yahweh's dwelling intersects with a person—a messiah, because Yahweh will "make you a house" and "He shall build a house for my name."

The divine discourse in 2 Samuel 7 legitimizes the typological relationship among the tent of meeting, the Jerusalem temple, and Jesus-the-temple. Nathan's vision from 2 Samuel 7 enables the reader of the Christian canon to retrospectively understand the trajectory of places of Yahweh worship. Whereas the point above is about reading forward in anticipation, this point is about reading the canon backward (and forward again). They are all united by virtue of being dwelling places of Yahweh's name. It is also noteworthy that the movable tent or tabernacle is defined as the place of Yahweh's personal presence from the time of the exodus. The reader of the Davidic covenant knows (or should know) that a physical temple in Jerusalem is but a step in the direction of God's final plan to have a person who will come from David's lineage who will be Yahweh's house.

In the Davidic covenant (2 Samuel 7), God's covenant-faithfullness hinges upon his act of building a "house" for his name so that his presence might dwell among his people, thus fulfilling all of his promises, in retrospect and in prospect.[17] The covenant promises to David that God would build him a "house" are especially important for the thesis that Jesus had to be conceived by a virgin mother through the immediate act of the Holy Spirit because of his identity as the heavenly temple of God. The ambiguity surrounding the use of the metaphor for building a "house" for David allows Yahweh to accomplish multiple intentions in and through this promise, including allowing Solomon to build a physical temple, establishing a Davidic dynasty, and ultimately establishing an eternal throne in the person of Jesus, the son of David. This point must not be missed: the person who fulfills the Davidic covenant is the "house" (*bayit*) of Yahweh—Jesus of Nazareth.

Cohesion with the Temple

Like the theophanies that attended the primitive altars of the patriarchs and the special presence of Yahweh in the tent of meeting, the *raison d'etre* of the Jerusalem temple was the presence of God among his people.[18] When the concept of "temple" is defined as God's personal and covenantal presence among his people in a cultic setting, then it is evident that the temple was not an invasion of Canaanite culture but a reflection of authentic Yahweh worship and obedience.[19] This sub-section focuses on the way in which the book of Acts presents the visitation of God in the person of Jesus as the building of David's "fallen tent."

The narrative scene of the Jerusalem council is at the literary center of the book of Acts and functions as its denouement. During this scene at the Jerusalem council, James presented a speech to the assembly to summarize the recognition that God was at work among the Gentiles. Here, James utilized the concept of cohesion when he stated, "And with this the words of the prophets agree, just as it is written" (Acts 15:15). James then quotes LXX Amos 9:11–12:

> After this I will return, and I will rebuild the tent of David that has fallen; I will rebuild its ruins, and I will restore it, that the remnant of mankind may seek the Lord, and all the Gentiles who are called by my name, says the Lord, who makes these things known from of old. (Acts 15:16–18)

The point of this passage is that it is *through* the restoration of David's dynasty that the Gentiles are included.[20] For the purpose of the argument, it is important that the arrival of Jesus is an act of divine rebuilding and restoration of the ruins of the Davidic dynasty. For James, Jesus is nothing less than the fulfillment of the divine promises according to the Davidic covenant (2 Sam. 7). The inclusion of the Gentiles reflects the expansion of God's kingdom as he conquers the nations through "inclusion, *not* domination."[21]

At this point, the theological, literary, and authorial unity of Luke-Acts offers more evidence as to *when* this act of divine rebuilding of David's fallen tent took place.[22] The introduction of Luke's Gospel points to the conclusion that this divine construction may include the resurrection but began at Jesus' conception.[23] This origination point is apparent as Luke stresses that Joseph was "of the house of David" (Luke 1:27). Luke makes the implications of Jesus' genealogy clear when he states:

> And the Lord God will give to him [Jesus] the throne of his father David and he will reign over the house of Jacob forever, and of his kingdom there will be no end. (Luke 1:31–32)

It is noteworthy that these words were spoken to Mary by the angel Gabriel while the baby Jesus was still in her womb (Luke 1:31). This timeline rules out any notion that Jesus' Davidic identity was based on his birth or any other event. For the reader of the Christian canon, or even of the two-volume set of Luke-Acts, Jesus is the Davidic king, and the restoration of the Davidic dynasty took place at his divine conception in Mary's womb by the direct power of the Spirit. In other words, the fulfillment of the prophet Amos, as quoted in Acts 15:16–18 to explain what God is doing among the Gentiles. God is expanding the Davidic "house" or kingdom-temple of God through the gospel.[24] The divine work of expanding the kingdom of David through the gospel is an extension of the restoration that began with the virginal conception.

These texts in Luke-Acts draw attention to the way that Jesus fulfills the covenantal promise to King David that God would build him a "house." The temple building in Jerusalem was in some sense a "house" for the Most High, but it was not *the* house for the Most High because it was made by human hands. This promise was progressively fulfilled through events and institutions such as Solomon's temple, but these were always partial, temporary, and contingent in nature. They pointed forward in salvation-history to the moment when God would directly build a house for his name to eternally dwell among his covenant people.

It is also important to observe how the language of construction was important for Amos as well as for James's interpretation of Jesus and the nature of his kingdom. The fulfillment of God's promises to Israel is directly tied to the divine act of building a house, drawing together the language of a divine person and construction. This reflects the way that the Davidic covenant intentionally uses wordplay based on David's desire to build Yahweh an architectural temple. The climax of the book of Acts focuses on the way the promised Messiah of Israel is the Messiah-temple or Messiah-tent who is from the line of David. Jesus' arrival has built the house of God so that God can dwell among his people forever, whether they are Jew or Gentile.

The act of reading the canon of scripture forward and backward draws attention to the centrality of the Davidic covenant in 2 Samuel and the promise of a Davidic king who would sit on the throne forever. There are three summary points. First, temples, tents, or places of Yahweh worship that were built by human hands anticipated a future fulfillment characterized by the merging of building a "house" and a person. Second, the divine discourse in Nathan's vision enables the reader of the Christian canon to retrospectively understand the trajectory of places of Yahweh worship. Third, the establishment of the Davidic covenant legitimizes the typological relationship between the tent of meeting, the Jerusalem temple, and Jesus-the-temple. The theological concept of Jesus' temple-conception as defined above is not only cohesive with the canonical data but also *required* by it.[25]

What can the Jerusalem temple and its antecedents teach us about Jesus? Much in every way. The point of this section is that the data of the New Testament demonstrates the legitimacy of moving from human-made altars, the tabernacle, and the temple to Christological doctrine. The data of the New Testament fit with the thesis of this study because it "sticks together" in unity. Unfortunately, while this idea may have been present among those in the early church (e.g., Athanasius), it fell out of favor as a heuristic device for Christology. The tide is slowly turning back. N. T. Wright laments that the "normal charge that first-century Jews had no idea of incarnation" might be answered by stating "of course they did; think of the Temple."[26] The argument at hand is a *categorical* syllogism, meaning that it is an argument about how the event of Jesus' incarnation should be categorized. Broadly speaking, the syllogistic argument addresses the question of which category best fits the virgin birth. According to the survey of places of Yahweh worship above, the answer to this question must include temple building.

For those who follow the storyline of the Christian canon, the ways in which places of Yahweh worship are constructed point to one reality: the heavenly temple to which they point must be created directly by the Spirit of God. The canonical descriptions of altars, the tabernacle, and temples all anticipate their climax in a heavenly temple because they were built by human hands. They could never truly or permanently be a house or dwelling place for the Most High. When considering the virginal conception of Jesus-the-Temple-Messiah, this divine act of construction occurred so that the Spirit of God was the instrument that united the divine Son of God with a human nature. For Jesus is God's temple and eternal dwelling place among humanity, and that is how an eternal temple that is heavenly, divinely made, eternal, and unshakable must be built.

The virgin birth (virginal incarnation) should be regarded within the tensions of the New Testament motif of "mystery" (*mystērion*). It stands alongside other doctrines such as election, redemption, covenant, and sacrifice. The virgin birth is something that is beyond human comprehension and expectations. But at the same time, God was progressively revealing a matrix of shadows, persons, institutions, and prophecies that functioned as types of the final temple—the Messiah-temple of Israel. The virgin birth was not a salvation-historical event *de novo*, nor was it an absolute *novum* in God's redemptive plan. Everyone (confessionally following the Apostles' Creed) agrees that it was new. But just *how* new was this event? Again, there are indeed texts that anticipated the incarnation in some nebulous manner, the future coming of God in human form to dwell among his people, that is, a God-man.[27] The entirety of this argument is as much about the nature of God's revelation and how he has revealed his plan of redemption as it is about the virgin birth. This argument rests upon the view (the assumption) that the canon of scripture progressively revealed God's divine plan to bring about salvation through the seed of a woman and to bring about an eternal place of God's dwelling among his covenant people.

This sustained interest in typology and salvation-historical significance is not at cross purposes with grammatical-historical interpretation. The relationship between these two readings is not only complementary but necessary. God's divine revelations in history were not only designed to address those in the past, but they were also designed to address those in the present, although the significance of such addresses may have changed.[28] Like the virgin birth itself, in each revelation and redemptive event, God was accomplishing multiple intentions through a singular action.

The argument of this study tries to follow the typological patterns of scripture by paying attention to what the writers of scripture were interested in. The writers of scripture in the Old Testament and the New Testament were keenly interested in the way in which places of worship were constructed or built because each type, whether altar, tent, or temple, was accompanied by divine commands that directed its construction. Those places made by human hands were sometimes attended by Yahweh's special covenant presence, but such events of divine dwelling were always temporary and contingent. They were always significant for salvation-history because they looked forward to a final and nonarchitectural temple made without human hands. It was only in this type of temple where God's personal presence could permanently dwell among his covenant people.

TEMPLE-CONCEPTION AND CONFESSIONAL
COHERENCE

The concept of *coherence* is a property of an argument determined by the reader or audience. This is often the quality in which a text "makes sense" to a reader. From the perspective of speech-act theory, this is the perlocutionary force of a text. Because this is an attribute that is decided by the reader, it is difficult to measure. Nevertheless, in this context, it is possible to measure the coherence of the present argument about the necessity of the virgin birth against the confessional ideas considered in the prolegomena section of this study. Inasmuch as ecclesiastical confessions and their traditions are the voice of the church, they may be used to measure coherence.[29] This study makes no claim to speak on behalf of others, but confessional voices of the church can be utilized through comparison to see whether certain views could or should be accepted. The concept of coherence refers to the way in which the argument (that Jesus had to be born in a virginal conception because of his identity as the heavenly temple of God) has qualitative attributes of being logical, consistent, and intelligible. The argument about the necessity of the virgin birth being based on temple Christology is not secured on the basis of merely being internally coherent, but it accords and coheres with Christian doctrine as found in the Apostles' Creed.

Additionally, the conclusion that Jesus' incarnation entailed a divine act of temple building or temple-conception follows in the path of Saint Athanasius's early Christological interpretation. As noted previously, Athanasius utilizes the analogy of Jesus as a temple in his description of the atonement: "by offering his own temple and bodily instrument as a substitute for all" (*De Inc.* 9). It is also important to point out that the argument for understanding Jesus, the Messiah-temple as being constructed as a temple in his conception, goes beyond the scope of the earliest catholic confessional tradition, but it does not go against it.

This study also directs attention to one of the key questions that the church must work to answer: "How, then, should we speak of God as born of a woman?" This study makes no claim that this question has been answered in any comprehensive way. However, this study does advance the discussion of the necessity of Jesus' virgin birth. This study began with a very specific question: why did the virgin birth (the virginal conception of Jesus) happen in the way that it did? Why did Jesus have to be conceived through the Holy Spirit in the womb of the virgin Mary? The divine intentions in the incarnation are certainly manifold. However, this study aims to extend the conversation about the scope of these intentions by adding the following thesis: *Jesus had to be conceived by a virgin mother through the immediate act of the Holy Spirit because of his identity as the heavenly temple of God.*

This proposition was defended and explained through the use of a deductive and categorical syllogism. The form of this deductive argument contained two major premises and a conclusion that logically and organically flowed from them. The major premise of the syllogism is that a heavenly temple must be constructed directly by the Spirit. Because this is a universal claim about the entirety of the canonical content, this major premise was considered in two separate chapters. It was explained and defended by demonstrating that primitive altars, the tabernacle, and Solomon's temple were made by human hands. All of these places of Yahweh worship were earthly, temporary, contingent, and anticipatory. Alternatively, all of the heavenly places of worship such as the Garden of Eden, the house of David, and Ezekiel's temple are all described as being constructed directly by the Spirit—by the hand of God.

The minor premise of this argument is that Jesus is a heavenly temple. This assertion is most easily demonstrated by the number and range of witnesses to Jesus' own statements about his identity. The conclusion is necessitated by the truthfullness and accuracy of the two premises. Jesus *had* to be conceived of a virgin directly by the Spirit because of his identity as a heavenly temple. The aim of this study was to demonstrate that this argument is one of necessity. Jesus, as the God-Man and Messiah of Israel, had to be born through the means of the Holy Spirit and the virgin Mary because he is the temple of God. This doctrinal formulation has the qualities of being catholic, canonical, and Christological, which are briefly summarized in the following sections.

A Catholic Doctrine

Although this study presupposes a Reformed and Protestant confessional foundation, the conclusions of this study are catholic in nature. Being born "without hands" or according to the instrumentality of the Spirit was a necessary condition of Jesus' status as the Temple *par excellence*. This study advances the catholic (little "c") and orthodox (little "o") understanding of the virgin birth by explaining its significance in relation to Jesus' status as the temple of God. This study also advances our understanding of the biblical motif of being "made without hands" as a description of creative acts of the Spirit achieved without mediating or secondary causes.

The introductory chapter of this study surveyed the *status quaestionis* within Protestant and Reformed theology regarding the reason for the virgin birth and found that there are many. This abbreviated survey attests to the fact that the purpose of the virgin birth in building God's temple does not stand alone and that there were many purposes achieved by the virgin birth. In other words, Catholic Christian doctrine has never demanded exclusivity of divine intentions with respect to the virgin birth. The enumeration of the various positions provides a certain cumulative effect that demonstrates the

legitimacy of considering further divine purposes, including the one presented here, viz., that Jesus had to be conceived by a virgin mother through
the immediate act of the Holy Spirit because of his identity as the heavenly
temple of God.

The doctrine of the virgin birth in the creedal tradition, perhaps even from
the Apostles' Creed, may have been an attempt to ward off heresies such as
Docetism. But it still succinctly captures an important historical and theological event as it liturgically teaches that Jesus was born of the Virgin Mary as
the Holy Spirit came upon her, just as the scriptures state. There is power
in such a simple approach. But this confessional minimalism is a double-
edged sword. It can lead to fideism about an event that the confessor does
not understand at all and cannot give any account of its necessity. Once the
church catholic is able to give an account of the historicity and the theological
necessity of the virgin birth, it can begin to engage with issues of practicality
and pastoral theology. Consider the following three possible areas of praxis.

*The doctrine of Temple-conception has implications for the praxis of wor-
ship.* This means that those who worship Jesus the Messiah-temple participate
in the same trajectory as those who worshiped Yahweh in the physical places
of worship in the Old Testament. Such places included primitive altars, the
tabernacle, and the Jerusalem temple. But now that Jesus has ascended into
heaven, the place of worship is in heaven and is thus accessible to all peoples
by faith in the power of the Spirit. The ascended Jesus is a temple who tran-
scends all geographic and physical boundaries. Jesus stands or sits at the
center of the created universe, including whatever might be seen and unseen.
The Spirit's presence at Pentecost was accompanied by sound, wind, and
fire—elements that evoke the filling of God's architectural temple in the past
era.[30] Those who enter into God's presence will encounter the same divine
presence that filled Solomon's temple, was kept behind walls and curtains,
and which previously scared those who saw remnants of it on Moses' face.

*The doctrine of Temple-conception has implications for the personal and
corporate identity of God's people as temples of God.* Christians are temples
of God because they are in union with Christ, who is himself the temple of
God. By faith, Christians participate in what God has done in Christ. As Lois
Farag explains: "Christians are temples of the Holy Spirit and so 'become
partakers of God.'"[31] Farag continues: "We were dead, and through the
incarnation we are 'made alive' and become temples of God. By making us
alive, he makes life, he grants us the renewal of life."[32] Peter Leithart offers
a rhetorical query along the same lines of thinking: "How else would we partake in God by partaking of the Son, if the Son were not himself that which
partakes wholly of, or is begotten by, the Father? And Scripture teaches that
we partake of divine nature by sharing in Jesus (2 Pet. 1:4) and thus are made
into temples of the living God."[33]

The doctrine of Temple-conception has implications for ministry. Specifically, this doctrine illumines the need for God's people to be "born again" in the sense that they must be "rebuilt" by the Spirit of God. Salvation from sin, death, and the power of darkness is only found through being united to Christ, who is God's temple. Walker explains, "Although the new Temple par excellence was Jesus himself, in a derivative sense that status was passed on to those who believed in him."[34] Faith is what unites a person to Jesus the Messiah-temple. And faith enables the temple of God's people to be built by the Spirit, by God's own hand.[35]

This study has followed the recent interest in going back to the early church fathers, such as Athanasius, who used typological studies of biblical images, persons, events, and institutions to develop their Christological formulations. While this approach fell out of favor, contemporary theologians have begun to probe the question: What might it do to our systematic Christologies to make the Temple, rather than theories about natures, persons, and substances, central to our reflection?"[36] Whereas this question might be read as introducing a choice between exegesis and dogmatic formulations, this study has sought to avoid the fallacy of unnecessary dichotomies. There is no need to presuppose that Nicaean categories of substance and person must be jettisoned in order to pursue a Christology based on the Bible's own agenda.

A Christological Doctrine

This study has sought to partially answer the recent call to "reintroduce" Christology and typology. Peter Leithart is one such voice; he laments that after the first few centuries, "Christology and typology have often gone their separate ways."[37] This study attempts to answer the call by trying to understand how the act of constructing the temple and its antecedents might shape how we understand the virgin birth (virginal conception) of Jesus. Beyond this study, it may also be fruitful to further probe the ways in which the virgin birth may have been understood by the earliest Christians as a direct act of God so that the virgin birth was achieved "without hands."

The collective answer of the church must start engaging this question through the words, images, patterns, and concepts of the scriptures themselves. It is for this reason that the study sought to pick up the mantel as laid down by the church father Athanasius, who diligently sought to explain the virgin birth and the incarnation of the Lord through the scriptural language of temple building.

The significance of this study first lies in its aim to reorient the study of the virgin birth toward Jesus' own identity as the "temple" of God. This self-identity is present in the historical record of Jesus' own statement, in the memories of his followers, and on the lips of his opponents. N.

T. Wright laments that certain scholars have been "looking in the wrong places" for understanding "the Jewish roots of very early and high Christology. They have been looking at angels, the figure of Melchizedek, and so forth, none of which have more than an occasional or tangential relationship to New Testament Christology."[38] But when "temple" is used as a dogmatic category, it enables us to rethink traditional systematic categories in terms of something that draws directly from the focal point of so many writers in scripture.[39]

Yet another point of significance lies in the direction that this entire study pushes toward: a return to the ancient paradigm in which Christology paradigms and typological relationships control dogmatic expressions. Peter Leithart explains that after the Nestorian controversy, extra-biblical categories and terms came to control creedal language.[40] This led to a "methodological inversion" so that extrinsic language came to control biblical language, categories, and terms.[41]

When discussing the theology of Jesus-the-temple, there are two Christological errors to avoid. The first error would be asserting that Jesus became a temple at some stage in his adult life, perhaps at the moment of his baptism in the Jordan River. This would be akin to the error of adoptionism or the view that Jesus' divine sonship was not essential to his identity and/or that his divine sonship was honorific only, and not ontological.[42] Against this notion is the position that Jesus became the temple of God at the moment of the incarnation. This means that Jesus did not become a temple. Second, the language of "dwelling," or being a "temple" does not imply the Nestorian error in which "the Word of God was joined to human nature only by an indwelling."[43] This means that the language of "indwelling" does not mean that the person of the Son of God is distinct from the person of the Son of Man.[44] Against this error, it is also essential to insist that any concept of God's indwelling in Christ as a temple is a reference to the Son of God taking upon himself a human nature in one united person.

This biblical agenda is best revealed through a robust hermeneutical spiral of canonical interpretation. The argument presented here argues for the necessity of the virgin birth of Jesus based on an intentional reading of the Christian canon of scripture. If one reads the scriptures backward, starting at and prioritizing the New Testament, it is patently clear that Jesus is the temple of God. Then the question arises: If Jesus is the temple of God, *how are temples built?* Correspondingly, if one reads the scriptures forward, the reader will learn that all places where Yahweh dwelt among his people after the Fall were temporary and contingent in nature. The question arises: *where is the final temple of God's dwelling with his covenant people?* Such a question should lead the reader to read the scriptures forward to find out that Jesus is the climax of God's temple-building activities in salvation-history.

There is an important sense in which the broad concept of "temple," when defined as a dwelling place of Yahweh among his covenant people, appears at the beginning, climax, and end of redemptive history. The typological thread of "temple" may be picked up at either side, with the same results. The use of temples in the Old Testament provided an element of antecedent theology out of which the virgin birth can be understood to be an organic development.[45] The virgin birth appears out of nowhere but only in the sense that it unifies a wide matrix of existing expectations. According to the view of this study, the reality and nature of the heavenly was revealed incrementally and progressively across the canon of scripture. Before the heavenly temple of Christ was revealed, a series of heavenly places (including altars, a tent, and temples) were constructed that anticipated a climactic final temple of God's dwelling.

The case for the necessity of the virgin birth is coherent with the canon and cohesive with the churches' confessional traditions. It is also simple. The simplicity of the argument provided here relies upon the nature of scripture so that those who want to understand Jesus the Messiah-temple need only to look toward the pattern of temples in the scriptures.[46] It follows the internal philosophical nature of the canon. The philosophical style of the canon reveals a sustained "accumulation of instances in patterned usages that point to an abstract principle."[47] The literary patterns in scripture form relationships that progressively increase how God would eventually fulfill all of his covenantal promises for redemption, salvation, shalom, and a new creation. The abstract idea of God's dwelling place among his people was formed through a sustained pattern of constructing places of Yahweh worship that were regulated by divine fiat as given through priests and prophets.

The abstract idea of the dwelling place of God with his covenant people is worked out through the telling and retelling of historical events in which Yahweh visited his people. These theophanies or Christophanies occurred at places that God himself designated through revelation as places where he should be worshiped, including altars, the tabernacle, and the temple. But these instances of temple-dwelling were always contingent and insufficient to be a "house" for the true living God who created all things. Any place of worship built by human hands was only temporary. Any place of worship that would be built by God's hand points to the promise of a person who would sit on God's throne forever. This means that the way in which the temple in Jerusalem and its antecedents were built explicates the mode of the Son coming into the world: he was constructed as a building would be for the full indwelling of God's presence, yet without human hands. The reader who pays attention to the way temples are built, when broadly construed, must arrive at such a conclusion.

This dogmatic construction of temple-conception explains the work of the Holy Spirit as the means of uniting the eternal Son of God with a fully human nature. It enabled the human body of Jesus to be a temple of God's presence among his covenant people and even the world. The virginal conception of Christ was an act of divine temple building in which the final and climactic temple of God's dwelling place was constructed. The temple of Jesus' body was destroyed by death for three days but was resurrected by God's power to publicly and cosmically legitimize Jesus as God's eternal temple.

To summarize this section, Jesus' temple-conception *coheres* with Christian doctrine. The thesis that Jesus had to be conceived by a virgin mother through the immediate act of the Holy Spirit because of his identity as the heavenly temple of God should be acceptable to a wide range of confessional traditions. The notion that the virgin birth was necessitated by Jesus' identity as the temple of God fits together with confessional catholic doctrine across a wide range of persons and Christian church traditions.

TEMPLE-CONCEPTION AND CATHOLIC CORROBORATION

This section draws attention to the way in which the church father Saint Athanasius (c. AD 290–373), bishop of Alexandria (328–73), viewed the incarnation as an act of divine construction. The use of this language, which likens Christ's incarnation to the establishment of a building, is so clear that Peter Leithart concluded that Athanasius "expounds the incarnation as a construction project."[48] Athanasius is a theologian who is still revered by a wide range of Christian traditions, from Protestants to Eastern Orthodoxy and Roman Catholicism. The language of divine construction is significant because Athanasius is one of the most well-known church fathers and because of his steadfast expressions of Trinitarian theology in the face of the Arian heresy.

Athanasius is a significant figure for this present study because of his exegetical methodology, which drew from typological relationships across the Christian scriptures.[49] Lois Farag comments that: "Athanasius interprets the Old Testament typologically: Old Testament prophecies are types pointing to Christ's incarnation and his work within humanity."[50] His theological method is marked by a focus on the scriptures.[51] Again, Peter Leithart's evaluation is helpful as he explains that Athanasius drew the substance of his Christology "from his elaboration of biblical paradigms."[52] Technical and more philosophical explanations of the Trinity were used when elaborating on their status as persons, unified nature, and consubstantiality. But biblical language was used to form and inform the heart of his Christology.[53]

Athanasius utilized a range of analogies to describe Christ, his salvific work, and his person. The analogy of light was used to "describe the relationship of the Son to the Father" as he sought to explain internal plurality within biblical monotheism.[54] Christ's status as the Last Adam and his act of incarnation is analogous to the work of restoring a decaying artwork: "Even the material on which it is painted is not case aside, but the portrait reinscribed on it" (*De Inc.* 14).[55] In another example, Athanasius uses a "clothing analogy" to describe the way in which redeemed humanity may participate in Christ's resurrection life: "the incorruptible Son of God consequently clothed all with incorruptibility in the promise concerning the resurrection" (*De Inc.* 9).[56] Within this very same paragraph, Athanasius utilizes the analogy of a temple in his description of the atonement: "by offering his [Jesus'] own temple and bodily instrument as a substitute for all" (*De Inc.* 9). It is especially relevant for this present study that Athanasius's intrinsicist approach used the category and term of "temple" to develop Christology.

As a matter of prolegomena, it is important to point out that Athanasius' own theological method is complementary to the use of categorical syllogism and logical argumentation, as found in this present work. In his work entitled *Against the Gentiles*, Athanasius identifies his scriptural reasoning as "doctrine" (*logos*) and denies that faith in Christ can be "irrational" (*alogos*).[57] Rational thinking is part of God's creation, which reveals beneficial knowledge. The human capacity for reason points to Christ, who is necessary and sufficient to reveal God to humanity.[58] Specifically, it is through the incarnation that Athanasius understands that "human beings are able to learn from humans more directly about higher things" (*De Inc.* 12).[59] This affirmation of rationality through faith provides confirmation that an analytical argument based on a categorical syllogism is appropriate for developing dogmatic formulations.

With respect to revelation, God has ordered creation so "that although he cannot be seen by nature, yet he can be known from his works" (*Gent.* 35).[60] Nevertheless, Athanasius affirms that the book of creation is insufficient and must be placed alongside the book of scripture so that the doctrines of Christ might be fully clear. At the end of the volume entitled *On the Incarnation*, which complements the first volume *Against the Gentiles*, he writes that his readers should go to the scriptures to "learn from them more completely and more clearly the accuracy of what has been said" (*De Inc.* 56). Grahame Rosolen concludes that in Athanasius' thought, "creation was insufficient for revealing God because it is only through Christ, as the Word taking form, that knowledge of God is possible."[61] There is one unified redemptive plan for the world so that the creative work of God cannot be separated from the salvific plan of God in Christ.[62] There are five aspects of Athanasius' temple Christology that are helpful.

First, Athanasius describes the incarnation as a divine "construction project" in his *Orations against the Arians (Orationes contra Arianos)*:

Therefore according to His manhood He is founded, that we, as precious stones, may admit of building upon Him, and may become a *temple* of the Holy Ghost who dwells in us . . . He is founded for our sakes, taking on Him what is ours, that we, as incorporated and compacted and bound together in Him through the likeness of the flesh, may attain unto a perfect man, and abide immortal and incorruptible. (*C. Ar.* 2.22.74)

According to this text, the ecclesial language of the membership of those united with Christ as a temple depends upon Christ's own status as a temple. This means that the status of Christians as "precious stones" who make up the temple of God is derivative of and dependent upon Jesus' identity as a "temple of the Holy Ghost."[63] Peter Leithart explains that for Athanasius, "In founding his Wisdom through the incarnation, the Father is also founding the temple of the Spirit that is the church. The temple of Israel thus serves as a double type, both of the body of the Son and of the body of the church."[64]

Second, Athanasius uses the language of construction to describe the incarnation of Christ as though it were a house built by a king:

For the race of human beings would have been utterly dissolved had not the Master and Savior of all, the Son of God, come for the completion of death. Truly this great work supremely befitted the goodness of God. *For if a king constructed a house* or a city, and it is attacked by bandits because of the carelessness of its inhabitants, he in no way abandons it, but avenges and saves it as his own work, having regard not for the carelessness of the inhabitants but what is fitting and appropriate for Himself. (*De Inc.* 9–10)

This quotation above is significant because it draws attention to the way in which Athanasius considered the incarnation as a construction event because of the way it drew attention to the importance of the builder—God himself. Whatever heretical dangers might attend a misunderstanding of this analogous language of construction, Athanasius shows no concern. It is precisely because God "built" Jesus that he does not abandon him, but rather avenges him and saves him.

Third, Athanasius uses the language of temple Christology to describe Jesus' atoning death:

For being above all, the Word of God consequently, *by offering his own temple* and his bodily instrument as a substitute for all, fulfilled in death that which was required; and, being conjoined with all through the like [body], the incorruptible Son of God consequently clothed all with incorruptibility in the promise concerning the resurrection. (*De Inc.* 9)

Here, Jesus' body is both offering and temple, so that Jesus fulfills the Mosaic law with its cultic sacrifices in multiple ways.

Fourth, Athanasius utilizes temple imagery to describe Jesus' resurrected body and its capacity to offer eternal life:

> Or what kind of end should befall the body, once the Word had come to it? It was unable not to die since it was mortal and afforded death on behalf of all, for which the Saviour had prepared it for himself. But it could not remain dead, because it had become *the temple of life*. So, it died as mortal, but came again to life because of the life which is in it; and the works are a proof of the resurrection. (*De Inc.* 31)

It is noteworthy to observe that within the same book (*On the Incarnation*), Athanasius has no qualms about describing Jesus' pre-passion body as a temple which was offered as a sacrifice and his resurrected body as a "temple of life." There is a sense in which Jesus was the temple of God, and a sense in which he became the temple of God.

Fifth, Athanasius connects Jesus' identity as the temple of God with the concept of God's "dwelling":

> He prepared for himself in the Virgin the body as a temple, and made it his own, as an instrument, making himself known and dwelling in it. (*De Inc.* 8.3)

Here above, Athanasius unites the concepts of God dwelling in the temple of Jesus' body. Jesus' body was a "temple" even from the time when he was in the womb. To be precise, Athanasius does not refer specifically to the medically accurate moment of conception, but there is also no reason to suggest another option. There is no condition laid upon Jesus' status other than the state of being hypostatically united to human nature.

These five aspects of Athanasius's temple Christology above are certainly not exhaustive, nor are they intended to be. They simply demonstrate the early and catholic resource that is to be found in his writings. Lois Farag explains that for Athanasius,

> The temple was a shadow created of stone and gold but when reality came the type ceased and the temple was destroyed. Thus, we worship the body of the Lord that was formed by the Holy Spirit and clothed the Word.[65]

These examples highlight the way in which Athanasius utilized biblical imagery to establish a set of dogmatic formulations from words, images, and language belonging naturally in the canon of scripture.

Unfortunately, this intrinsicist approach to using biblical imagery for constructive dogmatics soon fell out of favor. Peter Leithart explains that Christologies of divine indwelling were "dismissed as Christologies of *mere* indwelling."[66] While temple Christology may certainly be abused and deployed in favor of Arianism, this is not logically demanded by the present argument. The notion that Jesus was a temple of God who was indwelt by the Spirit does not require that he was *merely* a man. Argumentatively speaking, this would be a fallacy of non-sequitur. Nor does it follow that simply because a doctrine could be abused for the purposes of heresy, it is automatically wrong.

It is important to mention that Athanasius's use of "temple" language to depict the incarnation was followed by others such as Cyril of Alexandria (*c.* 375–444). Daniel King's translation of Cyril into English notes that "theologians of Cyril's day frequently use the term 'temple' to refer to the physical manifestation of the Logos on earth. Although it is not a term used by modern theologians it will be found throughout these treatises."[67] For example, Cyril stated in his letter *On Orthodoxy to Theodosius* that the Word was a "temple born of the Virgin."[68] Even when Cyril distanced himself from the error of Apollinarius, he did so by describing it as a mistaken view of the way in which "the Word dwelt in this temple" as this heresy denied Jesus a human rational mind.[69]

In conclusion, it is true that other early-church interpreters, such as Cyril of Alexandria, also used the imagery of a "temple" to describe Jesus' body.[70] However, Athanasius frequently and clearly used the language of construction when referring to the incarnation, especially as found in his *On the Incarnation*. His catholic status as a church father, his foundational work on Trinitarian theology, and his repeated engagement with temple Christology offer a substantial body of material to engage with. As such, the works of Athanasius continue to offer guidance for utilizing the language of construction to describe the incarnation of Christ. In conclusion, Athanasius corroborates the findings of this study, as he used temple Christology in the service of dogmatics when he described the incarnation of Jesus as an act of constructing a divine temple.

SUMMARY

The aim of this chapter was to explicate what temple Christology entails as a dogmatic construction that explains the necessity of the virgin birth. A fully robust doctrine of temple Christology requires understanding Jesus' unchanging person as the Messiah-temple who was born through an act of temple-conception, died, and rose again in three days so that he might be an eternal dwelling place of God's personal presence among his people. This chapter seeks to use biblical language to define Jesus and to explain certain aspects of his self-identity. There is a sense in which analogous language qualifies equivocal words such as "construction" and "conception" by bridging them together with shared characteristics. Accordingly, this chapter establishes the fact that Jesus' self-identification as the "temple" of God bridges the gap between building construction and human conception. Jesus' templeness is one of the major ways that he and his contemporaries understood his death (the destruction of a temple) and his resurrection (the raising of a temple). It should not surprise us, then, that temple ontology can also explain Jesus' conception.

Inasmuch as this study is a fresh proposal in its present-day context, it is also a return to an ancient method of studying Christology through the scripture's own themes and motifs. Following the trajectory set by Athanasius, it seeks to explicate a fresh catholic defense for the necessity of Jesus' birth by a virgin mother because of his identity as the temple of God.[71] The aim of this constructive study unites that which has fallen to the fallacy of false dichotomy: old and new, biblical theology and systematic theology, east and west, Hellenism and Judaism, proposition and story. In sum, Jesus had to be born of a virgin birth (virginal conception) through the direct act of the Spirit because he is the Messiah-temple, and that's how temples are built.

NOTES

1. Phelan and Reynolds 1996, 22.
2. Phelan and Reynolds 1996, 22.
3. Johnson 2021, 105.
4. For example, 1 John 2:2 describes Jesus as the "propitiation for our sins." Paul states that Christ was "a fragrant offering and sacrifice to God" (Eph. 5:2). Hebrews (9:12) describes Jesus as fulfilling the sacrificial offerings of the "blood of goats and calves." Hebrews (10:12) also states, "But when Christ had offered for all time a single sacrifice for sins, he sat down at the right hand of God."
5. I assume throughout this study that Moses was the substantial author of Genesis, although there may have been minor editorial emendations after Moses' death. The scholarship on this topic is voluminous. For a discussion of this particular view of substantial authorship in light of the Mosaic authorship of the Pentateuch, see Merrill, Rooker, and Grisanti 2011, 167, and Garrett 1991, 85–86.
6. Hamilton 1990, 68.
7. Compare this with the theology of Hebrews 9:12, where the author explains that Jesus has "entered the holy place once for all" through his own blood.
8. Harris 2015, 290–1.
9. Leithart 2013, 121.

10. The apocryphal Wisdom of Solomon (9.8) suggests that the temple was an imitation of the tabernacle. Additionally, the texts of 1 Kings 8:4 and 2 Chronicles 5:5 refer to the "tent of meeting" being brought into the temple, which suggests that it was incorporated into the temple building itself. For a discussion, see Beale 2004, 32 n6.

11. Kerr 2002, 373.

12. Hays 2016, 176, emphasis his.

13. For a similar line of argumentation, albeit one that moves directly to the tabernacle rather than through primitive altars for Yahweh worship, see Anderson 2017, 101.

14. 2 Samuel 7:5–7

15. 2 Samuel 7:6

16. Greene (2018, 767–84) discusses the fact that there is no canonical record of the glory cloud of Yahweh's presence filling the Second Temple like it did when Solomon's temple had been finished, for example, 1 Kings 8:10–13. Greene suggests that the concept of Yahweh "dwelling" in the temple had come to take on "less intense" ideas of God's presence in that present time while also awaiting a more intense "manifestation of God's presence in the future" (p. 769).

17. Note how the word choice of God's promises in relation to building a "house" justifies the move between the terms of human "conception" and building "construction" in the categorical syllogism. This relationship between construction and the human conception of the Davidic messiah is not an ancillary matter but is one of central importance in the covenantal promises of God's people.

18. Wright (2002, 56) comments,

> The Temple, from the beginning, had as its whole *raison d'etre* the dwelling of Israel's God in the midst of his people, and the daily and yearly sacrifices through which fellowship with this God, and forgiveness from this God, were assured.

19. So also Levenson 1984, 280.

20. Bock (2007, 503) argues that James's point is not limited to Amos but reflects "what the prophets teach in general, or what the book of the Prophets as a whole teaches. Other texts could be noted (Zech. 2:11; 8:22; Isa. 2:2; 45:20–23; Hosea 3:4–5; Jer. 12:15–16)."

21. White 2016, 198.

22. The scholarship on the unity of Luke-Acts is well known and voluminous. For recent work in this area, see Bird 2007, 425–47. Walters offers a dissenting view on the unity of Luke-Acts (2009).

23. Bock (2007, 504) comments, "The rebuilding of the [Davidic] dynasty does not refer just to the resurrection."

24. This expansion of the kingdom of God through the gospel is best understood as inaugurated (already/not yet) eschatology. The presence of God's kingdom in the present does not preclude future eschatological developments related to the Davidic covenant and the new covenant. Further discussion of inaugurated eschatology in

Luke-Acts may be found in Wenkel 2018, 7–11 with the classic treatment being found in Ladd (2000) and (1993).

25. Athanasius also viewed the incarnation as the only possibility through which humanity could be redeemed (Gemeinhardt 2011, 327).

26. Wright 2002, 56.

27. It is a "God-man" which Cole (2013, 113) denies is explicitly found in the Old Testament antecedent theology: "A returning Elijah? Yes! A coming Son of Man? Yes! A coming Davidic messiah? Yes! A God-man? No."

28. Woudstra (1981, 145) views that divine revelation and Israel's responses to it had multiple purposes even within the book of Joshua. Such a view can reasonably be expanded to the entire canon of scripture.

29. Wenkel (2019, 360–61) identifies confessions as "the communal voice" of the church.

30. Hays (2016, 177) comments, "the imagery of sound, wind, and fire from heaven filling the whole house is reminiscent of God coming to fill the tabernacle (Exod. 40:34–38) and the temple (1 Kings 8:10–11)."

31. Weinandy and Keating 2017, 33.

32. Farag 2020, 125.

33. Leithart 2011, 48.

34. Walker 1996, 170.

35. For a discussion of the people of God and the temple, see DeRouchie 2017, 16–45.

36. Wright 2002, 58 and also quoted by Leithart 2013, 121.

37. Leithart 2013, 121.

38. Wright 2002, 54.

39. Wright 2002, 56.

40. Leithart 2013, 120.

41. Leithart 2013, 120.

42. These two qualities of the heresy of adoptionism are from Bird 2017, 7.

43. Leithart 2013, 117. Nestorianism was condemned as heresy by the Council of Ephesus (AD 431).

44. Aquinas identified the heresy of Nestorius as using "indwelling" language, which made the person of the Son of God distinct from the person of the Son of Man (White 2015, 80–81).

45. "The ultimate divine intent of OT texts (with respect to both sense and referent) can and likely often does legitimately transcend any given human author's immediate written speech, while still organically growing out of it and never contradicting it" (DeRouchie 2020, 241).

46. Johnson (2021, 39) explains this "Hebraic style" of philosophy that characterizes the scriptures by using the example of chairs: "To illustrate it philosophically, by telling and retelling historical accounts of *chairs* in covenant relationship to Yahweh, *chairness* and its philosophical significance would be pointed up to the reader." Johnson concludes that this is "often how abstract ideas are worked out in the Hebrew Bible."

47. Johnson 2021, 39.

48. Leithart 2013, 116.

49. Here I want to acknowledge that Athanasius' canon may not have been identical to the present books received in traditional Protestant lists. For example, he calls the book of Judith "scripture" (*Four Discourses Against the Arians, C. Ar.* 2.35) and cites Tobit along with Matthew and Isaiah (*Defense of Constantius*, 17).

50. See Farag (2020, 39); Leithart (2011, 30, 43) also understands Athanasius to interpret the Old Testament typologically.

51. Farag 2020, 23.

52. Leithart 2013,116.

53. Athanasius relied primarily on biblical interpretations and only occasionally utilized philosophical arguments, according to Gemeinhardt 2011, 319.

54. Robertson 2007, 20; Gemeinhardt 2011, 297.

55. For a discussion of Christ renewing the image of humanity and the analogy of restoring a decaying artwork, see Rosolen 2020, 88, and Robertson 2007, 201.

56. Rosolen 2020, 89.

57. For a lengthy quotation from *Against the Pagans* (*Gent.* 1), see Athanasius, *On the Incarnation*, with an introduction by C. S. Lewis (2011, 12); for a discussion of this point, see Gemeinhardt 2011, 303.

58. Rosolen 2020, 87.

59. Rosolen 2020, 87.

60. Athanasius 2011, 18.

61. Rosolen 2020, 86.

62. Athanasius 2011, 18.

63. Hewitt (2020, 40) argues that Christians share "in the messiah's experiences *rather* than his identity."

64. Leithart 2011, 33.

65. Farag 2020, 70.

66. Leithart 2013, 120.

67. Cyril 2014, 47.

68. Cyril 2014, 47.

69. See Cyril's (2014, 40) letter *On Orthodoxy to Theodosius*.

70. Cyril of Alexandria, who inherited the tradition of Athanasius, states,

> for there was a union of the two natures, and this is why we confess One Christ, One Son, One Lord. According to this understanding of the unconfused union we confess that the holy virgin is the Mother of God [*theotokos*], because God was made flesh and became man, and *from the very moment of conception he united to himself the temple* that was taken from her. (*Acta conc. oec.* 1.1.4.17)

For a translation and discussion see Wessel 2004, 270. On Cyril's development of Athanasius's theology see Farag 2020, 60; Farag 2007, 124.

71. After all, as Vanhoozer (2016, 33) points out, "The only good Protestant is a catholic Protestant—one who learns from, and bears fruit for, the whole church."

Bibliography

Abernethy, Andrew. 2016. *The Book of Isaiah and God's Kingdom: A Thematic-Theological Approach.* NSBT 40. Downers Grove: InterVarsity Press.

Adams, Sean A. and Seth M. Ehorn. 2016. "What Is a Composite Citation? An Introduction." Pages 1–16 in *Composite Citations in Antiquity: Volume One: Jewish, Graeco-Roman, and Early Christian Uses.* Edited by Sean A. Adams and Seth M. Ehorn. LNTS 525. 2 vols. London: Bloomsbury T&T Clark.

Alexander, Loveday. 1999. *Jesus and the Heritage of Israel: Luke's Narrative Claim upon Israel's Legacy.* ed. D. Moessner. Harrisburg: Trinity Press International.

Alexander, T. Desmond. 2009. *From Eden to the New Jerusalem: An Introduction to Biblical Theology.* Downers Grove: InterVarsity Press.

———. 2018. *The City of God and the Goal of Creation.* SSBT. Wheaton: Crossway.

Allen, Leslie C. 1990. *Ezekiel 20–48.* WBC. Dallas: Word.

Anderson, Gary A. 2017. *Christian Doctrine and the Old Testament: Theology in the Service of Biblical Exegesis.* Grand Rapids: Baker Academic.

Arndt, W., F.W. Danker, W. Bauer, and F.W. Gingrich. 2000. *A Greek-English Lexicon of the New Testament and Other Early Christian Literature.* Chicago: University of Chicago Press.

Athanasius. 2011. *On the Incarnation: With An Introduction by C.S. Lewis.* Yonkers, NY: St Vladimir's Seminary Press.

Augustine of Hippo. 1968. *The Retractations.* Edited by Roy Joseph Deferrari. Translated by Mary Inez Bogan. Vol. 60 of The Fathers of the Church. Washington, DC: The Catholic University of America Press.

———. 1993. *Tractates on the Gospel of John 28–54: The Fathers of the Church.* vol. 88. Translated by John W. Rettig. Washington, DC: Catholic University of America Press.

Auer, Peter and Carol M. Easton. 2010. "Code Switching." Pages 84–112 in *Society and Language Use.* Edited by Jan-Ola Östman, Jef Verschueren, Jürgen Jaspers. Handbook of Pragmatics Highlights 7. Philadelphia: John Benjamins.

Averbeck, Richard. 2010. "Temple Building among the Sumerians and Akkadians (Third Millennium)." Pages 3–34 in *From the Foundations to the Crenellations: Essays on Temple Building in the Ancient Near East and Hebrew Bible*. Edited by Mark J. Boda and Jamie Novotny. Münster: Ugarit-Verlag.

Baker, David L. 1976. "Typology and the Christian Use of the Old Testament." *SJT* 29, no. 2: 149–150.

Barnes, William H. 2012. *1–2 Kings*. Edited by Philip W. Comfort. Vol. 4b. CBC. Carol Stream: Tyndale House.

Barron, Robert. 2016. *The Priority of Christ: Toward a Post-Liberal Catholicism*. Baker Academic.

Barth, Karl. 1957. *Church Dogmatics, II*. Edinburgh: T&T Clark.

———. 2010. *Church Dogmatics: IV.1 The Doctrine of Reconciliation*. Edited by T.F. Torrance and G.W. Bromiley. Translated by G.W. Bromiley. London: T&T Clark.

Bauckham, Richard. 1998. *God Crucified: Monotheism and Christology in the New Testament*. Grand Rapids: Eerdmans.

———. 2007. *The Testimony of the Beloved Disciple: Narrative, History, and the Theology of the Gospel of John*. Grand Rapids: Baker Academic.

Bavinck, Herman. 2006. *Reformed Dogmatics, Volume 3: Sin and Salvation in Christ*. Edited by John Bolt. Translated by John Vriend. 4 Vols. Grand Rapids: Baker Academic, 2006.

Bayer, Oswald. 2007. *Theology The Lutheran Way*. Edited and Translated by Jeffrey J. Silock and Mark C. Mattes. Grand Rapids: Eerdmans.

Beale, G.K. 1999. *The Book of Revelation: A Commentary on the Greek Text*. NIGTC. Grand Rapids: Eerdmans.

———. 2004. *The Temple and the Church's Mission: A Biblical Theology of the Dwelling Place of God*. NSBT 15. Downers Grove: InterVarsity Press.

———. 2008. *We Become What We Worship: A Biblical Theology of Idolatry*. Grand Rapids: InterVarsity Press.

Beale, Gregory K. 2014. and Benjamin L. Gladd. *Hidden But Now Revealed: A Biblical Theology of Mystery*. Downers Grove, IL: InterVarsity Press Academic.

Beckwith, Francis J. 1986. "Of Logic and Lordship: The Validity of a Categorical Syllogism Supporting Christ's Deity." *JETS* 29: 429–30.

Behr, John. 2015. "Saint Athanasius on 'Incarnation.'" Pages 79–98 in *Incarnation: On the Scope and Depth of Christology*. Edited by Niels H. Gregersen. Minneapolis: Fortress.

Begg, Christopher. 1997. "The Transjordanian Altar (Josh 22:10-34) According to Josephus (Ant. 5.100-114) and Pseudo-Philo (LAB 22.1-8)." *AUSS* 35, no. 1: 5–19.

Berkhof, Louis. 1938. *Systematic Theology*. Grand Rapids: Eerdmans.

Salisbury, Steve and Kirk Lowry (eds). 1996. *Biblia Hebraica Stuttgartensia: With Westminster Hebrew Morphology*. Electronic ed. Stuttgart; Glenside, PA: German Bible Society; Westminster Seminary.

Billings, J. Todd. 2011. *Union with Christ: Reframing Theology and Ministry for the Church*. Grand Rapids: Baker Academic.

Bingham, Matthew C. 2017. "English Baptists and the Struggle for Theological Authority, 1642–1646." *JEH* 68: 546–569.

Bird, Michael F. 2020. *Evangelical Theology, Second Edition: A Biblical and Systematic Introduction*. Grand Rapids: Zondervan.

———. 2007. "The Unity of Luke-Acts in Recent Discussion." *JSNT* 29, no. 4: 425–447.

———. 2017. *Jesus the Eternal Son: Answering Adoptionist Christology*. Grand Rapids: Eerdmans.

Blenkinsopp, Joseph. 1990. *Ezekiel*. Interpretation. Louisville, KY: WKJP.

Block, Daniel. 2013. "Eden: A Temple? A Reassessment of the Biblical Evidence." Pages 3–29 in *From Creation to New Creation: Biblical Theology and Exegesis*. Edited by Daniel M. Gurtner and Benjamin L. Gladd. Peabody MA: Hendrickson Publishers.

Bock, Darrell L. 2007. *Acts*. BECNT. Grand Rapids: Baker Academic.

Bockmuehl, Markus. 2006. *Seeing the Word: Refocusing New Testament Study*. STI. Grand Rapids: Baker Academic.

———. 2015. "The Gospels on the Presence of Jesus." Pages 87–104 in *The Oxford Handbook of Christology*. Edited by Francesca Aran Murphy and Troy A. Stefano. Oxford: Oxford University Press.

Branch-Trevathan, George. 2020. *The Sermon on the Mount and Spiritual Exercises: The Making of the Matthean Self*. NovTSup 178. Leiden: Brill.

Brannan, Rick (ed.). 1997. *Historic Creeds and Confessions*. Oak Harbor: Lexham Press.

Braun, Roddy L. 1986. *1 Chronicles*. WBC 14. Dallas: Word, Inc.

Bray, Gerald. 2012. *God Is Love: A Biblical and Systematic Theology*. Wheaton: Crossway.

Brown, Frank Markham. 2003. *Boolean Reasoning: The Logic of Boolean Equations, 2nd edition*. Dover Books on Mathematics. Norwell, MA: Kluwer Academic.

Brown, Raymond E. 1993. *The Birth of the Messiah: A Commentary on the Infancy Narratives in the Gospels of Matthew and Luke, New Updated Edition*. Anchor Bible. New York: Doubleday.

Bruce, F.F. 1988. *The Book of the Acts*. NICNT. Grand Rapids: Eerdmans.

Calaway, Jared C. 2013. *The Sabbath and the Sanctuary: Access to God in the Letter to the Hebrews and its Priestly Context*. WUNT 2/349. Tübingen: Mohr Siebeck.

Caneday, Ardel. 2019. "Biblical Types: Revelation Concealed in Plain Sight to be Disclosed: 'These Things Occurred Typologically to Them and Were Written Down for Our Admonition.'" Pages 135–156 in *God's Glory Revealed in Christ: Essays on Biblical Theology in Honor of Thomas R. Schreiner*. Edited by James Hamilton, Denny Burk, et al. Nashville: B&H Academic.

Carson, D.A. 2004. "Mystery and Fulfillment: Toward a More Comprehensive Paradigm of Paul's Understanding of the Old and the New." Pages 393–436 in *Justification and Variegated Nomism: A Fresh Appraisal of Paul and Second Temple Judaism, vol. 2: The Paradoxes of Paul*. Edited by D.A. Carson et al. WUNT 2/181. Tübingen: Mohr Siebeck.

Pope John Paul II. 1995. *Catechism of the Catholic Church: Second Edition*. New York: Doubleday.

Chang, Kai-Hsuan. 2021. *The Impact of Bodily Experience on Paul's Resurrection Theology*. LNTS. London: Bloomsbury T&T Clark.

Childs, Brevard S. 1979. *Introduction to the Old Testament as Scripture*, 1st ed. Philadelphia: Fortress.

Chyutin, Michael. 2006. *Architecture and Utopia in the Temple Era*. Translated by Richard Flantz. LSTS 58. London: T&T Clark.

Ciampa, Roy E. and Brian S. Rosner. 2010. *The First Letter to the Corinthians*. PNTC. Grand Rapids: Eerdmans.

Clark, John C. and Marcus Peter Johnson. 2015. *The Incarnation of God: The Mystery of the Gospel as the Foundation of Evangelical Theology*. Wheaton: Crossway.

Clements, Ronald E. 1965. *God and Temple: The Idea of the Divine Presence in Ancient Israel*. London: Basil Blackwell.

Coady, C.A.J. 1992. *Testimony: A Philosophical Study*. Oxford: Clarendon.

Cochrane, Arthur C. (ed.). 2003. *Reformed Confessions of the Sixteenth Century*. Louisville: Westminster John Knox.

Cohen, Shayne J.D. 1984. "The Temple and the Synagogue." Pages 151–174 in *The Temple in Antiquity: Ancient Records and Modern Perspectives*. Edited by Truman G. Madsen. Provo, UT: Brigham Young University Press.

Cole, Graham A. 2013. *The God Who Became Human: A Biblical Theology of Incarnation*. NSBT 30. Downers Grove: InterVarsity Press.

Collins, Adele Yarbro and John J. Collins. 2008. *King and Messiah as Son of God: Divine, Human, and Related Literature*. Grand Rapids: Eerdmans.

Coloe, Mary L. 2001. *God Dwells with Us: Temple Symbolism in the Fourth Gospel*. Collegeville: Liturgical.

Compton, Jared M. 2008. "Shared Intentions? Reflections on Inspiration and Interpretation in Light of Scripture's Dual Authorship." *Them* 33, no. 3: 23–33.

Kiffin, William et al. 1646. *A Confession of Faith of Seven Congregations or Churches of Christ in London, Which are Commonly (but unjustly) Called Anabaptists: The Second Impression Corrected and Enlarged*. London: Matthew Simmons.

Cormack, Robin. 1985. *Writing in Gold: Byzantine Society and Its Icons*. London: George Philip.

Cotnoir, A.J. 2019. "On the Role of Logic in Analytic Theology: Exploring the Wider Context of Beall's Philosophy of Logic." *JAT* 7: 508–528.

Crisp, Oliver D. 2010. *Retrieving Doctrine: Essays in Reformed Theology*. Downers Grove, IL: InterVarsity Press.

Croy, Nathan Clayton. 2022. "That They also Might Be [One] in Us." *NovT* 64, no. 2: 229–248.

Cyril of Alexandria, 2014. *St. Cyril of Alexandria: Three Christological Treatises*. Translated by Daniel King. Washington, DC: Catholic University of America.

Daley, Brian E. 2018. *God Visible: Patristic Christology Reconsidered*. Changing Paradigms in Historical and Systematic Theology. Oxford: Oxford University Press.

Davies, Todd. 1985. *Analogy*. CSLI Information Notes Series. Stanford: Center for the Study of Language and Information.

DeRouchie, Jason S. 2020. "The Mystery Revealed: A Biblical Case for Christ-Centered Old Testament Interpretation." *Them* 44, no. 2: 226–248.

DeSilva, David A. 2000. *Perseverance in Gratitude: A Socio-Rhetorical Commentary on the Epistle "to the Hebrews."* Grand Rapids: Eerdmans.

DeVries, Simon J. 2003. *1 Kings*, 2nd ed. WBC. Dallas: Word.

Dew, James K. and Ronnie P. Campbell Jr. (eds.). 2024. *Natural Theology: Five Views*. Grand Rapids: Baker.

DeWeese, Garrett J. 2007. "One Person, Two Natures: Two Metaphorical Models of the Incarnation." Pages 114–153 in *Jesus in Trinitarian Perspective: An Introductory Christology*. Edited by Fred Sanders and Klaus Issler. Nashville: B&H.

Dodson, Geran F. 2016. *The Impact Of Reason On Faith, Ethics And Belief*. Vernon Series in Philosophy. Wilmington: Vernon Press.

Dozeman, Thomas B. 2009. *Commentary on Exodus*. ECC. Grand Rapids: Eerdmans.

Duby, Stephen J. 2022. *Jesus and the God of Classical Theism: Biblical Christology in Light of the Doctrine of God*. Grand Rapids: Baker Academic.

Ducharme, Howard M. 1994. "A Critical Evaluation of a Classic Moral Scientist: Are there any Moral Facts to Discover?" Pages 25–46 in *Morality: Reasoning on Different Approaches*. Edited by Vasil Gluchman. Amsterdam: Rodopi.

Dunn, J.D.G. 2009. "Incarnation." Pages 519–23 in *The New Interpreter's Dictionary of the Bible: Volume 5*. Edited by K.D. Sakenfeld, 5 Vols. Nashville: Abingdon.

Edwards, James R. 2002. *The Gospel According to Mark*. PNTC. Grand Rapids: Eerdmans.

Ehrman, Bart D. and Zlatko Plese. 2013. *The Other Gospels: Accounts of Jesus from Outside the New Testament*. Oxford: Oxford University Press.

Ellingworth, Paul. 1993. *The Epistle to the Hebrews: A Commentary on the Greek Text*. NIGTC. Grand Rapids: Eerdmans.

Emerson, Matthew Y. 2016. *Between the Cross and the Throne: The Book of Revelation*. Transformative Word. Bellingham: Lexham Press.

Epsen, Edward. 2016. "Why God Had to Have an Immaculate Mother." *New Blackfriars* 97: 560–574.

———. 2020. *From Laws to Liturgy: An Idealist Theology of Creation*. SST 21. Leiden: Brill.

Erickson, Millard J. 1998. *Christian Theology*. 2nd ed. Grand Rapids: Baker.

Eslinger, Lyle. 1994. *House of God or House of David: The Rhetoric of 2 Samuel 7*. JSOTSup, 164. Sheffield: JSOT Press.

Farag, Lois M. 2007. *St. Cyril of Alexandria, A New Testament Exegete: His Commentary on the Gospel of John*. Piscataway, NJ: Gorgias Press.

———. 2020. *Athanasius of Alexandria: An Introduction to His Writing and Theology*. Eugene, OR: Cascade.

Fay, Ron C. 2006. "The Narrative Function of The Temple in Luke-Acts." *TrinJ* 27, no. 2: 255–270.

Feinberg, Charles Lee. 1935. "The Hypostatic Union: Part One." *BSac* 92: 261–276.

Finnis, John. 1992. "Legal Law and Legal Reasoning." Pages 134–157 in *Natural Law Theory: Contemporary Essays*. Edited by Robert P. George. Oxford: Oxford University Press.

Furlong, Dean. 2020. *The Identity of John the Evangelist: Revision and Reinterpretation in Early Christian Sources*. London: Lexington/Fortress Academic.

France, R.T. 2005. "Relationship Between the Testaments." Pages 666–672 in *Dictionary for Theological Interpretation of the Bible*. Edited by Kevin J. Vanhoozer et al. Grand Rapids: Eerdmans.

———. 2007. *The Gospel of Matthew*. NICNT. Grand Rapids: Eerdmans.

Frayer-Griggs, Daniel. 2013. "Spittle, Clay, and Creation in John 9:6 and Some Dead Sea Scrolls." *JBL* 132: 659–670.

Fyall, Robert. 2004. "A Curious Silence." Pages 49–58 in *Heaven on Earth: The Temple in Biblical Theology*. Edited by T. Desmond Alexander and Simon Gathercole. Carlisle: Paternoster Press.

Gaffin, Richard B. Jr. 2022. *In the Fullness of Time: An Introduction to the Biblical Theology of Acts and Paul*. Wheaton: Crossway.

Garrett, Duane A. 1991. *Rethinking Genesis: The Sources and Authorship of the First Book of the Pentateuch*. Grand Rapids: Baker.

Gawronski, Raymond. 2015. "Knowing About Jesus, Knowing Jesus: Christology and Spirituality." Pages 378–392 in *The Oxford Handbook of Christology*. Edited by Francesa A. Murphy and Troy A. Stefano. Oxford: Oxford University Press.

Geisler, Norman L. and Paul D. Feinberg. 1980. *Introduction to Philosophy: A Christian Perspective*. Grand Rapids: Baker.

Gemeinhardt, Peter (ed.). 2011. *Athanasius Handbuch*. Tübingen: Mohr Siebeck, 2011.

Gentry, Peter J. 2017. *How to Read and Understand the Biblical Prophets*. Wheaton: Crossway.

Giesler, Norman L. 2004. *Systematic Theology, Volume Three: Sin, Salvation*. Minneapolis, MN: Bethany House.

Glouberman, Mark. 2012. *The Raven, the Dove, and the Owl of Minerva: The Creation of Humankind in Athens and Jerusalem*. Toronto: University of Toronto Press.

Goad, Keith Wesley. 2010. "Trinitarian Grammars: A Comparison of Gregory of Nazianzus and Some Contemporary Models." PhD Diss., The Southern Baptist Theological Seminary.

Goldingay, John and Pamela J. Scalise. 2012. *Minor Prophets II*. UBCS. Grand Rapids: Baker.

Goroncy, Jason. 2013. "Review of *Barth's Interpretation of the Virgin Birth: A Sign of Mystery* by Dustin Resch." *JTS* NS 64, no. 2: 818–823.

Green, Bradley G. 2014. *Covenant and Commandment: Works, Obedience and Faithfulness in the Christian Life*. NSBT 33. Downers Grove: InterVarsity Press.

Greene, Joseph. 2018. "Did God Dwell in the Second Temple? Clarifying the Relationship Between Theophany and Temple Dwelling." *JETS* 61, no. 4: 767–784.

Greidanus, Sidney. 1999. *Preaching Christ from the Old Testament: A Contemporary Hermeneutical Method*. Grand Rapids: Eerdmans.

Gromacki, Robert. 2002. *The Virgin Birth: A Biblical Study of the Deity of Jesus Christ*. The Woodlands, TX: Kress Christian Publications.

Guarino, Thomas G. 2005. *Foundations of Systematic Theology*. London: T&T Clark.

Gurtner, Daniel M. 2007. *The Torn Veil: Matthew's Exposition of the Death of Jesus*. Cambridge: Cambridge University Press.

Gwynn, David M. 2007. *The Eusebians: The Polemic of Athanasius of Alexandria and the Construction of the 'Arian Controversy'*. OTM. Oxford: Oxford University Press.

———. 2012. *Athanasius of Alexandria: Bishop, Theologian, Ascetic, Father*. CTC. Oxford: Oxford University Press.

Habets, Myk. 2023. "Revelation, Rationalism, and an Evangelical Impasse." Pages 84–110 in *Thomas F. Torrance and Evangelical Theology: A Critical Analysis*. Edited by Myk Habets and R. Lucas Stamps. SHST. Bellingham: Lexham Academic.

Habets, Myk and R. Lucas Stamps. 2023. "Introduction: Torrance and Evangelical Theology in Conversation." Pages 1–7 in *Thomas F. Torrance and Evangelical Theology: A Critical Analysis*. Edited by Myk Habets and R. Lucas Stamps. SHST. Bellingham: Lexham Academic.

Hagner, Donald A. 2011. *Hebrews*. UBCS. Grand Rapids: Baker.

Hahn, Scott W. 2008. "Temple, Sign, and Sacrament: Towards a New Perspective on the Gospel of John." *Letter & Spirit* 4: 107–143.

Hall, Christopher A. 2002. *Learning Theology with the Church Fathers*. Downers Grove, IL: InterVarsity Press, 2002.

Hamilton, James M., Jr. 2006. "The Skull Crushing Seed of the Woman: Inner-Biblical Interpretation of Genesis 3:15." *SBJT* 10: 30–54.

———. 2015. *With the Clouds of Heaven: The Book of Daniel in Biblical Theology*. NSBT 32. Downers Grove: InterVarsity Press.

———. 2022. *Typology: Understanding the Bible's Promise-Shaped Patterns: How Old Testament Expectations Are Fulfilled in Christ*. Grand Rapids: Zondervan Academic.

Hamilton, Victor P. 1990. *The Book of Genesis, Chapters 1–17*. NICOT. Grand Rapids: Eerdmans.

Hammett, John S. 2015. "Multiple-Intentions View of the Atonement." Pages 143–193 in *Perspectives on the Extent of the Atonement: Three Views*. Edited by Andrew David Naselli and Mark A. Snoeberger. Nashville, TN: B&H.

Harrington, Daniel J. 2007. *The Gospel of Matthew*. Sacra Pagina. Collegeville: Liturgical Press.

Harris, Murray. *John*. 2015. EGGNT. Nashville: B&H.

Hart, D.G. 1995. *Defending the Faith: J. Gresham Machen and the Crisis of Conservative Protestantism in Modern America*. Grand Rapids: Baker.

Hays, J. Daniel. 2016. *The Temple and the Tabernacle: A Study of God's Dwelling Places from Genesis to Revelation*. Grand Rapids: Baker.

Hays, Richard B. 2002. "The God of Mercy Who Rescues Us from the Present Evil Age." Pages 123–143 in *The Forgotten God: Perspectives in Biblical Theology: Essays in Honor of Paul J. Achtemeier on the Occasion of His Seventy-Fifth*

Birthday. Edited by A. Andrew Das and Frank J. Matera. Louisville: Westminster John Knox.

———. 2016. *Reading Backwards: Figural Christology and the Fourfold Gospel Witness.* Waco: Baylor University Press.

———. 2018. *Echoes of Scripture in the Gospels.* Waco, TX: Baylor University Press.

Healy, Nicholas J. 2005. *The Eschatology of Hans Urs Von Balthasar: Eschatology as Communion.* Oxford: Oxford University Press.

Heger, Paul. 1999. *The Three Biblical Altar Laws: Developments in the Sacrificial Cult in Practice and Theology; Political and Economic Background.* BZAW 279. Berlin: de Gruyter.

Hensel, Benedikt. 2018. "Das JHWH-Heiligtum am Garizim: ein archäologischer Befund und seine literar-und theologiegeschichtliche Einordnung." *VT* 68, no. 1: 73–93.

Heppe, Heinrich. 2007. *Reformed Dogmatics.* Translated by G.T. Thompson. 1950 reprint. Eugene, OR: Wipf and Stock.

Hewitt, J. Thomas. 2020. *Messiah and Scripture: Paul's "In Christ" Idiom in Its Ancient Jewish Context.* WUNT 2/522. Tübingen: Mohr Siebeck.

Hjalmarson, Leonard. 2015. *No Home Like Place: A Christian Theology of Place*, 2nd ed. Portland: Urban Loft.

Hooker, Morna D. 1991. *The Gospel According to Saint Mark.* BNTC. London: Continuum.

Horton, Michael S. 2002. *Covenant and Eschatology: The Divine Drama.* Louisville: Westminster John Knox Press.

———. 2003. "Who Needs Systematic Theology When We Have the Bible?" *Modern Reformation* 12: 13–22.

Hoskins, Paul M. 2006. *Jesus as the Fulfillment of the Temple in the Gospel of John.* Milton Keyes: Paternoster.

Hubbard, David A. 1986. *1 Chronicles.* WBC. Dallas: Word, Inc.

Hurtado, Larry W. 2011. *Mark.* UBCS. Grand Rapids: Baker.

Inge, John. 2003. *A Christian Theology of Place.* Explorations in Practical, Pastoral and Empirical Theology. London: Routledge.

Itkonen, Esa. 2005. *Analogy as Structure and Process: Approaches in Linguistics, Cognitive Psychology, and Philosophy of Science.* Philadelphia, PA: John Benjamins.

Jipp, Joshua W. 2014. "Sharing in the Heavenly Rule of Christ the King: Paul's Royal Participatory Language in Ephesians." Pages 251–279 in *'In Christ' in Paul.* Edited by Michael J. Thate et al. WUNT 2/384. Tübingen: Mohr Siebeck.

Jenson, Robert W. 2009. *Ezekiel.* BTCB. Grand Rapids: Brazos.

Jobe, Sarah C. 2019. "The Monstrosity of God Made Flesh: Karl Barth on Leviathan." *JRT* 13: 238–256.

Johnson, Adam. 2011. "A Temple Framework of the Atonement." *JETS* 54, no. 2: 225–237.

Johnson, Dru. 2021. *Biblical Philosophy: A Hebraic Approach to the Old and New Testaments.* Cambridge: Cambridge University Press.

Johnson, Keith L. 2011. *Karl Barth and the Analogia Entis*. T&T Clark Studies in Systematic Theology. London: T&T Clark.

Jonker, Louis C. 2013. *1 & 2 Chronicles*. UBCS. Grand Rapids: Baker.

Joseph, Abson Prédestin. 2012. *A Narratological Reading of 1 Peter*. LNTS 440. London: T&T Clark.

Kaiser, Walter C. 1985. *The Uses of the Old Testament in the New*. Chicago: Moody.

Kelly, J.N.D. 2006. *Early Christian Creeds*, 3rd ed. London: Continuum.

Keener, Craig S. 2012–13. *Acts: Vol 1: An Exegetical Commentary & 2: Introduction and 1:1–14:28*. Grand Rapids: Baker Academic.

Kerr, Alan. 2002. *The Temple of Jesus' Body: The Temple Theme in the Gospel of John*. JSNTSup 220. New York: Sheffield Academic Press.

Kerr, Fergus. 2011. "Trinitarian Theology in the Light of Analytic Philosophy." Pages 339–348 in *The Oxford Handbook of the Trinity*. Edited by Gilles Emery and Matthew Levering. Oxford: Oxford University Press.

Kimble, Jeremy M. and Ched Spellman. 2020. *Invitation to Biblical Theology: Exploring the Shape, Storyline and Themes of Scripture*. Grand Rapids: Kregel.

Kinzer, Mark S. 2018. *Jerusalem Crucified, Jerusalem Risen: The Resurrected Messiah, the Jewish People and the Land of Promise*. Eugene, OR: Cascade.

Klawans, Jonathan. 2006. *Purity, Sacrifice, and the Temple: Symbolism and Supersessionism in the Study of Ancient Judaism*. Oxford University Press.

Klein, Ralph W. 1983. *1 Samuel*. WBC. Dallas: Word.

Knight, John Allan. 2013. *Liberalism versus Postliberalism: The Great Divide in Twentieth-Century Theology*. Oxford: Oxford University Press.

Koester, Craig R. 1989. *The Dwelling of God: The Tabernacle in the Old Testament, Intertestamental Jewish Literature, and the New Testament*. CBQMS 22. Washington: Catholic Biblical Association.

———. 2018. *Revelation and the End of All Things*. 2nd ed. Grand Rapids: Eerdmans.

Koehler, Ludwig, Walter Baumgartner, M.E.J. Richardson, and Johann Jakob Stamm. 1994–2000. *The Hebrew and Aramaic Lexicon of the Old Testament*. Leiden: E.J. Brill.

Köstenberger, Andreas J. 2004. *John*. BECNT. Grand Rapids: Baker Academic.

———. 2006. "The Destruction of the Second Temple and the Composition of the Fourth Gospel." Pages 69–107 in *Challenging Perspectives on the Gospel of John*. ed. John Lierman. WUNT 2/219. Tübingen: Mohr Siebeck.

———. 2021. *Signs of the Messiah: An Introduction to John's Gospel*. Bellingham, WA: Lexham Press.

Kusch, Martin. 2011. "Disagreement and Picture in Wittgenstein's Lectures on Religious Belief." Pages 35–57 in *Image and Imaging in Philosophy, Science and the Arts*, volume 1. Edited by Richard Heinrich et al. Paris: Ontos.

Kruger, Michael J. 2012. *Canon Revisited: Establishing the Origins and Authority of the New Testament*. Wheaton: Crossway.

Krueger, Karl. 2017. "Bible Translations." Pages 90–91 in *Dictionary of Luther and the Lutheran Traditions*. Edited by Timothy J. Wengert. Grand Rapids: Baker Academic.

Ladd, George E. 1993. A Theology of the New Testament, Revised Edition. Grand Rapids: Eerdmans.

———. 2000. *The Presence of the Future: The Eschatology of Biblical Realism.* 1977 reprint; Grand Rapids: Eerdmans.

Lakeland, Paul and Serene Jones (eds.). 2005. *Constructive Theology: A Contemporary Approach to Classical Themes.* Minneapolis: Augsburg Fortress.

Lanier, Gregory R. 2014. "Luke's Distinctive Use of the Temple: Portraying the Divine Visitation." *JTS* 65, no. 2: 433–462.

———. 2021. *Corpus Christologicum: Texts and Translations for the Study of Jewish Messianism and Early Christology.* Peabody, MA: Hendrickson.

Leim, Joshua E. 2015. *Matthew's Theological Grammar: The Father and the Son.* WUNT 2/402. Tübingen: Mohr Siebeck.

Leithart, Peter J. 2000. *A House for My Name: A Survey of the Old Testament.* Moscow, ID: Canon Press.

———. 2003. *A Son to Me: An Exposition of 1 & 2 Samuel.* Moscow, ID: Canon Press.

———. 2011. *Athanasius.* Foundation of Theological Exegesis and Christian Spirituality. Grand Rapids: Baker.

———. 2013. "We Saw His Glory: Implications of the Sanctuary Christology in John's Gospel." Pages 115–135 in *Christology, Ancient and Modern: Explorations in Constructive Dogmatics.* Edited by Oliver Crisp and Fred Sanders. LATCS. Grand Rapids: Zondervan.

Letham, Robert. 2019. *Systematic Theology.* Wheaton: Crossway.

Levenson, Jon D. 1984. "The Temple and the World." *Journal of Religion* 64, no. 3: 275–298.

Levinson, Bernard M. 1997. *Deuteronomy and the Hermeneutics of Legal Innovation.* Oxford: Oxford University Press.

Lieu, Judith. 1999. "Temple and Synagogue in John." *NTS* 45: 51–69.

Lincoln, Andrew T. 2013. *Born of a Virgin? Reconceiving Jesus in the Bible, Tradition, and Theology.* Grand Rapids: Eerdmans.

Louth, Andrew. 2002. *St John Damascene: Tradition and Originality in Byzantine Theology.* Oxford: Oxford University Press.

Longman, Tremper III. 2016. *Genesis.* SGBC. Grand Rapids: Zondervan.

Lunn, Nicholas P. 2014. "'Raised on the Third Day According to the Scriptures': Resurrection Typology in the Genesis Creation Narrative." *JETS* 57, no. 3: 523–35.

Luz, Ulrich. 2001. *Matthew: A Commentary.* Hermeneia. Minneapolis: Augsburg.

MacCulloch, Diarmaid. 2004. *The Reformation: A History.* New York: Penguin.

Machen, J. Gresham. 1930. *The Virgin Birth of Christ.* London: James Clark & Co.

Macintyre, Alisdair. 1981. *After Virtue.* Notre Dame: University of Notre Dame Press.

Mackie, Scott D. 2011. "Heavenly Sanctuary Mysticism in the Epistle to the Hebrews." *JTS* 62, no. 1: 77–117.

Mattson, Brian G. 2012. *Restored to Our Destiny: Eschatology & the Image of God in Herman Bavinck's Reformed Dogmatics.* SRT 21. Leiden: Brill.

Marga, Amy. 2022. "Reading Karl Barth's Römerbrief 1919 for a Postcolonial Era of Theology." Pages 349–366 in *Karl Barth's Epistle to the Romans: Retrospect and Prospect*. Edited by Christophe Chalamet et al. TBT 196. Berlin: Walter de Gruyter.

Martin, Benjamin (ed.). 2021. *Introduction to Philosophy: Logic*. Quebec: Rebus Community.

Martyr, Justin. 1948. *Writings of Saint Justin Martyr*. Translated by Thomas B. Falls. The Fathers of the Church 6. Washington, DC: Catholic University of America Press.

McCall, Thomas. 2021. *Analytic Christology and the Theological Interpretation of the New Testament*. Oxford: Oxford University Press.

McGlothlin, Thomas D. 2018. *Resurrection as Salvation: Development and Conflict in Pre-Nicene Paulinism*. Cambridge: Cambridge University Press.

McGlothlin, W.J. 1911. *Baptist Confessions of Faith*. Philadelphia: American Baptist Publication Society.

McGraw, Ryan M. 2012. *By Good and Necessary Consequence*. ERCT. Grand Rapids: Reformation Heritage Books.

McFarland, Ian. 2019. *The Word Made Flesh: A Theology of the Incarnation*. Louisville: Westminster John Knox Press.

McKim, Donald K. (ed.). 2014. *The Westminster Dictionary of Theological Terms, Second Edition: Revised and Expanded*. Louisville: Westminster John Knox Press.

McKeown, James. 2008. *Genesis*. THOTC. Grand Rapids: Eerdmans.

McNicol, Allan J. 1998. "Rebuilding the House of David: The Function of the Benedictus in Luke-Acts." *ResQ* 40: 25–38.

Merrill, Eugene H., Mark Rooker, and Michael A. Grisanti. 2011. *The World and the Word: An Introduction to the Old Testament*. Nashville: B&H.

Michaels, J. Ramsey. 2011. *John*. UBCS. Grand Rapids: Baker Books.

Migliore, Daniel L. 2004. *Faith Seeking Understanding: An Introduction to Christian Theology*. Grand Rapids: Eerdmans.

Miller, Douglas B. 2010. *Ecclesiastes*. BCBS. Scottdale: Herald Press.

Miller, Stephen R. 1994. *Daniel*. NAC. Nashville: Broadman & Holman.

Moltmann, Jürgen. 1990. *The Way of Jesus Christ: Christology in Messianic Dimensions*. London: SCM.

———. 2012. *The Tabernacle Prefigured: Cosmic Mountain Ideology in Genesis and Exodus*. BTS 15. Leuven: Peeters.

Moore, Nicholas J. 2015. *Repetition in Hebrews: Plurality and Singularity in the Letter to the Hebrews, Its Ancient Contexts, and the Early Church*. WUNT 2/388. Tübingen: Mohr Siebeck.

Moran, Richard. 2017. *The Philosophical Imagination: Selected Essays*. Oxford: Oxford University Press.

Moyise, Steve and Maarten J.J. Menken. 2005. *Isaiah in the New Testament: The New Testament and the Scriptures of Israel*. London: Bloomsbury T&T Clark.

Mounce, Robert H. 2011. *Matthew*. UBCS. Grand Rapids: Baker.

Mroczek, Eva. 2015. "How Not To Build a Temple: Jacob, David, and the Unbuilt Ideal in Ancient Judaism." *JSJ* 46: 1–35.

Murphy, Frederick J. 2012. *Apocalypticism in the Bible and its World: A Comprehensive Introduction*. Grand Rapids: Baker Academic.

Nelson, William B. 2013. *Daniel*. UBCS. Grand Rapids: Baker.

Neusner, Jacob. 2011. *The Babylonian Talmud: A Translation and Commentary*. Peabody, MA: Hendrickson Publishers.

Niehaus, Jeffrey Jay. 2008. *Ancient Near Eastern Themes in Biblical Theology*. Grand Rapids: Kregel.

Nobile, Marco. 2004. "The Theology of the Old Testament: A Contribution to Jewish-Christian Relations." Pages 88–99 in *Out of Egypt: Biblical Theology and Biblical Interpretation*. Edited by Craig Bartholomew et al. Grand Rapids: Zondervan.

Noble, Thomas A. 2023. "Thomas F. Torrance and the Evangelical Tradition." Pages 8–38 in *Thomas F. Torrance and Evangelical Theology: A Critical Analysis*. Edited by Myk Habets and R. Lucas Stamps. SHST. Bellingham: Lexham Academic.

Nolland, John. 2005. *The Gospel of Matthew: A Commentary on the Greek Text*. NIGTC. Grand Rapids: Eerdmans.

Norris, Frederick. 1997. "Gregory Nazianzen: Constructing and Constructed by Scripture." Pages 149–162 in *The Bible in Greek Christian Antiquity*. Edited by Paul M. Blowers. Notre Dame, IN: University of Notre Dame Press.

Oden, Thomas. 1992. *Classic Christianity: A Systematic Theology*. New York: HarperCollins.

O'Donovan, Oliver. 2011. *On the Thirty-Nine Articles: A Conversation with Tudor Christianity, Second Edition*. London: SCM Press.

———. 2019. "John Webster on Dogmatics and Ethics." *IJST* 21, no. 1: 78–92.

Osborne, Grant R. 2002. *Revelation*. BECNT. Grand Rapids: Baker Academic.

———. 2006. *The Hermeneutical Spiral: A Comprehensive Introduction to Biblical Interpretation*. Downers Grove: InterVarsity Press.

Pagán, Jonathan Warren. 2023. "Torrance, the Tacit Dimension, and the Church Fathers." Pages 39–63 in *Thomas F. Torrance and Evangelical Theology: A Critical Analysis*. Edited by Myk Habets and R. Lucas Stamps. SHST. Bellingham: Lexham Academic.

Parsons, Mikeal C. 2008. *Acts*. PCNT. Grand Rapids: Baker Academic.

———. 2015. *Luke*. PCNT. Grand Rapids: Baker Academic.

Pelikan, Jaroslav. 1996. *Mary Through the Centuries: Her Place in the History of Culture*. New Haven, NJ: Yale University Press.

Perrin, Nicholas. 2010. *Jesus the Temple*. Grand Rapids: Baker.

Phelan, Peter J. and Peter J. Reynolds. 1996. *Argument and Evidence: Critical Analysis for the Social Sciences*. New York: Routledge.

Pietersma, Albert and Benjamin G. Wright (eds.). 2007. *A New English Translation of the Septuagint: And Other Greek Translations Traditionally Included under That Title*. Oxford: Oxford University Press.

Piper, John. 2000. "Are There Two Wills in God?" Pages 107–132 in *Still Sovereign: Contemporary Perspectives on Election, Foreknowledge, and Grace*. Edited by Thomas Schreiner and Bruce Ware. Grand Rapids: Baker.

Porter, Stanley E. 1993. "Did Jesus Ever Teach in Greek." *TynB* 44, no. 2: 199–235.

Postell, Seth D. 2020. "Messianism in Light of Literary Strategy." *BSac* 177: 329–350.

Powell, Samuel M. 2011. "Nineteenth-Century Protestant Doctrines of the Trinity." Pages 267–280 in *The Oxford Handbook of the Trinity*. Edited by Gilles Emery and Matthew Levering. Oxford: Oxford University Press.

Provan, Iain W. 2012. *1 & 2 Kings*. UBCS. Grand Rapids: Baker.

Przywara, Erich. 2014. *Analogia Entis: Metaphysics: Original Structure and Universal Rhythm*. Translated by John R. Betz and David Bentley Hart. 1962 reprint. RRCT. Grand Rapids: Eerdmans.

Pummer, Reinhard. 2016. "Was There an Altar or a Temple in the Sacred Precinct on Mt. Gerizim?" *JSJ* 47:1–21.

Purves, Andrew. 2020. "The End of Ministry: Thomas F. Torrance and Eschatology." pages 277–290 in *T&T Clark Handbook of Thomas F. Torrance*. Edited by Paul D. Molnar and Myk Habets. London: Bloomsbury.

Randolph, Berkeley W. 1903. *The Virgin-Birth of Our Lord*. London: Longmans, Green, and Co.

Regev, Eyal. 2019. *The Temple in Early Christianity: Experiencing the Sacred*. AYBRL. New Haven: Yale University Press.

Renshaw, Julie. 2003. "Boolean Logic in the Corinthian Correspondence." Pages 177–193 in *Paul and the Corinthians: Studies on a Community in Conflict*. NovTSup 109. Leiden: Brill.

Resch, Dustin. 2012. *Barth's Interpretation of the Virgin Birth: A Sign of Mystery*. Barth Study Series. Surrey: Ashgate.

Reymond, Robert L. 1998. *A New Systematic Theology of the Christian Faith*. Nashville, TN: Thomas Nelson.

Richardson, Alan and Thomas Uebel (eds.). 2007. *The Cambridge Companion to Logical Empiricism*. Cambridge: Cambridge University Press.

Rico, Christophe and Peter J. Gentry. 2020. *The Mother of the Infant King, Isaiah 7:14: Alma and Parthenos in the World of the Bible: A Linguistic Approach*. Eugene, OR: Wipf and Stock.

Roberts, Kyle. 2017. *A Complicated Pregnancy: Whether Mary was a Virgin and Why It Matters*. Minneapolis: Fortress.

Rogers, Jack and Donald K. McKim. 1979. *The Authority and Interpretation of the Bible: An Historical Approach*. New York: Harper and Row.

Rosolen, Grahame. 2020. "The Incarnational Christology of Athanasius." *Phronema* 35: 85–95.

Rubin, Miri. 2009. *Mother of God: A History of the Virgin Mary*. New Haven, NJ: Yale University Press.

Rüpke, Jörg. 2014. "Historicizing Religion: Varro's Antiquitates and History of Religion in the Late Roman Republic." *History of Religions* 53, no. 3: 246–268.

Sargent, Benjamin. 2015. *Written to Serve: The Use of Scripture in 1 Peter*. LNTS 547. London: Bloomsbury T&T Clark.

Schaff, Philip. 1882. *The Creeds of Christendom, with a History and Critical Notes: The Evangelical Protestant Creeds, with Translations*. Vol. 3. New York: Harper & Brothers.

Schenk, Richard A. 2016. *The Virgin Birth Of Christ*. Milton Keyes: Paternoster.

Schiffman, Lawrence H. 1991. *From Text to Tradition: A History of Second Temple Judaism and Rabbinic Judaism*. Hoboken, NJ: Ktav.

Schnabel, Eckhard J. 2019. "Biblical Theology from a New Testament Perspective." *JETS* 62, no. 2: 225–249.

Schönborn, Christoph. 2010. *God Sent His Son: A Contemporary Christology*. Translated by Henry Taylor. San Francisco: Ignatius Press.

Schreiner, Patrick. 2016. *The Body of Jesus: A Spatial Analysis of the Kingdom in Matthew*. LNTS 555. London: Bloomsbury T&T Clark.

Segond 21. 2007. Genève: Société Biblique de Genève.

Selman, Martin J. 1994. *2 Chronicles: An Introduction and Commentary*. TOTC 11. Downers Grove: InterVarsity Press.

Simkovich, Malka Z. 2018. *Discovering Second Temple Literature: The Scriptures and Stories that Shaped Early Judaism*. Philadelphia: Jewish Publication Society.

Skarsaune, Oskar. 2002. *In the Shadow of the Temple: Jewish Influences on Early Christianity*. Downers Grove: InterVarsity Press.

Sleeman, Matthew. 2009. *Geography and the Ascension Narrative in Acts*. SNTSMS 146. Cambridge: Cambridge University Press.

Spaulding, Mary B. 2009. *Commemorative Identities: Jewish Social Memory and the Johannine Feast of Booths*. LNTS 396; London: T&T Clark.

Spong, John Shelby. 1992. *Born of a Woman: A Bishop Rethinks the Birth of Jesus*. New York: Harper.

Stanley, Timothy. 2010. *Protestant Metaphysics After Karl Barth and Martin Heidegger*. Eugene: Cascade.

Strauss, Mark L. 2014. *Mark*. ZECNT. Grand Rapids: Zondervan.

Strong, Augustus H. 1907. *Systematic Theology*. Philadelphia: American Baptist Publication Society.

Swain, Scott R. 2017. "The Bible and the Trinity in Recent Thought: Review, Analysis, and Constructive Proposal." *JETS* 60: 35–48.

———. 2021. *The Trinity and the Bible: On Theological Interpretation*. Bellingham, WA: Lexham Academic.

Tabb, Brian J. 2019. *All Things New: Revelation as Canonical Capstone*. NSBT 48. Downers Grove: IVP Academic.

Tappenden, Frederick S. 2016. *Resurrection in Paul: Cognition, Metaphor, and Transformation*. Early Christianity and Its Literature 19. Atlanta: SBL.

Tanner, Kathryn. 2001. *Jesus, Humanity and the Trinity: A Brief Systematic Theology*. Minneapolis: Fortress Press.

Taylor, John B. 1969. *Ezekiel: An Introduction and Commentary*. TOTC. Downers Grove, IL: InterVarsity Press.

Thatcher, Tom. 2007. "Remembering Jesus: John's Negative Christology." Pages 165–189 in *The Messiah in the Old and New Testaments*. Edited by Stanley Porter. MNTS. Grand Rapids: Eerdmans.

Thiselton, Anthony C. 2015. *Systematic Theology*. Grand Rapids: Eerdmans.

Thompson, Alan J. 2011. *The Acts of the Risen Lord Jesus: Luke's Account of God's Unfolding Plan*. NSBT 27. Downers Grove: InterVarsity Press.

Ticciati, Susannah. 2013. *A New Apophaticism: Augustine and the Redemption of Signs*. SST 14. Leiden: Brill.

Torrance, Thomas F. 1969. *Space, Time and Incarnation*. Edinburgh: T&T Clark.

————. 2008. *Incarnation: The Person and Life of Christ*. Edited by Robert T. Walker. Downers Grove: InterVarsity Press Academic.

Treier, Daniel J. 2016. "Incarnation." Pages 216–42 in *Christian Dogmatics: Reformed Theology for the Church Catholic*. Edited by Michael Allen and Scott R. Swain. Grand Rapids: Baker Academic.

Tuell, Steven. 2012. *Ezekiel*. UBCS. Grand Rapids: Baker.

Turner, Ian. 2018. "Going Beyond What is Written or Learning to Read? Discovering OT/NT Broad Reference." *JETS* 61: 577–594.

Turner, David L. 2008. *Matthew*. BECNT. Grand Rapids: Baker Academic.

Tyler, Kate. 2020. "Thomas F. Torrance and Ecclesiology." Pages 22–242 in *T&T Clark Handbook of Thomas F. Torrance*. Edited by Paul D. Molnar and Myk Habet. London: Bloomsbury T&T Clark.

Um, Stephen T. 2006. *The Theme of Temple Christology in John's Gospel*. LNTS 311. London: Bloomsbury T&T Clark.

VanderKam, James S. 2001. *An Introduction to Early Judaism*. Grand Rapids: Eerdmans.

Vanhoozer, Kevin J. 1998. *Is There a Meaning in This Text?: The Bible, the Reader, and the Morality of Literary Knowledge*. Grand Rapids: Zondervan.

————. 2016. *Biblical Authority After Babel: Retrieving the Solas in the Spirit of Mere Protestant Christianity*. Grand Rapids: Brazos.

Verrett, Brian A. 2020. *The Serpent in Samuel: A Messianic Motif*. Eugene, OR: Wipf and Stock.

von Balthasar, Hans Urs. 2000. *Theo-Logic: Theological Logical Theory: The Truth of the World*. trans. Adrian J. Walker; vol. 1; San Francisco: Ignatius Press.

————. 2004. *Theo-Logic: Theological Logical Theory: Truth of God*. Translated by Adrian J. Walker vol. 2. San Francisco: Ignatius Press.

von Campenhausen, Hans. 2011. *The Virgin Birth in the Theology of the Ancient Church*. 1954 Reprint. Eugene, OR: Wipf and Stock.

von Harnack, Adolf. 1898. *History of Dogma*. Edited by T.K. Cheyne and A.B. Bruce. Translated by Neil Buchanan. vol. 4. Boston: Little, Brown, and Co.

Vos, Geerhardus. 2003. *Biblical Theology: Old and New Testaments*. 1948 Reprint. Eugene, OR: Wipf & Stock Publishers.

Walker, P.W.L. 1996. *Jesus and the Holy City: New Testament Perspectives on Jerusalem*. Grand Rapids: Eerdmans.

Walters, Patricia. 2009. *The Assumed Authorial Unity of Luke and Acts: A Reassessment of the Evidence*. JSNTSup 145. Cambridge: Cambridge University Press.

Walton, Douglas. 1996. *Fallacies Arising from Ambiguity*. Applied Logic Series. Dordrecht: Springer.

Walton, John H. 2003. "Eden, Garden Of." Page 202 in *Dictionary of the Old Testament: Pentateuch*. Edited by T.D. Alexander and D.W. Baker. Downers Grove: InterVarsity Press.

Walton, John H. 2011. *Genesis 1 as Ancient Cosmology*. Winona Lake: Eisenbrauns.

Walton, John H., Victor H. Matthews, and Mark W. Chavalas. 2000. *The IVP Bible Background Commentary: Old Testament*. Downers Grove: InterVarsity Press.

Watson, Francis. 1997. *Text and Truth: Redefining Biblical Theology*. Grand Rapids: Eerdmans.

Webster, John. 2019. *The Culture of Theology*. Edited by Ivor J. Davidson and Alden C. McCray. Grand Rapids: Baker Academic.

Wegner, Paul D. 2014. "Review of Andrew T. Lincoln's *Born of a Virgin? Reconceiving Jesus in the Bible, Tradition, and Theology*," *Them* 39, no. 2: 367–369.

Weinandy, Thomas G. and Daniel A. Keating. 2017. *Athanasius and His Legacy: Trinitarian-Incarnational Soteriology and Its Reception*. Mapping the Tradition. Minneapolis: Fortress Press.

Wellum, Stephen. 2016. *God the Son Incarnate: The Doctrine of Christ*. Foundations of Evangelical Theology. Wheaton: Crossway.

———. 2020. "From Alpha to Omega: A Biblical-Theological Approach to God the Son Incarnate." *JETS* 63, no. 1: 71–94.

Wenham, Gordon J. 1979. *The Book of Leviticus*. NICOT. Grand Rapids: Eerdmans.

———. 1986. "Sanctuary Symbolism in the Garden of Eden Story." Proceedings of the World Congress of Jewish Studies 9: 19–25.

Wenkel, David H. 2021a. *Jesus the Dayspring: The Sunrise and the Visitation of Israel's Messiah*. NTM 43. Sheffield: Sheffield Phoenix Press.

———. 2021b. "The Gospel of Matthew and Apocalyptic Discourse." *ExpTim* 132: 259–270.

Wenkel, David H. 2009. "Matthew's Two-Age Eschatology: Toward Bridging Systematic Theology and Biblical Studies." *MJT* 7: 137–157.

———. 2011. "The Logic and Exegesis behind Calvin's Doctrine of the Internal Witness of the Holy Spirit to the Authority of Scripture." *PRJ* 3, no. 2: 98–108.

———. 2012. "The Most Simple and Comprehensive Script for the Theo-Drama of Scripture: Three Acts or Four?" *SBET* 30, no. 1: 78–90.

———. 2017a. *Jesus' Crucifixion Beatings and the Book of Proverbs*. New York: Palgrave Macmillan.

———. 2017b. "The Lord Will Reveal the Lord: God's Invisibility and Jesus' Visibility in 1 Timothy." *HBT* 39, no. 2: 197–210.

———. 2018a. "Abraham's Typological Resurrection from the Dead in Hebrews 11." *CTR* 15, no. 2: 51–66.

———. 2018b. *Shining Like the Sun: A Biblical Theology of Meeting God Face to Face*. Bellingham, WA: Lexham.

———. 2018c. *The Kingship of the Twelve Apostles in Luke-Acts*. New York: Palgrave Macmillan.

———. 2019. "The Doctrine of the Extent of the Atonement among Early English Particular Baptists." *HTR* 112, no. 3:358–375.

———. 2020. "Noah as a New Adam in the Narrative Substructure of Romans 5:12–21." *JTI* 14, no. 1: 74–86.

Westminster Assembly. 1851. *The Westminster Confession of Faith: Edinburgh Edition*. Philadelphia: William S. Young.

Wessel, Susan. 2004. *Cyril of Alexandria and the Nestorian Controversy: The Making of a Saint and of a Heretic*. OECS. Oxford: Oxford University Press.

White, Aaron W. 2016. "Revisiting the 'Creative' Use of Amos in Acts and What it Tells Us About Luke." *BTB* 46, no. 2: 195–206.

White, Thomas Joseph. 2015. *The Incarnate Lord: A Thomistic Study in Christology*. TRS 5. Washington, D.C.: The Catholic University of America Press.

Whitlark, Jason A. 2022. "Reading Hebrews in a Roman Vicus with Voluntary Associations." Pages 359–376 in *Greco-Roman Associations, Deities, and Early Christianity*. Edited by Bruce W. Longenecker. Waco, TX: Baylor University Press.

Widder, Wendy L. 2016. *Daniel*. SGBC. Grand Rapids: Zondervan.

Witherington, Ben III. 2017. *Isaiah Old and New: Exegesis, Intertextuality, and Hermeneutics*. Minneapolis: Fortress Press.

Wittgenstein, Ludwig. 1999. *Denkbewegungen: Tagebücher 1930–1932, 1936–1937*. Edited by I. Somavilla. Frankfurt am Main: Fischer.

———. 2001. *Philosophical Investigations*. 3rd Edition. Edited and Translated by G.E.M. Anscombe. Oxford: Blackwell.

Wood, William. 2021. *Analytic Theology and the Academic Study of Religion*. Oxford: Oxford University Press.

Woudstra, Marten H. 1981. *The Book of Joshua*. NICOT. Grand Rapids: Eerdmans.

Wright, N.T. 1992. *Who Was Jesus?* London: SPCK.

———. 2002. "Jesus' Self-Understanding." Pages 47–61 in *The Incarnation: An International Symposium on the Incarnation of the Son of God*. Edited by Stephen T. Davis, Daniel Kendall, and Gerald O'Collins. Oxford: Oxford University Press.

———. 2016. "Historical Paul and 'Systematic Theology.'" Pages 147–164 in *Biblical Theology: Past, Present, and Future*. Edited by Carey Walsh and Mark W. Elliott. Eugene, OR: Cascade.

Yee, Gale. 1989. *Jewish Feasts and the Gospel of John*. Wilmington: Michael Glazier.

Zacharias, H. Daniel. 2017. *Matthew's Presentation of the Son of David: Davidic Tradition and Typology in the Gospel of Matthew*. London: Bloomsbury T&T Clark.

Zachman, Randall C. 2007. *Image and Word in the Theology of John Calvin*. Notre Dame, IN: University of Notre Dame Press.

Zervos, George T. 2019. *The Protevangelium of James: Greek Text, English Translation, Critical Introduction: Volume 1*. London: Bloomsbury T&T Clark.

Scripture Index

193

Topical Index

199

About the Author

David H. Wenkel, PhD (Aberdeen), is Research Fellow in New Testament at LCC International University, Klaipeda, Lithuania. He is the author of *Jesus the Dayspring: The Sunrise and the Visitation of Israel's Messiah*.